More praise for *How to Market Books*

"This is excellent. The clarity of the whole thing is beyond praise – let alone the gargantuan task of compilation on such a comprehensive scale. Many congratulations. It deserves to become the 'bible' of marketing in publishing."
Professor Emrys Jones, LSE

"Year after year How to Market Books *features at the top of our recommended reading list for students of book marketing. The straightforward, sensible and practical nature of the advice found within it ensures that it is much trusted and respected, by staff and students alike."*
Dr Caroline Copeland, Programme Leader MSc Publishing, Napier University

"As a small publisher I've had to learn every part of the business on the hoof. This book is a godsend – first you read it right through for a full understanding of the marketing process, then you return to it time and again for techniques that really work in practice. And because Alison's style is so open and clear – it's like a personal helpline."
Heather Alabaster, Clever Clogs Publishing

"The urge to write and get published has never been stronger, and it's just wonderful to see the satisfaction people feel from getting into print and sharing their ideas. Whether you are organizing a single reading, a whole festival, trying to get a publishing deal or to self publish, this book is packed with wise and practical information. It's invaluable."
Sandy Williams, Director, Kingston Readers' Festival

"I would recommend this book wholeheartedly – not just to the new promotions assistant in the department, but to all the marketing, publicity and sales staff."
Learned Publishing

"I have been recommending How to Market Books *when talking to university students about publishing as a career, or at SYP conferences, ever since the first edition in 1990. Publishing has changed enormously over those years, with the increasing power of central buying and – most of all – the arrival of the internet. Successive editions have always reflected changing market conditions with detailed, accessible and practical advice on what to do and how to do it. This new edition more than keeps up the tradition."*
Nicolas Jones, Strathmore Publishing

HOW TO MARKET BOOKS

The essential guide to maximizing profit and exploiting all channels to market

4TH EDITION

Alison Baverstock

PARK LEARNING CENTRE
UNIVERSITY OF GLOUCESTERSHIRE
PO Box 220, The Park
Cheltenham GL50 2RH
Tel: 01242 714333

KOGAN
PAGE

London and Philadelphia

First published 1990
Second edition 1997
Third edition 2000
This edition 2008

120 Pentonville Road
London N1 9JN
United Kingdom
www.kogan-page.co.uk

525 South 4th Street, #241
Philadelphia PA 19147
USA

© Alison Baverstock, 1990, 1997, 2000, 2008

ISBN 978 0 7494 5020 5

British Library Cataloguing-in-Publication Data

A CIP record for this book is available from the British Library.

Library of Congress Cataloging-in-Publication Data

Baverstock, Alison.
  How to market books : the essential guide to maximizing profit and exploiting all channels to market / Alison Baverstock. — 4th ed.
       p. cm.
  Includes bibliographical references and index.
  ISBN 978-0-7494-5020-5
  1. Books—Marketing. 2. Selling—Books. I. Title.
  Z278.B38 2008
  002.068'8—dc22
                                  2007037085

Typeset by JS Typesetting Ltd, Porthcawl, Mid Glamorgan
Printed and bound in India by Replika Press Pvt Ltd

Contents

Acknowledgements

This book began in 1989, as a course handout for the Publishing Training Centre at Book House, but quickly became a compendium of things I wished I had known when I began in the industry. I kept writing and soon had a contents list and several chapters of a book, which Kogan Page promptly agreed to publish. The deadline was provided by pregnancy and my daughter timed her arrival perfectly. I completed the manuscript four days before she was born, and as she arrived on a Friday, promptly framed – and hung on her wall – the front cover of the edition of *The Bookseller* that carried her date of birth.

My guiding principle from the start was to include everything I would like to have known when I began work as a publisher; to set down a checklist of possible types of marketing activity that should be considered whatever the format or subject area of the list being promoted. This new edition has been written as an international guide, as I am convinced that the same problems and issues face publishers, wherever they are located.

I am delighted this book continues to fill a need. Its updating has relied heavily on various friends and colleagues drummed into commenting on sections. In particular I would like to thank Wendy Allen, Fiona Allison, Veronica Angel, Florence Ascoli, Alberto Barraclough, Jacqui Bass, Clare Baverstock, John Beale, Steve Bohme, Elaine Boorman, Susannah Bowen, Susan Brent, Hugh Bulford, Graham Bulpitt, James Carey, Rowena Carey, Dr Steve Carey, Irene Chalmers, Jill Chapman, John Cheshire, Jane Cholmeley, Sheila Christie, Chris Chrystal, Christian Ciullo, Lisa Ciullo, Desmond Clarke, Chris Cleave, Mike Coleman, Tracey Cooke, Robert Creffield, Dr Bill Crofts, Gill Cronin, John Davey, Roy Davey, John Davies, Simone Davies, Dr Michael de Souza, Nigel Dollin, Cathy Douglas, John Downham, Margaret Drabble, Nancy Dull, David Dutton, Wendy Cope, Debbie Cox, Gill Cronin, Justine Crowe, James Ellor, Mike Esplen,

Lorraine Fanin, Anne Fanning, Tim Farmiloe, Dr Frank Fishwick, Lindsay Fraser, Dr Alex Gibson, Dave Golding, Dr Stephen Hancocks, Holly Hardy, Brian Harper-Lewis, Jo Henry, Alan Hill, Jean Hindmarch, Caroline Hird, Talitha Hitchcock, Heather Holden-Brown, Steve Holland, Barbara Horn, Jo Howard-Brown, Kelly Howe, Robert Howells, Jeanette Hull, Matthew Huntley, John and Kate Hybert, Louis Ingram, Amy Irvine, Ian and Jan Jacobs, Liz James, Paula Johnson, Professor Emrys Jones, Nicholas Jones, Irene Jordan, Dr Elizabeth Katay, Louise Kaye, Barrie Kempthorne, Rob Langley, Clive Leatherdale, Tom Lee, June Lines, Simon Littlewood, David Lindley, Tammy Livermore, Catherine Lockerbie, Professor Wendy Lomax, Gian Lombardo, Dot Lubianska, Ursula Mackenzie, Nicholas Masucci, Jane Mays, Dr Christine McAuley, Finbarr McCabe, Hamish McGibbon, Sheila McGlassen, Miranda McKearney, Sally McKinnel, Sarah McNally, Alice Meadows, John Merriman, Peter and Jean Milford, Sue Miller, Roger Millington, Carol Monyios, Katherine Naish, Mary Lou Nash, Victoria Nash, Mary Nettlefold, Dr Kingsley Norton, Alice Noyes, Orna O'Brien, Pamela Oldfield, Chris Oliver, Bob Osborne, John Park, Dr James Parker, Madeleine Parkyn, Dharm Patel, Janette Paterson, John Peacock, Jane Pembroke, Brian Perman, John Purefoy, Margaret Radbourne, Deborah Rea, Sarah Rees Brennan, Dr Kimberley Reynolds, Joel Rickett, Jennifer Rigby, Julian Rivers, Dr Joan Rutherford, Gerald Scott, Pippa Scoones, Allan Shanks, Barbara Singh, Liz Small, Alan Smith, Dag Smith, Nicola Solomon, Clare Somerville, Andrew Sullivan, Jane Tatam, Graham Taylor, Ian Taylor, David Teale, Jonathan Tilston, Sara Tricker, Katherine Tozeland, Susan Turret, Jo van der Borgh, Mark Waite, John Walsh, Philip Walters, David Walton, Andrew Welham, Howard Willows, John Winkler, Wendy Woodley, Mark Wray and Martin Wyn-Jones.

Finally I would like to thank Martin Neild for his introduction to this edition, my publishers Kogan Page, and in particular Jon Finch, Martha Fumagalli, Helen Savill and Susan Curran, my colleagues at Kingston University, my agent Jenny Brown and my family who have been encouraging and patient throughout. A particular thank you to my eldest son Alasdair for his proofreading/ironic commentary. You really can start a sentence with 'and'. See *Genesis*, chapter 2.

Foreword

Publishing today, as Alison Baverstock says in this remarkable book, is totally driven by marketing. This is not, as the doomsday merchants would have it, a reflection of the end of culture and creativity as we know it because of the irrevocable rise of the 'suits'. It is, quite simply, that in the challenging markets of the 21st century, publishing will not survive unless its marketing is totally effective which means it needs to be professional, relevant, properly targeted, creative and innovative.

There are several reasons for this, all of which are well covered in Alison Baverstock's book. The first, as Alison puts it so succinctly, is that 'books compete for both consumer and business spend with a whole range of other products'. In consumer publishing, these are music, computer games, films (including DVD), newspapers and magazines, all of which sit together under the same 'entertainment' code in mass market retailers, and all of which are competing for the same leisure pound. The marketing of our author brands must compete with the marketing of brands in all of these other areas. While publishers can never hope to operate the same marketing budgets as these competitors, our marketing has to be at least as professional and even more imaginative. This book provides the best possible tools to start tackling these issues.

On the consumer side, supermarkets are now a significant and growing market for our books. We are engaging fully with Tesco, Asda and the others, dealing with buyers outside the traditional book business whose only expertise is in fast moving consumer goods and who will simply laugh at sloppy, unconvincing, traditional book campaigns as not worth the badly produced presenters they are printed on. High street booksellers and independents also rightly have much higher expectations of publishers' marketing, as do many authors and agents.

And, of course, in all areas of publishing, we are now either selling through and, in some cases, competing with the internet where marketing is reaching new heights of sophistication.

Alison's book teaches us how to approach all this in a thorough, calm, rational and totally comprehensive way. Crucially, the book's focus throughout is on what consumers *want*, whether they are general readers or students, and how to target marketing accordingly. A key point she makes is that you cannot take any reader's interest for granted, particularly in an environment of 24/7 media when there is so much competition for our attention. This is a fact too often overlooked by publishers.

The book demonstrates that in spite of these daunting challenges, there are more opportunities than ever before for the marketing of books. What other industry has as much 'free advertising' as we do in the form of book pages, and acres of column inches in newspapers; TV and radio chat shows crying out for the sort of copy that books and authors can supply? What other industry can use 'talking heads' to the same extent as we can use authors to engage directly with the reading public through signings, festivals, library events etc? The internet, e-mail, mobile phones, 'guerrilla marketing' and electronic devices not yet invented give us a unique opportunity to reach out directly to consumers to promote books.

None of this can be effectively done, however, without a complete understanding of the basics required for every aspect of the book marketing process, whether it be acquiring books from authors and agents, selling to the trade or the consumer. Successful publishing is and always will be about attention to detail. Alison Baverstock's book is the best possible exponent of this.

It should be required reading not just for aspiring marketers but for anyone wishing to enter or understand publishing. There is no satisfaction either culturally or commercially in publishing books which do not sell. I hope that reading this excellent book will enable more of tomorrow's publishers to understand this and it will certainly give them the tools to do something about it.

Martin Neild
Chief Executive
Hodder & Stoughton

Marketing in publishing: what it means and what is involved

Publishing today is driven by marketing. The search is on for markets with specific needs and the ability to pay, for which resources can be developed and sold.

Marketing at its most effective appears simple: the slogan so appropriate that it is instantly memorable; the sales letter that makes a product sound so desirable the reader fills out the order form immediately. Yet this simplicity is not easily achieved. It depends on a complete understanding of both designated market and product, an understanding that emerges only through detailed planning and research.

All too often in publishing, immense pressure on the time available means that planning and research tend to get forgotten in the rush to get something ready. The habit of planning marketing strategies – aims and objectives – is an important one to acquire. Drawing up a marketing plan acts as a mind-focusing exercise, encouraging clarity of thought and helping you to prioritize. And, of course, carefully planned campaigns stand a very much better chance of achieving their goals.

It is increasingly the case that an effective marketing plan is vital in acquiring as well as selling books. Agents or authors offering titles to prospective publishers will place considerable importance on the suitor companies' various abilities to present (and deliver) coherent marketing plans.

WHAT YOU ARE UP AGAINST

How many books were published worldwide in 2006? How many are currently available? These are deceptively simple questions with complicated answers.

If the new *Harry Potter* gets translated into 50 languages, is that 50 titles or just one? If a book comes out as a hardback, then a trade paperback, then a B format paperback, then an A format paperback, is that one title or two or four titles? What about the export edition or the airside edition (sold in duty-free bookshops at airports)? Then there are print on demand (POD) titles: some are new books, some are old books prevented from going out of print by going POD (with an old or new ISBN, depending on the status). And there are 'publish yourself facilitators' such as Ellora's Cave and Lulu.com – which boast 30 new publishers every week (publishers, mind, not books).

Looking away from print, how should you count audiobooks – cassette/ CD/download? And what about e-books? If an e-book is available in 10 different e-formats, is that one book or 10 – or is it none because it is available as a printed book and counted as that? What about novels disseminated as podcasts or as text messages straight to your mobile (the latest thing in Japan)?

The UK publishing industry produces about 130,000 new titles each year (two per head of the population); the United States offers roughly half a book per head. So far, so good, but trying to establish how many books are published in other specific territories is a logistical (and political) nightmare. What about China, Japan, India, North Korea, Malawi, the Turks & Caicos Islands?

In short, there are no available numbers – or, to put it another way, there are too many. Google your question and you get lots of interesting leads. One thing is universally accepted to be true: the number of books published (however you define it) increases every year, and has surely done so every year for the last 10 and possibly 20 years.

Even if no one agrees it completely, a working total is useful. Bowker (North America's leading provider of bibliographic information) estimated that in 2004 English-speaking countries published 375,000 new books worldwide, and that with a further 75,000 imported titles available in multiple markets, this gave a grand total of 450,000 new English-language books available for sale in the English-speaking world. In just one year.

An understanding of the breadth of the market should help you to guard against complacency. You may be very familiar with the impending publication of a forthcoming title, having seen it on the production schedule for so long, but can you think of any reason why the book retailer or consumer should be equally familiar with it? (If you want instantly convincing and depressing proof, take a trip along to your nearest bookstore and examine the shelf on which the forthcoming title will hopefully sit, and in what company. The answer is usually lots.)

In the United Kingdom, over half the books sold each year are sold through bookshops (according to BML's Books and the Consumer Survey 2005–07), so time spent in them trying to understand more about the market for your titles is seldom wasted. If you can get a local bookstore to take you on, a couple of days helping out will teach you a huge amount. Try to find out how many e-mails are received each day, or arrive when the post is being opened one morning to see how much information a store receives in a single day; notice how much gets deleted/rejected, without even being looked at, as simply inappropriate. Even if you cannot work in one, do acquire the habit of visiting bookstores at regular intervals. See how busy they are (particularly in the run-up to holiday/festival seasons); watch how customers peruse the stock (browse in depth but take a fresh copy to the counter); listen to the scanty information they have about the titles they want. ('Do you have a book that was on the radio within the last month? I think the author was Joanne someone.')

The aim of all this is to encourage you to stop viewing your list of titles as an interesting whole, united by its single publisher, and to see it rather, as the book retailer will see it, as a series of individual products. For each title, rejection is the easiest option, and reasons for stocking need to be fully spelt out. Your eventual customer meanwhile will probably be more familiar with your authors' names than that of your publishing house or imprints.

What is more, books compete for both the consumer and business spend with a whole range of other products, not just other books. A manager may select an online consultancy service rather than an expensive reference work; a windsurfing enthusiast may prefer a DVD on technique to a new book; a school principal decide on a morale-boosting staff training day rather than new teaching resources. And the amount of advertising trying to direct our pattern of spending is enormous.

So where do you start in trying to develop coherent plans for your marketing? Perhaps by considering what marketing means.

THE MEANING OF MARKETING

There is a more detailed examination of the meaning of marketing, supported by full explanation of techniques for conducting a company audit and drawing up a detailed marketing plan, in the companion volume to this one, *Are Books Different?*, also published by Kogan Page.

No one is entirely sure what marketing is. Each industrial trailblazer has his or her own personal philosophy (and vocabulary to describe it). Even the academics teaching and studying the subject cannot agree. My own opinion is that over-concentrated discussion has compounded the problem. Boil down all the seminal texts and jargon and you are left with a simple concept: marketing means effective selling. So if marketing appears in your job title, it means you are involved with selling what your company produces. Whether or not you count the cash, you help prepare customers to part with their money.

WHAT MARKETING MEANS IN PUBLISHING

Marketing in publishing has a more recent history; in the last 25 years there has been a complete revolution. Publishing companies used to be run by editors; today they are run by marketers. Indeed, the pendulum has swung so far the other way that many argue high editorial standards are being sacrificed as firms spend ever-increasing amounts on pushing the product.

CHECKLISTS FOR ACHIEVING GOOD MARKETING

Here are two short summaries of what marketing is about. The first is a six-part definition of what marketing means in practice (the first four parts of which come from Professor Baker of Strathclyde University); the second, a checklist for ensuring your marketing is on track:

Marketing means:

■ Concentrating on the customer and their needs; being market oriented rather than product oriented.

■ Taking a long perspective. Allocating a huge marketing budget won't produce enormous sales the next day. Effective understanding of markets and products takes detailed study and hence time.

■ Making full use of all the resources available. Marketing won't work if it's only seen as important by the marketing department. The whole organization needs to be involved and committed.

■ Innovating and being flexible. Markets and customers change all the time; their only abiding loyalty is to their own interests. Even best-selling products can become boring. If you want to stay ahead you have to think ahead.

■ Managing relationship. Effective marketing is not something that can be carried on in isolation. Stone Age people learnt that as they bartered basic commodities, crops for hides. Today relationships are just as important, both within and without the firm: with employees and those who might consider becoming your employees; with the market; with shareholders; with the next generation of customers.

■ Being logical. Marketing often suffers from an image problem; it can be viewed as forcing unwanted goods on the unwilling. True marketing means planning what you want to achieve and how to do so, then implementing and monitoring it.

The second useful checklist of ideas has been credited to a variety of different gurus. Marketing is about offering:

■ the right people
■ the right product by saying
■ the right things in
■ the right way
■ at the right time and
■ in the right place.

Applying this checklist to publishing is a useful way to start thinking about how to plan your marketing.

The right people

For the marketing-orientated publishing company, the customer's needs should come before product or service development; products should grow out of an understanding of consumer requirements. In exploring customer needs, a variety of different sources of information may be used: specialist knowledge from your authors; socio-economic data; website and mailing list research; relevant directories; the sales pattern of related products, general knowledge; talking to people and observation of trends.

The right product

The right product is the one that customers want, or one that they will be prepared to want – and pay for – once they have been informed of its existence. The manufacturer's initial concept should be refined until it meets this standard.

Applied to publishing, this means considering the best format (which is not necessarily a book – the market might find more useful a magazine or a website, or a combination of elements such as textbook, teachers' notes and supporting website). It can include changing the level at which the product is pitched, the cover or number of illustrations, or price to meet the anticipated needs and preferences of the market. Although active involvement in this process may well occur only higher up the publishing tree, you should bear in mind that the author's first submission of text is not necessarily what finally appears in published form (whatever medium is chosen). Appropriate and professional presentation to the market is a very important part of the publishing process.

The right things

The right things are those that need to be said to convince the potential buyer to purchase. That does not mean listing every possible sales benefit, but concentrating on those most relevant to the market. For example, tyre manufacturers could stress a variety of different product benefits: competitive price, road-holding ability, value for money and longevity. They usually concentrate on a single one: safety.

Taking the selection of sales benefits a stage further, what offer in combination with your product is more likely to persuade the buyer to purchase? General advertising yields lots of examples: the free extra if an order is over a certain value; the complimentary voucher that accompanies student bank accounts; the cast-iron guarantee of a refund if the customer is not completely satisfied.

The right way

This means the right creative strategy (style of copy, format, design, typography and so on) that allows the message to speak clearly to the market. For example, when selling business information to companies your tone probably needs to be clear, professional and centred on the potential competitive advantage you are offering. If writing copy for point-of-sale material to be used in children's book departments, the image chosen must both attract children and sell through to those who will make the buying decision. The visual appeal must be instant.

The right time

The right time is the best time to be selling. Advertising fireworks in April or Christmas decorations in July may achieve sales but will probably not produce the best possible results. Pharmaceutical companies producing drugs for seasonal illnesses frequently secure the best response if they time their marketing to doctors carefully, for example by sending information on hay fever remedies when the pollen count is high.

The best time to contact teachers with information on an educational publishing programme is when they are thinking about how to spend their forthcoming budget or at the beginning of the new school year. If you send out during the long holidays there will be no one there to read your material. On the other hand, contacting university academics at the same time will frequently find them still at their desks but, in the absence of their students, with more time to absorb and consider your sales message.

The right place

The right place is the selection of the most appropriate sales vehicle; the place where the largest number of your prospective customers will read your message. For example, to doctors you may decide on an e-mail campaign, space advertising in a relevant publication or to instruct a team of freelance reps to take your product into medical centres. All three are different ways of reaching the same market.

HOW TO DRAW UP A MARKETING PLAN

The basics

A good starting point for a marketing plan is to make a list of all the standard promotional boosts received by every product published by your house. Not only will compiling such a list give confidence, it will also be useful when you have to speak to authors or agents about promotion plans for a specific title. (Often these standard promotional processes are so familiar that they are easily forgotten.)

If the task of setting up these procedures is yours too, the following list will be helpful.

A website entry

Once a title has been decided on, information will usually be added to the organization's website (unless there are strategic reasons for keeping quiet – perhaps you do not wish to let your competitors know what you are doing). This will include basic title and author details, an outline content and expected price and publication date.

An advance notice or advance information sheet

This is usually in the form of a single sheet (sent by e-mail and in printed format) and includes all the basic title information: a brief description (blurb) and author profile; bibliographical details, price and expected publication date; key selling points and features. The 'AN' or 'AI' is sent to reps, booksellers and other interested parties, normally six to nine months ahead of publication. Available in print and electronic format.

Inclusion in catalogues and seasonal lists

Most general publishers produce two six-monthly catalogues (spring and autumn); others produce a new books list three times a year or even quarterly. Academic and educational firms usually produce a separate catalogue for each subject for which they publish. Catalogues generally appear six months before the books featured are due to be published, and are available in print and electronic format.

Advertising

Are there any standard features in which all your firm's titles are listed? For example, are there standard space bookings for the export editions/on the websites of the trade or professional press?

Despatch of covers to major bookshops and libraries

Your production department can arrange for extra book jackets and covers to be printed. If you have these stamped on the back with price and publication date they can form useful display and promotional items when sent to bookshops. A basic mailing list could consist of buyers at your key accounts (ask the sales manager for contact names). Alternatively, professional associations representing traders can rent a list of names to you. The best time to circulate is four to five months before publication. Similarly, jackets can be sent to large public libraries.

'Silent salespeople'

This term was coined by Tim Farmiloe, former editorial director of Macmillan. There are a number of other possible homes for your material, which take varying amounts of effort to reach but may result in extra sales. These include sending information to:

■ Relevant websites and bloggers, who may write/enthuse about your product. Some of these sites get huge audiences. For ideas on which sites to use, start with your authors, who are often bloggers themselves. See also Chapter 6 on using the internet to sell.
■ Governmental and other relevant organizations: for example the British Council promotes titles from UK publishers abroad.
■ Professional organizations and trade bodies. If for instance you are producing a title on writing, there are many organizations that would-be writers can join, and each has a useful book list on its website.

- Organizations listing titles available (eg Nielsen Book Data, www.nielsen bookdata.co.uk).
- Web retailers such as Amazon and Play, and in particular, encouraging purchasers to use the mechanisms provided for reviewing what they have enjoyed.
- Various booksellers who produce their own catalogues.
- Relevant associations and groups (many have websites that list recommended publications).
- Appropriate media and press to stimulate features or the demand for review copies (see Chapter 7).

The marketing manager of one major academic publishing house concluded that 95 per cent of its sales were achieved through such intermediaries.

Marketing plans for individual titles

The checklist above should apply to all your titles. For marketing plans for individual titles, a number of considerations need to be thought through before you start planning.

What is your strategy?

What is your company trying to achieve through marketing? To launch something new, to raise the profile of an existing product, or to probe and eventually break into a new area of publishing? You need to know the goals to stand a chance of achieving them.

The very best marketing is grounded in a clear understanding of both the product and target market. Only if you have this will your copy be relevant and personal, and your advertising be seen by those who need to read it in order to buy. Research is the only way to achieve this.

Researching the market ('the right people')

Market research should have been of fundamental importance to the commissioning and development of your company's products. You now have to find the groups of people who need what you have to offer and persuade them to buy.

Segmenting, targeting and positioning

Marketing theory emphasizes the importance of segmenting the market into different groups of people, and then targeting those most likely to purchase (or influence a purchasing decision). The marketing for a product can be segmented as follows in decreasing levels of interest:

▪ people who have bought/used such a product or a related product before;
▪ people who need such a product now;
▪ people who used to but do so no longer;
▪ people who have never done so.

Your best strategy is to think carefully about what kinds of people are to be found within the first category (what other products have they bought; how much do they need what you have now?); investigate how to reach them (eg through mailing lists, societies and memberships that reveal an affinity with what you are promoting), and then target them with a marketing approach. Once you have targeted them, and hopefully persuaded them to buy, you can then move on to trying to motivate them to enthuse about, or recommend, your product to others known to them.

Lastly marketers consider a product's 'positioning'. This is the emotional relationship that the would-be consumer has with your product and your brand. This impression created by the words you use, and the image you create through design and promotional format.

Always be aware of the impression you are creating. Large promotion budgets do not necessarily lead to better sales – indeed, over-lavish material can directly contradict your sales message. For example, full-colour material to promote a product supposedly offering good value for money can lead the consumer to conclude that the price is unnecessarily high, pushed up by the cost of the sales message. On the other hand, when selling a high-price product through the mail, attractively produced promotion material, giving an impression of the quality of what is available, and the beauty it will add to the customer's home, is essential. Look out for the advertisements for multi-volume encyclopaedia sets or other collectables which show the products beautifully lit in prestigious surroundings and often provide the appropriate shelving as part of the deal.

Sometimes it may be advantageous to use cheaper materials or to make your message look hurried. Stockbrokers who produce online 'tip sheets' deliberately go for a no-frills approach. If time has to be allowed for design and professional layout, the information is stale by the time it is received. Similarly, look at the fund-raising mailshots sent out by charities: they are usually printed on recycled paper, stressing an urgency and need that would be entirely defeated were full-colour brochures enclosed. But when it comes to their gift catalogues they print in full colour to put the merchandise in its most advantageous light.

What is the market like?

What kind of people are they? Is the purchaser likely to be male or female; are there socio-economic indicators, or area biases (most mailing lists are selectable in these respects)? Database and software companies can now offer very sophisticated socio-economic analysis of your mailing lists. This is mostly done by postal or zip code analysis but can also draw on additional information such as the examination of house name or first name of householder.

Try to read publications the market has access to, both general interest or professional, and to meet some of the market. Can you go along to a professional meeting or annual conference? Once there, observe what goes on. Gathering this kind of information will help you to decide on the right promotional approach.

Other questions to ask yourself about the market

■ What needs does the market have? How will the product you offer improve people's lives? How much will they benefit? How much do they want it or need it?
■ Who is the product for? Who will buy it?

These two sets of questions are not identical. Think of the advertising of children's toys on television at Christmas, designed to encourage children to ask for the products that parents and other adults will buy. Equally for educational publishers, new materials may be preferred and recommended by classroom teachers, but it is departmental heads or principals who make the buying decisions, and someone else will usually place the order.

■ How big is the potential market? How does this compare with the title's print run? What percentage of the market do you have to sell to in order to make the project profitable?

■ How much will the market pay and how will they pay? If they are buying for the organization they work for, how much can they spend on their own account without having to get a second signature to approve the purchase?

■ How much does your product cost? Will price rule out any important markets? For example, academic libraries are more likely than individual lecturers to buy high-priced monographs, but are there enough libraries in the market to make publication worthwhile? Corporate libraries may be able to afford the latest information, but can public libraries? By targeting your message to one market will you alienate another (and possibly larger) one?

■ For an existing product, how has it been marketed in the past and with what success? If the product has come to your house from a competitor, try to get copies of the promotion material it used. Was marketing one of the reasons the author decided to change houses? If so, what were his or her chief complaints?

■ Once you have established the primary market, ask yourself who else might need the product. Is there anyone who certainly won't buy it? (You can perhaps capitalize on this in your promotional information – 'If you think $500 is too much to spend on ensuring your children have the most up-to-date information to support their homework, read no further.')

Researching the product ('the right product')

This means finding out all you can about the product you are to promote. Who is the author/provider of content: best-selling or unknown; always published by your house or new to the list; available at the time of publication for interviews; with other titles in print? Look at the title. *Confessions of a Showgirl* will give you an idea of the content.

If the title exists in typescript form, try to get sight of it. The number of titles you have to look after will dictate the amount of time you are able to spend on each one. For example, a major new English scheme brought out by a primary education publisher should be examined in detail. If you have 15 monographs a week to promote, looking closely at them all will be impossible. You will have to rely on what the editors have said about them.

Even if you don't have access to the manuscript, search the editorial and marketing files for information. Not everything of relevance finds its way from one department to the other.

Most publishing houses have an evolutionary cycle of forms, altered product details passing on to second- and third-generation versions of the original. As you look through these you will acquire an understanding of the title and how it has developed. At one stage in the cycle (perhaps with the 'presentation' form or 'A' form, the name varies from publishing house to house) it will have been brought before a formal marketing/editorial meeting and approved. On this form a note of the anticipated print run and first- and second-year sales will have been made. These are your targets.

Study the contents list. Ask yourself (or the editor) why the book was commissioned. What market needs does it satisfy? Are there any readers' reports in the file (reports on the manuscript before a decision to publish was taken)? There should also be an author's publicity form. The amount of time authors spend on compiling these varies, but a fully completed one can be an excellent source of information. Who could be better than the author to tell you who should buy the book?

If you are promoting a book that is already·published, look at previous advertisements. Find out from the customer services department what the sales and returns patterns have been. Ask the reps what the market thinks of your product, and in particular, what they call it. You may be surprised.

Study the competition. Early in-house forms and the author's publicity form should list any major competitors to a forthcoming title, or say if a publishing project has been started to meet a major market opportunity. Bearing in mind that the competition may not just consist of other books, start gathering information on what your product competes with and how the alternatives are promoted. Book fairs are a good time to collect other publishers' information and catalogues. Consult their websites and see what they say, and scan the relevant press for ads. You can pay a press agency, to clip the advertisements of your competitors for you, but you will get a better general idea of the market, as well as early warning of any new competition, if you scan the relevant media yourself.

Look on retail websites and see rankings. Find out whether any tele-selling has been done on this product, or a related title, in the past. As well as yielding orders you can gain a great deal of product information. If the market is easily identified, try ringing a few prospects, or consult a directory for contact numbers. You will be surprised how many people find it flattering to have their opinion sought about the need for a new product. Librarians can be particularly helpful.

If there are still unanswered questions, ask the book's editor about contacting the author. Be prepared; ensure that you have read all the information the author provided about the book before you ring. There is nothing more annoying for an author than to spend valuable time filling in a questionnaire only to be rung by a marketing person who has clearly not read it. It may also be helpful to get the author to check your promotional copy. Similarly, can the author help with testimonials or suggest individuals who might give the book a recommendation that you can quote in your advertising material? The recommendation of one expert will be worth 10 times what you can think of to say.

A word of warning. Just because you don't understand the subject matter of the product does not mean you are an inappropriate person to handle the marketing. I maintain you often do a better job if your understanding is incomplete, because you are forced to take nothing for granted, and to ask basic questions: who is it for, what does it do, and so on.

By now the project should be starting to come alive. Start refining your thoughts by answering the following questions about the book or project.

- What is it?
- What does it do?
- Who is it for?
- What is new about it?
- Is it topical?
- Does it meet a new or rediscovered need?
- What does it compete with?
- What does it replace?
- What are its advantages and benefits?
- How much does it cost? What value does this provide?
- Are there any guarantees of satisfaction?
- Are there any testimonials and quotes you can use?
- Does the product satisfy any human needs?

Several copywriting gurus have outlined basic human needs, in the belief that any piece of advertising copy should aim to appeal to at least one. For example:

- to make money;
- to save money;
- to save time and effort;
- to help your family;
- to be secure;
- to impress others;
- to belong, or emulate others;

- to be popular;
- to attract attention;
- to improve oneself;
- to avoid loss or trouble;
- to further your career;
- to gain pleasure.

A new business information title may offer the reader a valuable competitive edge and the chance to make money, a new novel a temporary escape from reality. Take this a stage further by making a list of selling points (features and benefits: see Chapter 3 for more information on the difference between the two) and putting them in order. Successful advertising comes from making the message credible and comprehensible: there may be lots of benefits but the potential buyers need only two to be convinced. The important thing is knowing which two. If you include them all you might confuse people.

Store a copy of your list in the title file; it will be useful later if you have to acquaint yourself with the product in a hurry, perhaps before meeting the author or having to write an advertisement or press release at short notice. This will save you reinventing the wheel.

What you say ('the right things')

The words used in a marketing campaign are often referred to (when combined with appropriate design) as the 'creative strategy'. The next chapters will provide ideas on how to make your approach relevant and effective, suggest new promotional themes and much more. For now I would just recommend that you nurture a general interest in all advertising copy. Don't confine your study to the publishing trade press alone. Start looking out for copywriting techniques that do and do not work, and think why in each case. Keep two files, one of ideas you like (and can copy), the other of mistakes to avoid. It is daunting to realize how much advertising effort (and expenditure) goes entirely unnoticed. Get on as many mailing/e-mailing lists as possible to see how other firms are selling.

Keep file copies of every piece of promotional material you produce, along with a note of how they performed. This will help you to plan marketing strategies in the future, and save you repeating expensive mistakes. Reading through such a file from time to time also acts as a valuable lesson in objectivity. You will quickly spot things you would like to change, and in time come to wonder if it really was you who wrote them.

The following checklist may be helpful to get you started:

1. Think about where and when your promotional material is to appear/be read and what it is trying to achieve.
2. Plan your schedule. Where does marketing material have to be and when?
3. Think about the market. What needs do people have that will be fulfilled by your product? What will motivate them to buy?
4. Draw up a list of product benefits to the market.
5. Put them in order of importance.
6. The most important should form the basis for your theme.
7. Start thinking about the headline, bullet points and paragraph headings for your body copy.
8. From them on it's a lengthy process of writing and rewriting, reading aloud and putting to one side to read later. Remember to intersperse your writing with plenty of breaks. You can't keep up an intensive concentration for long and still be working at your best.
9. When you think you have finished there are several ways of testing your copy. You can buy a computer program to analyse the complexity of your sentences, the number of personal words used and the readability level. A less expensive option is to try your copy out on colleagues at work. Get them to read it aloud to you. Better still, show it to someone completely unconnected with your work and ask if they find it:
   - interesting?
   - persuasive?
   - clear?
   - believable?
   - motivating? And in particular do they know what to do next and how to fill in the order form?

The format ('the right way')

Deciding on whether to produce a cheap two-sided flyer or set up a bespoke website is often where most marketing plans start. It's a much better idea to allow the decision on format to grow out of an understanding of the market and the product. For example, given absolute creative freedom to change format and words of an existing direct marketing piece you would be lucky to put up your response by more than 0.5 per cent. You'd be far better off reviewing the selection of lists, thinking through the product benefits in fuller detail or coming up with a new offer.

Nevertheless, armed with a marketing strategy to reach your customers, there is a lot of scope for lateral thinking on promotional format. Bear in mind that it is the slightly unexpected that secures attention. There are various ways to attract, such as different offers through e-mail, variously sized envelopes for mailshots, new sizes for space advertisements and so on.

Getting your timing right ('the right time')

When is the best time to promote to your market? When do you need your marketing materials to be ready by? Start working back through your diary, allocating time to all those involved such as designers and printers. See the example schedule in Chapter 5 on direct marketing.

Planning too far ahead can be as bad as leaving too little time; it allows everyone the chance to change their mind and the project to go stale. Responding and rising to the challenge of occasional crises for copy is good practice, but in the long term it is best not to survive on ulcer juice alone. Even if you are desperately short of time, try to let the copy sit overnight. What seems very amusing at 5.30 one evening may appear merely embarrassing the next morning.

Media planning ('the right place')

What are the best media through which to convey your promotional message? Should you use e-mail, press advertising, posters, cinema, television and radio advertising, direct mail, display material, public relations, stunts, free samples? All are elements of the promotional mix, tools at your disposal.

Let's take press advertising as a specific example for further examination. Which magazines and journals does your target market read? Consult the author's publicity form and note where he or she suggests review copies should be sent. Talk to editorial and other marketing staff. Do you know any members of the market personally? If so, ask them what they think. Make a short list and look up the rates on a commercial directory or the magazine's advertising website. If they are within your budget, ring up and ask for sample copies as well as details of the readership profile (useful ammunition when the publication starts pestering you for a booking and you want a reason to say no).

Before you make the decision to pay for space, consider whether it could come free. Is there an associated website or chatroom? Could you start a discussion about the subject of your book? Alternatively, is the magazine looking for editorial copy? Might it run something on your book as a feature article, perhaps offering free copies for readers to write in for?

If you decide to advertise, do you plan to take a single space or a series? If there is one magazine or paper that reaches your target market, you will probably get better results from taking a series of advertisements, perhaps featuring a different product benefit each time, rather than spreading the same message over several different magazines. If you go for a series of adverts you should get a discount.

Having decided which media you will use, study them. Can you get yourself added to the free circulation list? Look through the pages. Which adverts do you notice? Is this because of effective copy and design, or placing? Where is the best place to be? In general, go for right-hand side, and facing text, never facing another advertisement (most people skip past double-page ads). Can you get space next to the editorial, or another hot spot such as the crossword or announcements of births, marriages and deaths? Space on book review pages may be cheaper than on news pages, but by opting for the former, will you escape the notice of a large number of your potential buyers? If you are planning to offer a coupon, can it be cut out easily?

Read the letters, and look at the job adverts – a close examination of these will tell you who is reading the magazine. If it is a weekly, is any advertiser writing topical copy? Does the lead time allow for this? Is it paid or controlled circulation? When you start writing you should be aiming your message at one individual reader. Can you picture him or her?

How much can you spend on marketing?

Chapter 10 on budgeting will look at costing promotion campaigns in more detail, but before you start sketching out your plans you need a rough idea of how much can be spent. This is usually based on one of these:

■ A percentage of anticipated revenue from the project.
■ A percentage of the firm's turnover.
■ A sum unrelated to these but designed to get the promotion off to a good start. For example, to launch a large reference work, a new journal or to celebrate the arrival of a new author at your publishing house, you may

be offered a sizeable budget in the hope that future sales will repay the initial investment.

Who to tell in-house

The last part of drawing up an effective marketing plan is letting the right people know what you are doing. First of all, inform the reps. If your marketing plans are likely to result in increased customer demand, it is vital that they know. As a result they may be able to persuade bookstores to take more stock and hence produce more sales. Even if your plans are simply up to schedule, do send a copy of each forthcoming promotion piece to the reps. It is embarrassing if the customers they visit know more about marketing plans than they do.

Second, inform all those on whom you rely. If you offer e-mail, website, telephone and fax numbers for direct orders (and you will probably reduce the response to your direct marketing by at least 50 per cent if you don't), make sure they are up and running before the adverts appear or the mailing goes out. Do the receptionist and people manning the switchboard know what you are offering? If calls come through to your department, does everyone who might answer your phone know what to say? Persuading other people to answer your telephone can be difficult. Try offering an incentive, such as a points systems resulting in chocolates or wine for every order taken in the department. Leave a basic list of prices or details of the current promotion next to your phone.

If the magazine you are advertising in offers a reader-reply scheme, do you have something ready to send out to those who respond? Is there a telesales script for following up a mailshot? All these things – and more – need thinking through beforehand.

FINAL SUMMARY FOR MARKETING PLANS: A CHECKLIST OF WHAT YOU MUST COVER

1. What are you trying to achieve and by when? What are the management expectations for this product/campaign? These are vital bits of information that will shape everything you do.
2. What is the product and how does it work/compete/improve with other solutions?

3. Who is it for? What are its key benefits to the market?
4. What is the company doing already? What standard promotional processes will take place to get this product better known?
5. How, in addition, can you reach the market? Make a list of all possible vehicles including those you could not possibly afford (because you may be able to think of other means to achieve the same thing).
6. What's the budget available? Is there any possible overlap with other titles, which means that budgets can be pooled, and wider publicity gained for the backlist?
7. What promotional methods will you use? What other mechanisms do you have at your disposal (such as free and negotiated publicity)?
8. What can the author/content supplier do? Who else can you encourage to be an ambassador/enthuser for the book?
9. Plan your schedule. What are the key dates? What must you have done by when?
10. Who must you inform about what you are up to, for both pragmatic and political reasons? Those who will be handling the resulting orders (customer services) as well as those dealing with any possible flack (PR staff) need to know what to expect, and you should always keep your line manager informed of what you are up to.

2

'The medium is the message': how to reach the market and different types of promotional format

One of the difficulties of promoting books is that there are just so many other products competing for the market's attention. Other publishers' wares are one form of competition, but there are also all the other, non-book products and services that compete for the same leisure or professional spend. The problem is exacerbated by two other issues, first money and second location. There is seldom as much money available as publishers would like to get titles better known, and the market's whereabouts can be very hard to pin down, for general titles in particular. It follows that marketing materials must be as multi-purpose as possible, encouraging recipients to be aware of, and promote a title on to others possibly interested, while paying sufficient attention to the specific buying messages that each market sector needs.

A variety of different mechanisms have evolved for publishers to inform those they rely on to talk up, review, recommend or simply buy their titles.

This chapter is intended to help you to understand their various functions, and to decide which are the best routes to the market for the titles you have to promote, and how to communicate most effectively through them. While the names of meetings and forms change from house to house, all seem to have similar procedures.

MARKETING INFORMATION FOR THE COMMISSIONING MEETING

The decision on which titles to publish is taken at a formal meeting, attended by representatives of all departments (editorial, sales, marketing, production, rights etc) as well as senior managerial staff. For this meeting the commissioning editor will prepare an overview of all proposed titles, and this will include a market breakdown, an analysis of the competition and an estimate of sales. The marketing department will be asked to help with the preparation of this (although authors and agents are increasingly involved in this too).

While you may not hear the presentation of this information, you may well get involved in its preparation. Even if you have a hand in neither, it is vital that the information collected is passed to the marketing department, for use in future. The commissioning meeting is a time when enthusiasm and optimism are flowing, and they need to be distilled for future use. As time goes on, competitors emerge, deadlines slip and the author may prove difficult to deal with – and publishers can start to wonder why they commissioned the title in the first place. So a look back to the initial rationale can be very helpful.

FIRST IN-HOUSE ALERT TO ALL

The very first information the marketing department receives will probably be the initial in-house alerting form, often sent by e-mail, to say the product is definitely going to be published. This may be accompanied by a copy of the author's publicity form (usually sent out to the author when the contract is signed, and filled in to varying standards). The short description or 'blurb' offered will probably have been written by the author or editor, perhaps a combination of the two. This initial mention of compromise should ring warning bells.

Take note: the more you become familiar with copy you don't understand, the more you will come to assume you know what it means. So if your initial reaction is one of bafflement or confusion ('What on earth is this about?' 'I thought it was about x, the current title is really misleading'), this will probably be the exact response of all other non-specialists – sales reps, general book retailers, librarians and others who may consider ordering the title on someone else's behalf. Never assume, either, that English will be every recipient's first language.

So get involved early. If you don't understand the blurb you are sent, or feel it is too wordy, lengthy or overly pretentious, attempt to unravel the meaning now rather than accepting that, at this stage, the information is still 'for in-house use only'. (There is no such thing: once a description is written you cannot control how it gets used.) Ask yourself whether you really understand the key features of the book. Are they lost in the description? Even for a highly technical title, the key selling points or reasons the book has been commissioned should be instantly obvious.

Remember that the results of your efforts will last. Information prepared at this stage will be stored on the company computer database for retrieval and use in a variety of other guises, ranging from catalogue copy to an advance notice to the trade.

ADVANCE NOTICES OR ADVANCE INFORMATION SHEETS

An advance notice is usually the first opportunity to alert both the firm and the wider market to the forthcoming publication of a new title. It is sent to bookstores, wholesalers, the company's reps and agents dealing with international markets, and any other parties interested in the firm's publishing programme. Ideally despatched six to nine months ahead of publication (less in the case of 'perishable' titles), it needs to be with wholesalers and bookshops to allow time for the subscription of orders. It should be sent further ahead if the information contained is to be catalogued and included in the recipients' own promotional material, or is the subject of a special publisher-retail promotion.

Because an advance notice is usually drafted by the editors it is often viewed as an editorial document. Forget that: its task is to sell.

How to write an advance notice that people will read

The proposed text is usually sent to the marketing department before it is printed. If this is the first chance you have had to take a detailed look at the proposed title copy, it is vital that you do so. Make sense of what you read, edit and amend, and submit your efforts for approval. Try to improve readability by shortening sentences or adding bullet points to highlight key features. If your efforts at simplifying are rejected on the grounds that the author is a specialist on the subject and he/she wrote the blurb you are attempting to unravel, gently remind critics that bookshops and reps receiving the information will not be specialists. Like you they should understand what they receive.

Relevant brevity is best. An advance notice serves to tell busy bookstore buyers why they should stock the title, and to provide the rep or agent with sales ammunition. Don't feel every inch of space has to be covered: densely packed copy is very off-putting.

Information that should be included in an advance notice

- Author, title and subtitle (actual, not a working approximation).
- Format (actual dimensions, not in-house jargon) and binding or protective packaging (if special).
- ISBN (complete: include your publisher prefix, however well known you think your firm is).
- Extent (ie number of pages and number of illustrations, colour or black and white).
- Imprint (ie which part of your company's organization, eg Puffin is an imprint of Penguin).
- Whether part of a series (and if so, the ISSN).
- Publication date and price. Be realistic, not optimistic: publishers get a name for the accuracy of their predictions.
- Short blurb.
- Brief author information. Concentrate on why the author is qualified to write this title, and include a brief sales history of previous titles and editions if relevant. Where the author is based? (The rep for that area will want to persuade the local bookshop to take stock.)
- Who is it for? *Briefly* outline the market.

■ Key selling points. What is new about it? What needs does it meet? Why did your house decide to publish? Why should the bookseller stock the title? Why is the book better than the competition? (These are probably best set out as a series of bullet points.)

■ Scope – ie broad description of what the book covers.

■ Contents. If they are long and complicated, stress 'main features/papers' first.

■ Key promotional highlights arranged so far. If you have already arranged for the title to be serialized in a major newspaper at the time of publication, say so. If it is a book with a strong regional flavour, say you will be targeting the local radio station. If the book is one of your lead titles for the season and so has an enormous promotion budget, pass on the information.

■ The availability of any point of sale material, eg if you are offering a dumpbin, state quantity, mix, price and ISBN.

■ The publisher's contact details: website, office address, telephone number and e-mail address (of the sales department).

Some publishers put the title in bold or underline it, and then repeat as often as possible on the grounds that they are reinforcing the words in the readers' mind (the same technique used in radio advertising). The reader, on the other hand, gets used to recognizing a familiar block of copy and skips past. It may never get read. It's far better to use the space to explain why the book is being published.

WEBSITE ENTRY

Most publishing houses now have a website, but they often tend to be managed by different people from the printed marketing materials a house may put out. In general, this is helpful: websites get read in a different way from printed materials. The reader tends to have a much shorter span of attention when reading on screen rather than on the page. However it can mean, if you are not careful, that your website entries bear no relation to the other information you put out. It should be clear that both printed and website materials are talking about the same titles!

If it falls to you to write copy for the website, the list of useful details for writing advance notices will be a good starting point. But there will probably be room for much less information, and you will need to think carefully about how to present it. Keep it short and use headlines, boxes with key

HOW TO MARKET BOOKS
The Essential Guide to Maximizing Profit and Exploiting All Channels to Market
4th Edition

Alison Baverstock

www.kogan-page.co.uk
120 Pentonville Road
London N1 9JN
Tel: +44 (0) 20 7278 0433
Fax: +44 (0) 20 7837 6348

- **International edition of authoritative text, with new information on digital marketing**
- **Practical and straightforward with easy-to-apply advice**
- **New foreword by Martin Neild, MD of Hodder Headline**

"This is the one book we recommend to all marketing staff. The information it contains is always sensible, realistic and reliable."
The Oxford Publicity Partnership

"The most comprehensive and useful tome on book marketing available. It is an indispensible teaching tool and guide."
Gian Lombardo, Publisher-in-Residence, Emerson College, USA and Director, Quale Press

Description

How to Market Books, now in its fourth edition, has for many years been the place to turn for professionals in the industry charged with maximizing revenues and minimizing costs. In recent years the selling and marketing of books has come under more and more pressure. The industry has become dominated by the larger chains, by new channels to market, by new players such as supermarkets, and by consumer demand for different product formats. This book provides the answers for the marketer whose job it is to sell and market books in today's increasingly competitive bookselling environment.

Whether you are a marketing or sales director, manager or executive, *How to Market Books* shows you best-practice ways to maximize marketing ROIs and deliver top-line growth for your publishing company. Written by Alison Baverstock, Senior Lecturer in Publishing Studies at Kingston University, the new edition has been brought right up to date to include: digital and online marketing; professional and STM publishing; leveraging international sales; and low-cost "guerrilla" marketing. Used throughout the industry, the new edition will ensure that the book maintains its well-earned status as "the bible of book marketing".

Author Information

Alison Baverstock began her career in publishing before setting up a marketing consultancy. She was heavily involved in setting up both the Kingston Readers' festival and the MA in Publishing Studies at Kingston University, where she is a Senior Lecturer. She regularly gives seminars on Publishing Studies at various universities and also lectures on Creative Writing. She has written several books, including *Marketing Your Book: An Authors Guide* and *Is There a Book In You?*

ISBN 13: 9780749450205
Publication: January 2008
Price: £25.00
Binding: Paperback
Extent: 336 pages
Format: 234x153mm

Territory: World
Band: 02
Author residence: London, UK
Subject: Marketing

READERSHIP
Students on publishing courses and graduates just entering the profession, marketing practitioners and directors in publishing houses, independent publishers and booksellers, authors

Previous ISBN 13:
9780749431059

Figure 2.1 A sample advance notice

features, lots of space and relevant 'click-throughs' to encourage browsers find out more. Try to organize your information in a logical manner. Putting the product specifications under 'how to order' may seem logical to you (because they both relate to the information that used to go at the end of catalogue entries), but the customer in a hurry might not think to look there! For more information, see Chapter 6 on using the internet to sell.

BOOK JACKET/COVER COPY

The information on a cover is usually drafted by the editor in consultation with the author. What appears is very important: it often forms the basis of a decision to buy. If you watch how customers in a bookshop assess a new title, you will see that the typical sequence is to look at the front cover, turn to the back for basic information on the title, and if this looks sufficiently interesting, flick through the contents or read the first couple of pages.

The copy should cover all essential sales points:

- why it is interesting (often achieved through a sentence on the front cover – or 'shout line' that is either atmospheric or pithy);
- what is new/unique about the book;
- what it is about (briefly);
- who it is for;
- the scope;
- the author's aim in writing it;
- the author's credentials for doing so (previous well-known titles);
- any quotable extracts from reviews/experts;
- bibliographic details.

The words you use should also give a flavour of the kind of book inside. So don't make a highly complicated textbook sound like an easy read for everyone, or a 'beach read' sound like a contender for a major literary prize. If someone has been misled by one of your cover blurbs before and felt let down by the contents, he or she might be wary of buying from your imprint again.

As regards layout of jacket blurb, do make the text easy to read. Don't centre the text or fit it around 'cut out' pictures so that the reader has to work hard to understand. Keep both sentences and paragraphs short and punchy.

A 'shout line' on the front of the jacket will draw further attention to the title. This is best handled as a summary of the feeling you get from reading the book, rather than as a quick outline of the content. Your best guide for writing effective shout lines is to begin a study of film posters. Thus rather than describing the details of a plot that featured an unknown creature attacking the staff of a spaceship, the poster for *Alien* read: 'In space no one can hear you scream'. Short shout lines work best.

How much of your jacket blurb will actually be read is debatable. Most readers will home in on the beginning and perhaps the end of the text, as Wendy Cope brilliantly captured in a blurb that appeared on the back cover of a promotional piece to advertise *Making Cocoa for Kingsley Amis*:

> Brilliant, original, irreverent, lyrical, feminist, nostalgic, pastoral, anarchic, classical, plangent, candid, witty – these are all adjectives and some of them can truthfully be used to describe Wendy Cope's poems. Very few people bother to read the second sentence of a blurb. Or the third. Most of them skip to the end where it says something like this: a truly spectacular debut, an unmissable literary event.

CATALOGUES

The production of catalogues is one of the main regular activities of those marketing books. Successful management of their preparation and production is vitally important. Not only do they stimulate orders by presenting the firm's wares in an attractive light, they are part of the regular selling cycle which the trade is used to responding to and hence expects. Catalogues are also a lasting form of promotion: once the initial ordering has been done, few are thrown away. For example, in bookshops they continue to function as reference material for enquiries and specific requests, and in schools they act as the reference point for topping up stock levels.

Amassing title information (including all the last-minute entries that will suddenly appear), checking publication and bibliographical details, rounding up illustrations, dealing with design and production – all involve a tremendous amount of detailed work.

How often catalogues are produced depends on the type of list being promoted. Many general houses produce six-monthly catalogues (usually autumn/winter and spring/summer) to fit in with their marketing cycles. The catalogue forms the basic document for presentation at the sales conference that precedes each new selling season. Mass-market paperback houses may produce catalogues or stock lists every month, usually three months ahead of the month of publication. Educational, academic and reference publishers often produce a separate annual catalogue for each subject area in which they publish. In addition, most houses produce a yearly complete catalogue which lists title, author and bibliographical information for their entire list. Most firms produce printed versions but also amend the copy for their website.

The copy contained in a catalogue should vary according to the anticipated readership and use, with the marketing department adapting the basic title information as appropriate. To get ideas on how to present information clearly and attractively, study both the catalogues of your competitors and those of firms which have nothing to do with publishing (eg consumer goods sold by direct mail). The following tips will also be useful.

Space for major titles

Ensure that the allocation of space in your catalogues reflects the relative importance of your various publishing projects. It's very reassuring to customers to know they are buying a successful product. A major scheme or series should stand out as such to the reader: reviews, illustrations and sample pages can all be added to impress. The same goes for backlist titles that are still widely used by the market. If the publisher gives them a poor allocation of space the market will conclude they are scheduled for extinction. Catalogues selling consumer goods often repeat key items within the same edition, so however quickly the potential customer flicks through, the chances are they still note the products the firm really wishes to push.

As a guide to how much space to allow for different titles, try comparing sales figures (real or anticipated) with the available space. At the same time, do try to avoid a rigid space allocation, which is very boring to the reader. For example, the common practice of giving all the big titles a double page at the front of the catalogue, a page each in the middle to the midlist and then putting the 'also rans' as a series of small entries at the back carries a clear message about what is and what is not important.

What most interests the recipient will probably be what is new or revised, so make clear use of flags and headlines to attract attention.

Ordering mechanisms

Include an ordering mechanism with each catalogue (order form, large print reference to the website or telephone number/postcard for obtaining an inspection copy), and monitor the response. Not all orders will come back directly to you, but if you take a note of the recorded sales before a catalogue goes out and a second reading a certain time after most orders have been received, you will have a reasonably accurate picture of how effective the material was. Some publishers take their monitoring a lot further, comparing space allocated with trackable orders (asking customers to quote a reference – or the 'long number next to your address' – before taking the order – standard practice in many industries), to produce an analysis of revenue per page. Such information over a number of years will enable you to assess the merits of different layouts and the effect they have on sales.

Offering a variety of different ordering mechanisms also gives useful feedback. Don't assume that the easiest method of ordering for you also meets the needs of your customers. You can test the benefits of order forms that are bound in as opposed to loose inserts or stiff order forms that fold out from the cover; those that require the customer to list titles selected against those that provide the information, requiring only a tick to purchase. Similarly do your customers prefer to use your website, and how easy do they find it to navigate? (A quick question at the end of the ordering process – perhaps incentivized with free entry into a prize draw – can help you find out.) Different methods of payment too can be tested against each other. One final tip: have you noticed how consumer mailings often enclose two order forms with any catalogue? In so testable a medium it must be working. What other tricks can you learn from them?

Layout

The presentation of information within a catalogue should be clear. On each page (or screen) it should be instantly obvious which section is being referred to, perhaps by the use of 'running heads' showing section titles along the top (eg imprint and fiction/non-fiction). Educational publishers often use 'running heads' to indicate the age for which material is designed or the curricular subject area.

Ensure there is both a table of contents (highlighting key new products with page references) and an index. Both are vital for accessing information in a hurry.

Cover

Put photos of your product(s) on the front of your catalogue. It is far more interesting to the recipient than 'new autumn books from Dodd and Co'. Can you imagine consumer mailers putting only the words 'new items from us' on the front of their catalogue? They want you to start reading product information as soon as possible. If you don't use a product, try a really attractive and appropriate illustration. Educational publishers have been known to produce posters for schools of popular catalogue covers.

For catalogues that will be used in one-to-one selling, for example by the rep visiting schools or bookshops, a light-coloured background on the front cover allows notes to be written, and noticed later on by the recipient.

For lists aimed at a particular vocational market (eg school books, ELT materials) a letter, perhaps from the editor, on the inside front cover of the catalogue can attract wide readership. It should always have a signature and look like a letter. Such a start to the catalogue can serve to introduce the list, attract attention to particular highlights and express an interest in the readers' ideas for publications (always a good way of ensuring the catalogue gets retained!).

Illustrations

Include as much illustration as possible. Covers are the first choice, particularly for a series. However prominently you write 'series' in the copy, the sight of a group of covers is more eye-catching and hence effective.

Avoid featuring covers that are too subtle and 'designer' in appearance. What you see at full size will disappear when reproduced at postage-stamp size. Similarly, check that the titles on reduced covers are still legible. You can also use illustrations (always with a selling caption), sample pages, photographs (perhaps of the materials in action) and line drawings.

Academic catalogues

Full author affiliations and contents are vital. Which qualifications/academic level do the various titles prepare students for? A mixture of different types of institution and author location always helps sell a title more widely. Can the authors also recruit endorsers for you?

Try to keep entries to a single page, avoiding the practice of taking a few lines over to the next one. The fate of catalogues mailed to academics is often for specific entries to be cut out or photocopied and circulated with a view to purchase. Carrying over copy makes the task more difficult and is annoying.

Last-minute entries

However well posted your catalogue deadlines are, last-minute copy on titles that simply must be included will always appear. Bear in mind that if you wait for every last correction you will never get to the market, and getting to the market when the market is expecting your information (and when your competitors' details will be there) is what really matters.

If your deadline is past and the costs of remaking pages to include a particular important extra title are unjustified, try including the copy on a 'stop press postcard'. This can also function as an order form/inspection copy request card – and the author may welcome stock for handing out at speaking engagements.

What else to do with your catalogue copy

Finally, a word of warning. Whilst most publishers need both website copy and catalogue copy, it seldom works to just load the catalogue information, as it is, onto the website. It needs first to be reworked for a different medium, to which viewers offer a much shorter attention span.

LEAFLETS AND FLYERS

Flyers are cheaply produced leaflets. In general, I would count anything with a fold or more than two colours as a leaflet, and single sheets as flyers. If you are producing a range of flyers for insertion in mailings and handing out at exhibitions, do make them look different. I once produced a range of slim leaflets advertising science titles. Each one was printed in black ink on yellow paper, one-third A4 size. The results were very eye-catching, but when attending a conference I noticed that delegates examining our stand, where they were laid out in separate piles, clearly assumed that they all advertised the same title. Thereafter I used a different colour stock for each leaflet.

The information you provide will depend on the purpose for which the leaflet/flyer is to be used, but in general try to make the format suit as many possible anticipated needs as you can. You can then add a letter to turn it into a mailshot, enclose in journals as a loose insert, send out with a press release to provide further title information, or insert in parcels. Give details of how to order; the space can be left blank on a bookstore version for over-stamping with the shop's name and address.

DIRECT MAILSHOTS

See Chapter 5, Direct marketing.

PRESS RELEASES

See Chapter 7, 'Free' advertising.

PRESENTERS AND BROCHURES

Many trade publishing houses produce these for reps to use when presenting new titles to bookstore buyers, and in particular to impress their key accounts. Presenters often form substantial (from four to six sides of card) glossy summaries of media and promotional plans, and anticipated spend for individual titles and their supporting backlist. Usually produced in full colour, they are often laminated or at least varnished.

When bookstore buyers are busy and reps have little time in which to attract their overstretched attention, such promotion pieces can play a key part in getting the importance of the title and its associated image across quickly. With luck, a corresponding commitment to take stock will follow.

Copy for these needs to be short and market focused: you are trying to persuade the bookstore to stock rather than to tell them details of the plot. Thus information relevant to the bookstore should have priority (what promotional highlights have been arranged, how the author's previous title sold and so on).

POSTERS, SHOWCARDS AND POINT OF SALE

These are produced by publishers and distributed to bookstores to attract customers' attention to major books, series or imprints at the place where they are available for purchase. The market's understanding should be instant, so such material should not be too copy-heavy or clever (eight words on a poster site is usually plenty). Sometimes they are not even put up in stores that accept them, but they still serve to demonstrate to the bookshop that a publisher is highlighting a major product, and so form an effective method of ensuring advance orders. The most attractive items may be put up in the staff room, or taken home, so it's a good idea to include a few copies rather than just one.

Dumpbins, which carry multiple copies of a key title, are often produced to encourage booksellers to take a large quantity of stock. These usually have a header which slots into the top of the box to attract attention. Use this space creatively. Avoid repeating the book title here, as it will feature on every cover beneath.

The days of one-size-fits-all for dumpbins have gone forever. Several bookshop chains now refuse to take them altogether, on the grounds that they interrupt the shop's designed environment and they have their own material. You may be required to produce dumpbins to the exact space requirements of other outlets such as supermarkets – usually worth it if a large stock order results.

Other point of sale items may include give-away items such as balloons, bookmarks, badges, shelf wobblers and mobiles. Sometimes these prove so popular as branded items that they can become a product range in their own right, and of course this has the hugely valuable function of further promoting the list, while producing income. For example a fiction house produced T-shirts for a sales conference with the image of the first covers it put out, 50 years before, and they proved so popular that it ended up marketing a range through shops. As a guide to whether you have a winner on your hands, anything that other people try to purloin (or steal) is usually a good investment.

SPACE ADVERTISEMENTS

For advice on promoting to specific interest markets, see Chapter 11. For advice on whether or not advertising can pay, see Chapter 10.

Classified ads

Classified advertising is one of the cheapest methods of promotion. Copy is usually typeset by the publication in which it is to appear. With little space, no illustration and lots of similar advertisements to compete with, try to use the variables that are at your disposal to attract attention. Experiment with different type densities, capital and lower-case letters. Quote established authorities such as those with professional qualifications. Give an incentive to do something now, such as look up the website or ring for a free catalogue.

For ideas on how to handle the medium well, consult the classified section of a magazine that is well known for its amusing and effective entries.

Semi-display ads

A step up from classified advertising, semi-display allows borders and illustrations. Don't take the permission to use reversed-out text too seriously, it is hard to read. Do allow plenty of white space around the advertisement – it serves to draw the eye in. Have a look through your local trade directories to see how effective – or otherwise – the use of a small advertising space can be.

Advertorials

Advertorials are advertisements that masquerade as editorial copy. In an editorially biased magazine or paper, advertising guru David Ogilvy reckoned six times as many people read the average editorial feature as the average advertisement.

Use the same typeface, caption illustrations in the same way, and use the same 'editorial' style as the rest of the publication. You may find that 'Advertisement' or 'Advertisement Feature' is printed by the magazine at the top of your space, but your message will gain in authority and readership and more people will remember it. For precisely these reasons some magazines do not allow advertorials. One word of caution: be careful that you don't end up paying for what the magazine would have printed free, as a feature.

Along similar lines is 'sponsored editorial', whereby the customer takes advertising space in return for a commitment from the magazine to provide editorial coverage.

INFORMATION FOR TELESALES CAMPAIGNS

See Chapter 5, Direct marketing.

RADIO ADS

Radio ads have been used very successfully for books in recent times. The launch of new commercial radio stations has offered cheap opportunities to reach highly targeted groups of people. Tying the commercials up with promotional offers such as competitions can secure a wealth of coverage at very competitive prices. Listening to the radio creates a cosy empathy between audience and station, and this can work particularly well in the promotion of books. Most memorable ads tell a story.

TELEVISION AND CINEMA ADS

The chance to prepare these will occur rarely in the lives of most publishing marketers. When publishing houses can afford to mount television campaigns they usually assign them to specialized agencies. But there is no harm in knowing the tricks of the trade: it will make you a more discerning buyer of out-house services, and you may get a crack some time. Small budgets can pay for regional television and radio advertising, and new channels may offer further opportunities.

If you are choosing between press and television as the best medium for a campaign, in general the less there is to explain about a product, the better suited it is to television. Cheaper, mass-market products too work better on television; if customers are being asked to spend a lot of money they need a fuller explanation of benefits than is possible during an average-length advertisement. An alternative is to give a telephone number or website address for further information at the end of the commercial.

3

Techniques for writing effective copy

Promotional copywriting is the art of producing the words that make up the campaign. It means selling through words, whether they are circulated on screen or in print. A copywriter's key objective is not to show they have a novel in them or display a noteworthy style, which perhaps drew particular praise from their English teacher at school, but to get customers to buy the product; to put across what I believe is our main aim:

> A believable promise aimed at the right audience.

So if you have been asked to write copy for a product and don't know where to start, or if you want to improve your writing techniques, this chapter will provide guidance.

NO RULES

The first rule for would-be copywriters is that there *are* no rules. The very practice of laying down rules for writing would result in wooden and stilted copy, 'formula writing'. Nor is past skill at literary criticism any guarantee of success. You may have thought a degree in English literature, or a high

A-level grade, excellent grounding for a future to be spent writing copy, but many such worthy candidates find freedom from linguistic rules off-putting.

Suddenly you have an immense amount of freedom: to start sentences with 'and' or 'but'; to use dashes rather than colons and semi-colons; to miss out the verb in a phrase altogether if the message is clear without it; to ignore the skills acquired during precis lessons and repeat your basic sales message again and again, each time in slightly different words. All become techniques at your disposal in the wider aim of attracting attention to the product you are promoting.

WRITING ABOUT THINGS YOU DON'T LIKE OR DON'T UNDERSTAND

Along with a consciousness of your own writing style, out must go your partiality for particular products. The copywriters' job is to do an effective sales job for whatever they are promoting, even if they personally think it is not worth reading. It is your job to put yourself into the frame of mind of would-be readers, and to think what they might look for from the product. It can also be very difficult writing about something for which you have a great passion, as whatever you draft does not seem praise enough.

Given that publishing attracts more arts than science graduates, marketing staff often find themselves working on scientific and technical products of which they have no understanding. I have been in this position myself, and I think people often do a better job writing about something with which they are unfamiliar, as they are forced to ask a series of questions: who is it for, what does it do, how does the customer benefit?

Although I said there are no general rules for successful writing, this chapter makes plenty of suggestions. We shall start with five basic principles and then continue with ad hoc suggestions.

FIVE BASIC PRINCIPLES

Think in detail about the market and the product before you start working out what to say

The best copywriting starts with thinking rather than writing. However tempting it is to get started, and however many other priorities you have competing for your time, if you do the thinking as you write, what you produce will be more muddled, and it will take you longer.

So before you start, immerse yourself in an understanding of the market you are writing to and the product you are writing about. Why do people need it? How does it compete on price with the competition? How will people pay for it? What other options do they have (not necessarily all books – they may find buying a DVD just as relaxing as reading a novel)? Can you picture a member of the market? Your copy is far more likely to be effective if it is personal. Summon up an image of a typical member of the market and then explain to that person one-to-one.

You will find it easier to get on to other people's wavelengths on a regular basis if you start varying your own reading and listening habits. So don't just read the same newspaper/news website or watch/listen to the same news programme every day (it will simply confirm your impression that everyone is as reasonable as you are). Read different ones, tabloid and broadsheet, commercial and public service, and see how different media report the same stories.

Similarly, try to widen the opinions you hear. You can probably guess the opinions of your close friends and family on a wide range of issues, but how about those outside your immediate circle? The most useful asset for any would-be copywriter is a strong curiosity.

Avoid grammatical howlers

If you are promoting the written word it's vital that your sales message is error-free. Check your work carefully for mistakes such as the combination of singular verbs and plural subjects, misspellings, and in particular, avoid the split infinitive (see glossary). This is not because it is wrong, but because most people believe it to be so. The split infinitive will attract the attention of many who ignore far more casual uses of the English language; they will stop reading your message and start congratulating themselves on catching you out. Their conclusions will be that if a publisher can't get such a basic grammatical point right its books must be unreadable.

Watch out, too, for the confusion of similar words with different meanings, such as accept and except, principle and principal, affect and effect.

Avoid 'isms'

Make no assumptions about the market you are writing to. You will offend part of it when (not if) you get it wrong. For example, ensure your copy is not sexist. Do not write to the business community as 'Dear Sir' or assume all nurses are female. You must qualify every 'him' with an 'or her' to show that what you say is equally applicable to both sexes. Alternatively, it is now acceptable to use plural pronouns (eg they, their, them) with singular subjects (eg anyone).

Some markets are particularly sensitive. Schools today are at the forefront of promoting equality of opportunity. All teacher training courses emphasize its importance, and schools are required to have a range of written policies on the subject. You might write a brochure to schools of complete sexual equality, yet include in your accompanying letter a couple of references to the masculine pronoun alone, and your material will start arousing the wrong kind of reaction. People who might have ordered will use the reply envelope to let you know how strongly they disapprove. (That does not mean that sexist language is offensive only in mailshots – just that direct mail is one of the few advertising methods that gives you direct feedback.)

The same rule applies to all the other 'isms' of today: racism, ageism and so on, although in these cases, as it is harder to offend through words alone, you should pay particular attention to the illustrations that accompany your text.

Avoid the predictable

Do not write exactly what the market expects: we do not bother to read an advertisement if from a cursory look we already know (or can guess) the content. This does not mean that you have to compensate by tending towards obscurity or outrageousness, just that to be interesting – and therefore get read – advertising should be slightly unexpected. And just to prove that rules exist only to be broken from time to time, an occasional cliché can be the copywriter's best friend, if skilfully used.

Never forget that the market has a choice

The assignments you wrote at school or university had to be read in order to be given a mark. Not so with copy: the market has plenty of other options and will only read what you send if it is interesting and relevant. Or to put it another way, as advertising creative director Andrew Sullivan said, 'The only people waiting to see your next ad are you, your client and your Mum.'

HOW TO LEARN MORE ABOUT WRITING WELL

Many publishing houses offer courses in copywriting, and there is also distance learning available (see the Bibliography for suggestions). Your principal option however is to learn on the job, from other people you work with/for and from the wider world of advertising. Teach yourself by gaining access to all the promotional material you can. Watch what your competitors are producing, and compare it with the past and current efforts of your own publishing house. Build an awareness of what makes for good and bad advertising. Learn to recognize good copy and formats that get frequently repeated, in particular those that are used in direct response advertising: they must work. Read a good book on the subject (again see the Bibliography).

Although there are no rules for writing copy, there are some useful acronyms for thinking about what you write. I think these work particularly well as mantras to keep in your head, or as a readily available method of judging what you have written. Slavishly working through them, letter by letter, is more likely to result in predictable copy. These acronyms are followed by a discussion of other techniques and ideas worth considering. This chapter finishes with a look at two parts of the promotion piece for which the copy is particularly vital, the headline and the ordering device, followed by a discussion of how to unscramble particularly difficult copy.

ACRONYMS

Acronyms are words formed from the initial letters of other words, for example NATO, SWALK (sealed with a loving kiss) and the more recent TLI (three-letter initials). The publishing industry seems to embrace the use of initials with particular enthusiasm; each house has developed its own terms.

AID(C)A

AIDA has been around for over 50 years: it is one of the best-known copywriting acronyms. Originally it served as a structure for writing direct mail letters, but it works equally well as a guide to writing e-mails, press advertisements, leaflets, telemarketing scripts and other promotional formats. It was recently updated with the addition of a 'C', and so now stands for Attract, Interest, Desire, Conviction, Action.

Attract

What is it about an advertisement or piece of promotional material that first attracts the reader's eye? It may be a stunning photograph, an attractive layout, the subject line on an e-mail, a message on the envelope of a mailshot, a personalized name and address at the start of a sales letter, a headline or slogan on a space advertisement or billboard. Whatever it is, if you start thinking about the process of attracting attention and start noticing what grabs yours, you are well on the way to writing successful copy yourself.

Interest

Once you have secured the reader's attention, your next task is to keep it: advertising guru David Ogilvy reckoned five times as many people read the headline as the text beneath. You must develop the copy in such a way that the reader stays with you, absorbing the sales message as he or she goes.

Explain the benefits of the product; use subheadings to assist readers who want to 'skim' before they read in detail. Talk logically through the sales points in a tone that is friendly without being either condescending or patronizing.

Desire

As you stimulate interest, create a desire to own or benefit from the product you are describing. Be enthusiastic: it's worth having! Will the reader be one of the first to benefit from this new kind of information source? Are stocks limited? Is there a pre-publication offer so that the reader will save money if the order is placed before a particular date? Has it already taken the United States by storm? Provide all the reasons you can to create the desire to purchase.

Conviction

Provide proof: testimonials, review quotes, how long it took to develop and trial the material now about to be published, the current sales trends, your cast-iron guarantee which shows your company's great confidence in the product.

Action

Lastly, direct the reader to take the action necessary to secure the product you have described. What is the publication date and where is it available? If you take direct orders make it easy to do so: offer freepost, the chance to order by telephone, fax or computer link and pay by credit card. Restate the comforting guarantee: your security procedures; if the buyer is not completely satisfied there is a full refund.

Look at the example in Figure 3.1 and notice how every stage is catered for, from the headline that attracts, to the additional proofs that provide objective feedback on why the qualification is worth taking. The telephone number and website are very clearly marked for action, and in the hot spot, the bottom right-hand corner, are all the reassuring brand logos that confirm the message.

FAB

This stands for Features, Advantages and Benefits: a useful checklist to ensure that your copy is relevant and interesting to the market. Many copywriters get no further than listing features. These need to be converted into what really interests the reader – benefits. Here are two examples, one from general advertising, the other from publishing:

New Snibbo toothpaste contains newly researched ingredient XPZ2. (feature)
Which reaches the plaque that covers your teeth, even in hard to reach places. (advantage)

Figure 3.1 Sample advert from the Open University Business School

Which means you and your family need fewer fillings. (benefit)

This new maths course has been extensively piloted in schools to ensure it meets the needs of a wide range of abilities. (feature)
Which means the whole class can be using the same material at the same time. (advantage)
Which means you get more time to concentrate on individual needs. (benefit)

The same principle was also neatly summed up as 'Sell the sizzle, not the sausage.'

Publishers are rather prone to describe how their systems work: how particular products came to be developed or how they are available for inspection. The market is far more interested in what benefits come from the product or service being offered than what product features help the publisher distinguish it from all the other titles available. Too often publishers simply state that a product is available rather than saying either how the market could benefit, or how else people could use their time.

For example, consider the advertisement in Figure 3.2. Rather than just offering a mown lawn, the writer makes an imaginative leap to talk about what else the happy recipient of the service could be doing with his or her time. This is easily replicable within publishing. Sometimes I read books because they are what other people are talking about, or because I feel I ought to, but more often it's because of the way I want to feel: relaxed, excited or involved. When reading stories to children, it's the shared time, the cuddle that is important, and when reading the same story again and again (which is what very small children like), the language is particularly vital. I find this is something publishers rarely mention.

USP

The search for a Unique Selling Proposition for every product was at its height in America in the 1950s. A USP is what makes a product different from everything else on the market; if one was not immediately apparent it had to be invented. Here are some examples of a USP providing an identity for products that are in reality very similar to others on the market:

Minstrels: 'The chocolates that melt in your mouth, not in your hand.'

AVAILABLE SHORTLY

BY

BPM GRASS CUTTING SERVICES

A superior grass cutting service at an affordable price. Save yourself all the hassle. Just think of all the things you could do with your family instead!!!

Yes I will cut your grass for only £7.50, and leave your lawn in a neat & tidy state.

No more hard days at the office followed by a hard couple of hours struggling with that five-a-side pitch out the back.

Let me do all the graft while you count out a mere £7.50 in freshly minted coins of the realm.

<u>Please annotate your preference below:</u>

❑   Yes please, come and save me from the tortures of mowing the lawn (as I can't afford any goats)

❑   No thanks, I find gardening hard graft and a bit of a pain, but it'll save me £7.50

Name

Address

I WILL COLLECT THESE FLYERS IN THE NEXT COUPLE OF DAYS. MANY THANKS FOR YOUR RESPONSE.
BEN McDANIEL

Figure 3.2   A sample ad for a grass-cutting service

Esso: 'Put a tiger in your tank.'
easyJet: 'Come on, let's fly.'

Today the practice is no longer obligatory. Some products are deliberately very similar to their competitors (known as the 'me too' market) and are best promoted on the basis of similarity, value for money or simply how strongly people feel about a product. John Hegarty of advertising agency Bartle, Bogle and Hegarty commented, 'Advertising has moved from the USP to the ESP, or emotional selling proposition. Product quality differences are far less, because technology has moved forwards so much. So today it's a matter of how you feel about a brand' (quoted in the *Sunday Times*, 18 April 1999). Nevertheless, if your early product investigations make you aware that the title you are promoting is unique (new to the market, a completely new look at the subject, new format, etc), make the most of it.

WIIFM?

Everyone reading promotional material or responding to advertising has this question in mind, and if the question is satisfactorily answered they will keep reading, right to the end. The message is: What's In It For Me?
And lastly:

KISS

Explain yourself clearly. Don't be over-complicated or verbose. In other words: Keep It Simple, Stupid!

FURTHER TECHNIQUES FOR EFFECTIVE WRITING

Write clearly and logically

Once you have established all the sales benefits of the product you are promoting, rank them and use them in order: one idea per sentence, one theme per paragraph. Use short sentences. David Ogilvy reckoned that the first sentence of advertisement body copy (the text that follows the headline) should contain no more than 11 words. Thereafter ensure sentence length is varied to avoid monotony. Use words from everyday speech (demotic language), and don't use long phrases where single words would do. For example:

> Use 'most' instead of 'a great deal of'.
> Use 'respected' instead of 'widely acclaimed'.
> Use 'consider' instead of 'take into consideration'.

Writer Georges Simenon (the creator of the detective Maigret) deliberately stuck to a vocabulary of just 2,000 words so that his books could be understood by everyone. Dr Seuss's famous book for children *Green Eggs and Ham* has just 50 words, and yet is never dull.

Use short words (often Saxon in origin) rather than long ones (often from Latin). For example:

> Use 'news' or 'facts', not 'information'.
> Use 'find' not 'discover'.
> Use 'show' not 'demonstrate'.
> Use 'now' not 'immediately'.

On the other hand, the occasional use of long words can attract attention, particularly if they are surrounded by monosyllabic terms that throw them into further relief. Prince Charles' use of 'carbuncle' at a speech to the Royal Institute of British Architects was well chosen. Positioned among short familiar words it had an added bite: 'what is proposed is a monstrous carbuncle on the face of a much-loved friend'. If he had instead described 'a monstrous carbuncle on the frontage of an elegant and familiar 19th-century Palladian-style building in a much-visited central London attraction', the words would have received much less emphasis.

Similarly, the linking of very different words (oxymorons) can be most effective. For example:

> Dangerously romantic
> Ridiculously bloodthirsty

Try to use vivid words, rather than stale ones:

Vivid	Stale
hate	dislike

adore	love
cash	money

Use active verbs, not passive. For example:

Use 'You can see' not 'It can be seen ...'.

Better still, use an imperative:

See how ...
Watch!

The present tense implies action, for example:

Use 'Research shows' not 'Research has shown ...'.
Use 'The author talks to' not 'The author was interviewed'.

Steer clear of over-used words. I am grateful to bookseller Justine Crow (www.booksellercrow.co.uk) for the following list of words that make her yawn. They appear in order of frequency:

unique ('almost unique' is even worse and makes no sense)

major	moving
timely	exciting
a must	heart-rending
outstanding	hilarious
exceptional	invaluable
revolutionary	essential
brilliant	remarkable
eye-catching	compelling
absolutely fabulous	original
unputdownable	wicked (in particular of children's books)
author at the height of his/her powers	... and nothing is quite what it seems

... nothing will ever be the same again
... she is left holding the baby, literally
... this book is bound to be a success
... more frightening than anyone could have imagined in their worst nightmares.

So as not to be negative, here are words from recent campaigns that did catch her eye and got her reading the rest of the copy:

high-rolling	enrapturing
twizzling	engrossing
exuberant	vital
banal	frisky
bizarre	striking
abrasive	inestimable
eye-washing	incomparable
delirious	

Justine commented, 'I believe the secret of good copy is enjoyment. If I, as a buyer, find that I am relishing what I read, I will enjoy actually selling the product and buy more from you.'

You should also avoid publishingese – words that mean different things to those involved with books from the rest of the population. For example, the heavily over-used 'accessible' means to the rest of the world that you don't have to stand on a step ladder to reach it. Similarly, avoid using in-house jargon – most of the population haven't a clue what a 'C format paperback' is.

Get to the point. Avoid long flowing sentences of introduction. Home straight in on the main benefits to the reader. When dealing with complex subjects with which they are not wholly familiar, many copywriters use the first paragraph to work their way into the subject, to demonstrate their understanding. Readers are not interested – get on with what is in it for them. It is remarkable how often simply deleting the first paragraph will improve the readability of copy.

Don't be clever or pompous, even when you are writing to an audience that is either or both. Imagine you were explaining the benefits to a prospect face to face: you would be concentrating on the product, not your presentational style. Many people assume that when writing to academics or high-powered business people they should produce a suitably lofty tone. Avoid this. It slows the reader down and impedes access to benefits. What is more, if you are not expert in the subject, you may get the jargon wrong or sound patronizing. Academics get enough tortuous prose from their students (usually downloaded from the web).

Don't drone on about your company. The average reader could not care less; it is the specific product that has attracted their attention. If there is information that is relevant to the product give it, but spare the reader the rest of the potted company history. The following is plenty:

This new 20-volume work comes from the publishers of the respected *Everyperson Encyclopaedia*, and was researched and written with the same accuracy and attention to detail.

Avoid flowing passages of purple prose, even if you are particularly pleased with them. Indeed, your own admiration for sections of your work should be your guide to what needs deleting. If it stands out to you as a particularly good use of words it will probably strike the reader in the same way, and slow down reading flow. Or as G K Chesterton put it, 'Murder your babies.'

Cut down on your sentence length

Long sentences are tiring on the eyes, and the market has plenty of other things to get on with. Cut down your sentence length and you make your message easier to read.

Here is an example of publishing copy:

An introductory survey of the history and the principles and practice of citizenship, based on the premise that the current conditions and debates about citizenship cannot be fully understood without a knowledge of the historical background.

By amalgamating the ideas, and dividing the content into two sentences, you make the message easier to absorb:

Citizenship is impossible to understand without a grasp of its historical background. Here is a complete introductory survey of its principles and practice.

Tell a story, talk to the reader, adopt a tone of sweet reason

This is best achieved by completing the research on the product, noting down the main sales points and then writing from memory. By doing this you explain the benefits to yourself as you write, and your copy is more likely to be convincing.

Overcome any objections the reader may think of while reading, perhaps by using question and answer panels, for example:

Why is this new biography needed?
Who will use this manual?

While a controversy may raise interest, it's not a good idea to be confrontational in copy, or to provide material for readers to argue with. The result will be that they stop reading altogether, either to analyse their reaction in more detail or through sheer annoyance. Your sales message is wasted.

Let the copy flow. Use linking phrases so that the text reads fluently. Copywriter Roger Millington calls these phrases 'buckets and chains':

And of course …	For example …
At the same time …	This includes …
Not to mention …	In addition …
Did you realize…	On the other hand …
After all …	Finally I must mention …
Just as important …	Two final points …

Make your copy personal. This means using 'you' rather than 'one' or 'they', and relating the examples you use to the interests of the reader. For example, instead of:

One-third of the population will develop cancer at some time in their lives; for 20 per cent of the population it will eventually be terminal.

try:

One in three people get cancer; one in five die from it.

or:

You have a one in three chance of getting cancer, and a one in five chance of dying from it.

Quote actual people rather than statistics. For example, instead of:

20,000 copies sold

try:

> 20,000 art lovers have already bought this book.

Keep editing

Write long and then cut back to the essentials. Are there still words that are not really necessary to the sense and which you could manage without? Delete extra adverbs and adjectives: they slow the reader down. Avoid the language of property sales: a bland and predictable prose, where one adjective is never used where two can be squeezed in (a practice that seems to be spreading with alarming rapidity). For example:

> this perfect and handy ground floor apartment
> a convenient and well-positioned house
> a useful and timely book.

You don't need both; one, three or none might attract more interest.

Structure the layout of benefits and selling points

Don't oversell: don't provide more selling points than the reader needs to reach a buying decision. One or two may be plenty. Your final copy doesn't need to make use of everything you have thought of: use too many selling arguments and the market can feel bullied.

Don't end the page or column of copy with a full stop. Make the text 'run over' so that the reader is encouraged to continue.

Writers of mailshots often save the biggest benefit for the end of the sales letter, perhaps putting it in the PS (regarded as one of the most highly read parts of the letter). There will be hints that this big benefit is coming for those who read from the start, to encourage them to keep going.

Divide up your copy

If you walk along a street of terraced houses with no front gardens you will find your eye is automatically attracted to the first gap, perhaps a side street or a house set back from the road. Look at a page of text and the effect is the same: see how your eye is sucked into the spaces.

There is another reason. Most of us are short of time, and faced with a page of text (even if we have written it) we 'skim read', homing in on the features we find most interesting. Use this information to manipulate your readers, encouraging them to be attracted to the sections and features most crucial to your message.

For the same reason, think carefully about asking for text to be set 'justified' (with both right and left margins vertically aligned). Use a ragged right-hand margin to attract the reader's eye into white space. Aim for visual variety. Ensure your paragraphs and sentences are of varied lengths. Short sentences attract attention: try this technique at the beginning or end of paragraphs. It works.

Use bullet points (heavy dots at the beginning of each line) for a list of short selling points. Beware of over-bulleting just because you can think of a large number of benefits to highlight: the text can end up looking riddled and the effect of sharpening the reader's attention is lost. The magic number is three, and five or six is the maximum you should ever use. However many you use, ensure they are different shapes – a long list of identically shaped short lines does not invite the reader in.

Subheadings attract attention to your main selling points. Each one can be fully explained in the paragraph that follows.

> Try indenting paragraphs for extra emphasis, using both the right hand of the page and the left for maximum effect.

Number your paragraphs. Use underlines and CAPITAL LETTERS (sparingly though). Print in bold or in a different typeface. Your software will allow you to produce a variety of wonderful effects, but do be careful that your finished text doesn't resemble a sampler designed to show the machine's capabilities rather than an advertisement. If you put copy in a box, try putting a tint behind the box, or reverse the text out (that is, making it paler than the background, but use reversed-out text sparingly as it is harder to read).

Many readers who cannot be bothered to read a whole page of text will have their attention caught by illustrations. So ensure every picture has a caption, and that the captions pass on the main sales benefits. Tables and bar charts divide up the copy and, armed with captions, reinforce your message.

Give facts, not opinions. Qualify every statement you make. If you don't, doubt may creep into the reader's mind as to the validity of your arguments. So instead of:

widely used in major companies

say where (with permission):

in extensive use at Astra Zeneca and BP.

This prize-winning book …

Winner of the 2008 Belling prize for scientific research.

This new work is based on extensive research.

These two volumes are the result of over 20 years' research in the Wedgwood family archives, the British Museum and other sources. Publication marks the first time that the subject has been explored in such detail.

Review quotations are more valuable to the reader than your opinion, but when deciding which ones to use, choose those from journals best known to the market, even if the comments are slightly less complimentary than those that appeared in less well-known journals.

Don't make the reader sound stupid

You probably don't realize that this new research has been published.

That is not a good line to take: it sounds patronizing and may alienate, particularly if the reader does realize! How about:

Market research showed us that many people did not realize that this new research was available. I am therefore writing …

This shifts the blame from the reader to the publisher.

Using the negative

The use of the negative can confuse your message. You risk your reader missing the negative or associating the negative with your product. So, instead of:

> If you do not find this title essential to your everyday work we will refund your money

try:

> You will find yourself consulting this title every working day or we will refund your money.

Using humour

Avoid humour unless you are a very good writer. As copywriter Claude Hopkins said, 'No one buys from a clown.'

Repeat yourself

Someone once spelt out the basic theory of writing a direct mail sales letter, and the practice can be extended to many other promotional formats where there is space to develop an argument, such as brochures and press releases:

■ Tell them what you are going to tell them.
■ Then tell them.
■ Then tell them what you have just told them.

Although it makes sense to repeat yourself, do so in different words each time. Don't be boring. Probably the dullest start to any advertisement is to repeat either the title of the book or the headline. Equally boring are:

> This new book is …
> This new title is …

It's often best to start in the middle of a sentence, with the present participle.

For example:

> Brings a whole new understanding to …
> Offers readers a completely new experience …

Get used to using a thesaurus

The most difficult word to find a synonym for is 'book'. Try the following: new edition, title, report, work, text, study, or qualify the book as a casebook, sourcebook or reference book. In some circumstances, describing a title as a book may sound insufficiently expensive or well researched, in which case you could try volume, compendium, dossier or other alternatives.

Other ideas for attracting attention

Feature the author. Is he or she controversial, newsworthy, interesting in his or her own right? Allow the new book to be promoted on the back of the name; to the media the personality is often more interesting than the fact that he or she has written a book.

Invent/use a character to use in the promotion. Several school publishers have lifted characters from their software programmes and illustrated schemes to enliven their promotion material.

Offer a firm guarantee. It shows complete confidence in your product and can compensate for asking for money up front. Challenge the reader. Are you offering the best value for money, a fantastic read or your money back? You'll be surprised how very few people claim refunds; far more will be impressed by your immense certainty that your product is excellent.

General advertisers can link their promotions to themes the public will find interesting. In *The Craft of Copywriting* (1987), Alastair Crompton lists the following:

■ animals;
■ cars;
■ entertainment;
■ holidays;
■ royalty;
■ sport;
■ weddings.

■ babies;
■ disasters;
■ fashion;
■ money;
■ sex;
■ war;

Think how closely this list follows the chief headline interests of the tabloid press.

See also Chapter 5 on direct marketing, and Chapter 8 on other promotional ideas: competitions, incentives, free samples, news sheets and much more.

TOPPING AND TAILING YOUR PROMOTION MATERIAL

When looking at an advertisement or promotional feature most readers instinctively do two things. First they look at the headline, then they look at the bottom of the page to see who is advertising. This means that the information presented in these two places is absolutely vital. A good headline can grasp the reader's attention and set the tone for an interesting advertisement; an effective 'signing-off block' can restate the main sales benefits and urge the reader to buy.

Yet still many publishers' advertisements start with information that is interesting to themselves rather than their customers. 'New from Snodgrass and Wilkins' is accurate, and may even be interesting if the firm has a world-renowned geography list and the feature appears in the *Geography Teachers' Review*. Too often, though, this approach is the inevitable start to a huge range of advertisements, simply because the copywriter doesn't have time or – dare I suggest – can't be bothered to think of anything else.

Similarly, if you were a rep and had just spent 20 minutes selling a product to a potential customer, the very last thing you would forget would be to ask for the order. Yet many publishers forget the Action stage of AIDCA. What is the point of stimulating interest, desire and finally conviction that your product is the one for them, if you then fail to make it clear how to obtain it?

Here follow some ideas for getting advertising material off to a good start, and for rounding it off to ensure that it produces the right results: orders.

Headlines

■ At the risk of stating the obvious, the headline should go at the top of the page or space. Flick through any recent newspapers or magazine and you will see how your eye is attracted to the bold headline, wherever it appears. If it is sited in the middle of the page and is sufficiently interesting for you to carry on with the rest of the text, you will find yourself reading what is immediately beneath the heading, even if that point is halfway through the explanatory copy.

■ Advertisements attract attention if the copy or look of the material is personal and relevant. So if you are writing for a specific market, name it:
  - Calling all mothers!
  - Important information for all maths teachers.

■ Target benefits to the audience as specifically as possible. Which of the following headlines would be of most interest to Sally Brown, new promotions assistant at Harcourt?
  - How all promotions departments can work more effectively.
  - How all new promotions assistants can do their jobs better.
  - Promoting books? How you can do *your* job better.

■ Don't be ambiguous or clever. Blind headlines (which can only be understood once the rest of the copy has been read) are best avoided. If the meaning is only semi-apparent most readers won't bother to investigate further.

■ One of the most reliable techniques for starting a headline is to ask a question:

> Why? What? Where? How? Who? When?
> How will this book save you time and money?
> Why is everyone talking about this new novel?

■ Start your headline by saying something controversial (preferably something that stimulates debate rather than causes an outright denial and the reader to stop!).

■ Feature a strange word.

■ Use catchwords that are instantly interesting: now, free, introducing, announcing, secret, magic, mother, unique, money off, save, sale, offer closes, guarantee, bargain.

■ Include a promise, for instance, 'A completely new kind of DIY manual: satisfaction or your money back.'

■ Feature news or a new way of using the product you are promoting:

> Why each year over 100,000 new businesses fail.

Use a quotation

David Ogilvy reckoned if you put the headline in quotation marks you increase recall by 25 per cent. So if you have testimonials at your disposal, use them at the top of the ad, or put a comment of your own in inverted commas. Large-size inverted commas attract more attention.

‘How your company can benefit from the latest techniques in marketing’

For backlist titles, are there any favourable reviews that will serve as headlines?

The envelope

If you are mailing your information, put an eye-catching headline on the envelope. State your best offer, or start a story but don't finish it so the reader is encouraged to open the envelope and read on.

How spending £100 on a new reference work will help your company save thousands more ...

If your budget won't stretch to overprinted envelopes a cheaper solution is to have a message that sits on your office franking machine and is reproduced every time an envelope is stamped. The cost is small and the technique works well for simple slogans:

Out now
Who's Who 160th edition
32,000 biographies
From A&C Black

Ask the person who looks after your company's outgoing mail about having one produced.

Coupons and order forms

■ Once you know how much advertising space has been booked, or how big your leaflet is to be, the order form should probably be the first thing to be designed. If potential customers are motivated to buy, it is essential that they find it easy to order. If your order form or coupon is difficult to complete you will reduce response.

■ Learn from the experts how to compile a form that is easy to use. Insurance proposal forms and the annual tax return are excellent examples of clarity. Both provide reversed-out white space for anything the customer has to complete; you can see at a glance whether all the required information has been given.

■ An order form should be a mini version of the advertisement, restating all the main selling points. Start with the chief one:

> Yes, I would like to save on a set of the new *Children's Encyclopaedia*.

■ Do be aware of the number of people reading the magazine or journal in which your advertisement will appear; it may have a far wider circulation than just the original subscriber or purchaser. So if you are providing a tear-off card or coupon for response, ensure that your address and number for telephone orders appear elsewhere on the advertisement. It can happen that people cut out an order form to send, and then find the address is not provided on it, but is back in the advertisement, in the magazine – wherever that is.

■ It is essential to provide addresses for your website, e-mail and telephone numbers, preferably freefone if you are targeting consumers at home. It is reckoned that as many coupons get cut out but don't get sent as do come back. Make sure the system for answering is up and running by the time the promotion goes out. (Ring/try out all the numbers on your order form before you pass for press, just to make sure they are what you say they are.)

■ Consider the position of the order form. 'How to order' should be clearly signposted on the website, and if on the printed page, preferably the bottom right-hand edge of a right-hand page so that it can be accessed with the minimum of disruption to the text. A better option is to ensure your coupon backs on to another ad (rather than text) as readers may be unwilling to chop up journals that are kept for reference. Do ensure your coupon does not back on to another coupon.

Here is a checklist of useful tips on preparing orders forms that produce results:

- Call the form something different: entitlement opportunity, invitation to a demonstration, estimate, hotline, information request, free sample request form.
- Include an envelope so the recipient does not have to hunt for one. Use freepost or business reply for offers to consumers. For business-to-business mail it does not make much difference.
- Put a time limit on the offer.
- Offer a free gift for a prompt response. (Your warehouse is probably full of suitable items.)
- Keep the shape simple – no complicated cut-outs, however pretty they look. You may have seen coupons the shape of the maps or telephones but I bet not many get returned.
- Give e-mail, telephone, fax hotlines. Put little diagrammatic symbols next to them to attract attention, so customers can find the numbers in a hurry and don't ring the wrong one by accident.
- Leave plenty of space for the customer to write his or her name, address and postcode. (It's expensive for your customer services department to have to question the information given. Ask customers for a contact telephone number in case of query.) Always fill in your order form yourself before you finalize it, and ask your customer services staff which questions those filling it in misunderstand or routinely do not have room for.
- Repeat the benefits on the order form.
- Repeat the terms of the offer.
- Test cash up front versus approval.
- Announce which credit cards you accept by showing little pictures of the cards – it attracts attention. Provide enough space to write the whole number, legibly. Avoid little boxes. Be sure to ask whether the card name and address are the same as the orderer's. Provide a space for writing the additional information if necessary.
- Name your product on the order form and show a picture of it if you have room.
- Test third-person copy against first person ('readers have found' rather than 'you will find', which may be a little too close for comfort if the product is of a sensitive nature), and vice versa.
- Test putting all the facts (ISBN, number of pages, etc) against minimal facts.
- Use rushing words to encourage the reader to act immediately – 'rush', 'express', 'now'.

- Personalize the order form by pre-addressing; printing all the recipient's details on the order form. If this is too labour-intensive, or expensive, try sticking the address label on the order form and use a window envelope so it shows through for posting.
- Test integral coupons against separate coupons.
- Test charging postage and packing against giving it free, or make it conditional on the size of order. Similarly, test offering free insurance for larger purchases.
- Add extra tick boxes: for a catalogue, or to hear about future titles in the same field so that customers keep in touch with you even if they do not want to order now.
- Try different colour order forms, or use spot colour on an integral one.
- If your order form is not being perforated, print a dotted line with scissors around the order form to show where it should be detached. Write 'cut here' next to it. Guide people to help you get the order back.
- Include a second order form.
- Stick real postage stamps on the reply device and ensure they are visible through the window of the envelope before it is opened: this increases the reader's perceived value of your mailing package.
- Ask for all the information on your order form that you think you may need in future when you come to contact your customers again. (But beware: if you ask for too much information you may put your customers off responding.)
- Make it clear to whom cheques should be made out.
- Offer the option to buy on standing order (less hassle; no obligation to purchase; a possible discount).
- Code the order form so you can see which list gave you the customer.
- Ask for the name of a friend to whom information on your products should be sent.

WRITING PROMOTIONAL COPY FOR BOOKS YOU DON'T UNDERSTAND

Having to write copy about a product you don't understand, or for a market you don't relate to, is very common in publishing. First, be assured that you don't have to develop a special way of writing if this happens to you. Publisher information is best presented as simply as possible, so avoid long sentences and paragraphs and complicated syntax. Never reprint a lengthy and highly complex advance notice drafted by the author or book's editor, assuming that once it reaches the right market, it will be understood. Remember that your title information will also be read by a range of other people who are not subject specialists: booksellers, reps, librarians and those standing in for academics on leave of absence or maternity leave. One further point: remember that English may not be the recipient's first language.

Before you try to decipher an incomprehensible blurb provided by your editorial department, think about what the market needs to know about the book you are promoting. The market is probably more interested in the treatment of a subject and the up-to-dateness of the content than either publisher reputation or the speed of supply. Asked to rank other information needed in order of importance, repeated surveys of academics have confirmed the following list (in order), and this shows what your priorities should be.

■ list of contents;
■ brief summary of the main features;
■ detailed description of the contents;
■ designated readership and level;
■ information on the author;
■ extracts from review coverage;
■ sample pages;
■ photograph of the cover.

The last item always scores low – I suspect few professionals would admit to being influenced by the look of the jacket – but I still try to feature a book-shot if the budget permits. A well-produced item will always win admirers (and possibly new authors). What is more, if it is a substantial tome that you are promoting, a picture conveys both value for money and the impressiveness of the publication.

The other reason for including the cover is the impression it will make on would-be users. I regularly note how students tend to make quick purchasing decisions on the same basis as they would were they buying clothes or CDs – the look and feel of the product matter hugely. Should not perhaps, but do.

Bibliographical information must be correct, and accurate, not optimistic. Ensure you cover the following:

■ author;	■ title;
■ series (if any);	■ publisher;
■ publication date;	■ page extent;

- ■ illustrations;
- ■ binding;

- ■ ISBN;
- ■ size.

Disentangle long and difficult blurbs

If the first information you receive on a forthcoming title is a long and complicated essay by the book's editor or author, the temptation to reproduce it whole in your leaflet rather than try to simplify it can be enormous, particularly if you have no inkling of the subject matter and are short of time. Remember that most academics can tell by looking at the title and contents whether or not a title is relevant to them, so a detailed list of the contents is always preferable to a long description.

The more you become familiar with the difficult blurb, the more you will come to think you too know what it means. Your first reaction is the one to hang on to. Remember there will be many other non-specialists who need to understand the key selling benefits too.

Where to start? I'm fond of quoting modern artist Cornelia Parker blowing up a garden shed – she then measured the distances to which the pieces fell, threaded each one onto chicken wire and hung them in a corresponding pattern, from the ceiling of the Tate Gallery in London. In the centre there were lots of tiny pieces, but around the edge of the room were all the major chunks (roof, walls, door, window frame). Do the same with the text facing you. Rather than edit it (which simply produces something more complex and even less flowing, a bit like a poor translation), blow it up. Read it slowly, looking out for all the main ideas. Try dividing up long sentences, lifting out the main features and highlighting them as bullet points. Divide up long paragraphs so the copy looks more readable. Explain to the editor (or author) what you are trying to do and ask him or her to check your results.

Avoid starting your copy with a general sentence or paragraph: generalities are usually more concerned with demonstrating your understanding of the subject matter than with the academic's need to know. If it helps you to get started by all means write one, but delete it once you have finished; your arguments should hold water without it. Try to answer the following questions:

- ■ If it is a new edition, what has changed since the previous one? Do you have factual information on the number of items in the index and the number of chapters completely rewritten?

■ If it is a textbook, what course is it for? For what level of students?
■ Who has reviewed or endorsed it, and in what publication? Your own opinion will carry far less weight than that of the academic's peer group.
■ Who is it by? Include qualifications, current position, special areas of research that are relevant to the subject and book.
■ Have you made it clear whether the book is a collection of the writings of several authors or an entirely new book? Make sure you distinguish conference proceedings as just that.
■ How does the recipient get in touch with the publisher? Is there a website or reply mechanism for requesting inspection copies, an e-mail or telephone number for ordering?
■ How will the recipient who wants to order, pay for the title? Is an institutional sale more likely than one to an individual?
■ What payment facilities and what guarantees do you need to offer?
■ Is your copy too 'hard sell'? It is a practice best avoided: it will not be convincing and probably makes the recipient suspicious.

Get rid of all academic 'publishingese' – words that are familiar within the industry but sound bland and unconvincing to the rest of the world. Particular words to look out for are 'prestigious', 'unique' and 'completely comprehensive'. Instead, try defining these terms and explaining precisely how they apply to the product you are promoting, and you will find your description is far more convincing. The following example of academic publishing jargon ironically describes an updated textbook on communications:

> It is written in a clear and accessible style by well-known authors who have used a new streamlined organization and a fresh teaching style.

There are four ideas in this sentence:

■ clear writing style;
■ well-known authors;
■ reorganized content;
■ offering a fresh teaching style.

By running the points into each other, as part of the same sentence, the copywriter has ensured none of them really gets noticed. Instead, you could home in on the more important one, and talk about it in more detail:

This is a famous textbook, but while you may be familiar with the name, the new edition has a completely fresh feel to it.

Alternatively, present the different ideas as bullet points (as noted above).

Academic jargon is more problematic. There may be certain words that you have to include (eg 'postmodern'), as a flag to show that the book deals with current issues! As a final check, have the editor, or author, check what you produce.

An example of unscrambled copy

The following copy reached me in a publisher's catalogue. The author details have been changed.

Cultures of Consumption
Commerce, Masculinities and Social Space in Late Twentieth Century Britain
Geoff Deade

Cultures of Consumption examines the construction of images of masculinity and the effect they have on identity, sexuality and sexual politics. It opens with the public face of male sexuality in consumerism, as represented in the street fashions of hip-hop, rap and house, which encourage men to see themselves sexually. This is followed by an exploration of a range of influences from black and white culture, where men are recreated in the postmodern landscape of the city.

Geoff Deade captures the energy and intertextuality of urban, postmodern culture and those who create its subcultures. He explores the ironies of class, colour and sexuality which he sees represented in it.

I would certainly recommend a more readily understood title or subtitle – the book's major concern seems to be masculinity and that is hardly evident from these. Starting the book blurb with a repetition of the book title is both repetitive and boring; it's far more engaging to begin with a question. And this is a wonderful example of academic jargon, using words that will be familiar to subject specialists but could arouse no more than 'switch off' from those who are not similarly enlightened, but who nevertheless make buying decisions about the book.

This is a title that would feature on the 'recommended reading' part of a reading list; it is not a textbook. The copywriter must therefore try really hard to get the title noticed. You could use questions to engage interest. A quotation is a particularly good ploy for attracting attention. Pre-publication, there will be no reviews to quote, so your best option is to find an academic teaching in a department well known for courses/research in this area. In this case, the title is one of a series, and so the series editor could usefully be asked to provide an overview of the title's significance.

Here is my suggested rewrite:

Cultures of Consumption
How men are seen in late 20th-century Britain
Geoff Deade

Where does today's popular image of men come from? And how does it affect both how men see themselves, and relations between the sexes?

This radical new book begins with an examination of the male image in advertising and how this has encouraged men to see themselves sexually. An exploration of a whole range of influences follows, from both black and white culture, drawing out issues of class, colour and sexuality. The result is a crucial study that reflects the ever-changing face of urban culture and sub-culture.

'An exploration of post-modern issues that is both subtle and dynamic. Fascinating.' David Evans, Silversmiths College, London

PRESENTING AND DEFENDING YOUR COPY

The urge to alter someone else's copy must be one of the hardest temptations to resist. Faced with almost any piece of text, people can always think of a better way of wording it. As part of the management process, copy shown for approval tends to mean copy changed (otherwise there is no evidence of managerial input). So how can you deal with this difficult problem? Here are some suggestions.

■ Try to influence how others will read your copy. I always send copy with a covering e-mail or letter describing my research into the product and market, and why I have written it the way I have. If the recipient understands that what has been drafted is the result of detailed thought, he or she may be less inclined to change it. The points need to be written down, though, not just said (people will be busy reading and may not listen).

■ Keep the approval committee as small as possible. The more people you send it to the more changes you get, and if you make them all, the flow of your argument will be ruined.

■ If you give a deadline by which changes must be received, never chase those who have not replied.

■ Often changes cancel each other out; you cannot make everyone's and still have a piece of copy that hangs together.

■ Remember that few people keep a copy of their corrections!

Novelist Fay Weldon, formerly an advertising copywriter herself, had a very effective technique for dealing with corrections. She would research, write and circulate the copy and then wait for the corrections. When they came back, she would include absolutely all of them, and then re-circulate. When the recipients responded with horror, she would re-circulate the original, which this time would meet with unanimous approval.

If you have persistent difficulties with a manager being negative about copy try these ideas:

■ Gently remind the person that if comments are always negative, it is demotivating to staff. Ask whether as well as putting a red line through things he or she does not like, he/she could also put ticks and comments next to things that *are* liked. This will boost confidence; most of us respond better to encouragement than constant evidence of our failings.

■ You could tactfully point out that providing this level of corrections must take a long time, and that you want to work together towards improved performance, to make better use of everyone's time.

■ Start an in-house discussion about the tone of voice you are trying to create, and how you want to come across (this is 'positioning'). Ask for samples of organizations or individuals whom the manager feels represent the core values of the organization, and work towards them. It's helpful to have a shared understanding of what is acceptable, and to be part of the debate about what this is, rather than a constant awareness that nothing is ever right.

■ Finally, try to keep a sense of perspective. When others try to change what you have written, do try to distinguish between valid criticism (it really is a better alternative) and the desire to meddle. But hang on to how it feels to be corrected. Being objective about your own work, and precise about your own reactions, will help you when you come to commissioning copy from freelances and in-house staff.

4

The layout and dissemination of marketing materials

DESIGN

Once copy has been written it needs to be presented in a suitable way for wider dissemination. This usually involves the services of a designer. You may have an in-house design department which will work for you. The advantages are speed and accessibility – you can go from draft copy to on-screen approval of the final image in one afternoon. Alternatively, it may be left to you to commission the work out of house, by using either a firm of designers or one of the local freelances that serve your company.

Whereas at one time every publishing house had its own in-house design department, today many are finding it more cost-effective to recruit such services out of house when they are needed rather than pay for them all the time. Publishing tends to be a very seasonal industry, which results in some equally frenetic promotional cycles. A firm may require the services of several designers one month, but only a month later have very little for them to do. Standard promotional items (web pages, catalogues, advance notices) are often managed by in-house staff. But the assumption that effectively laid-out information can be produced by those without proper training on the equipment they are using is usually a mistake.

Whomever you decide to use, do remember that the brief is yours. You may not have a design qualification, but nor will the market, and your common-sense ability to distinguish between what is easy to read and what is not is just as relevant. Remember the story about the Emperor's new clothes – it was the little boy in the procession, with no training in court etiquette, who pointed out that the king was not wearing anything.

WHAT IS GOOD DESIGN?

In the context of the preparation of marketing information, effective design encourages the designated market to read, absorb the sales message and act on the recommendation to buy. Good design should stimulate without swamping, and be implicit rather than explicit. Kate Hybert of Hybert Design commented, 'A well designed piece looks as if it was really simple to lay out, like it always had to go that way.' If readers start admiring decorative borders that frame text, will they remember to return to reading the list of product benefits?

Prepare yourself to recognize good design. Start scanning both the publications you are likely to advertise in and the general media for advertisements, and assess their impact. Observe your own habits as you surf the web – what kind of pages are hard to read and why? Read Ernst Gombrich's *The Story of Art* (1995) and David Ogilvy's *Ogilvy on Advertising* (2007). Visit art galleries, ask to look through designers' portfolios or your company's promotional archives, read relevant magazines such as *Creative Review* and *Design Week,* and let your awareness of design grow. I am afraid this is not a one-off exercise, but must become a habit – it is important to try to keep up to date. Design is as volatile as clothing and car style – fashions change and design styles can look just as outdated as last season's fad.

HOW PROMOTIONAL TEXT GETS READ

The designer needs copy. As the person who either wrote it or commissioned it, you will probably do a final check before you pass it on. You will start to read at the top of the page and work your way methodically through, looking out for spelling mistakes or verbs that have been used too often. (You may well miss some: it is very difficult to proofread your own work, particularly on screen.)

If, on the other hand, you can imagine yourself coming upon the text cold, or perhaps seeing it for the first time in its final form as an advertisement, you will realize that your reading habits are in reality much more haphazard. Uninvolved readers wait for their attention to be attracted, allow their eyes to flit around the page looking for something of interest and certainly do not feel duty-bound to read everything that is provided. They may look at the headline or picture, and perhaps at the caption. Their eye may be drawn in by quotation marks – someone else's opinion is much more interesting to them than the view of the advertiser. If their interest is stimulated they may look to the bottom right-hand corner or the back of a brochure to see who is advertising. Only then will motivated readers start on the main text (or body copy). The vast majority will not get that far. If people are reading on a screen their boredom threshold may be even lower. Today we all seem to want ever-quicker access to information; if we are not engaged we move on, and quickly. Advertising material has to work hard to draw a response.

The message is clear. You cannot take your readers' interest for granted, and so must use all the means at your disposal to encourage them to get involved: through the words you use, the illustrations you provide and the design layout that unites them.

For most publications there is also a style and order in which the articles and features are read. Awareness of this can help you present your sales information in the position or way most likely to ensure it gets noticed. Start observing your own reading habits.

So how do we read? In search of a quick review of what a magazine includes, many people flick through from the back forwards, so the inside back cover is a very hot spot for would-be advertisers. Similarly, it is common to start reading a newspaper with a speedy trawl through the pages, allowing your attention to be grabbed by particular headlines. Some people pause to read the articles beneath, others return to them later after having scanned specific sections of the paper where they habitually find items of interest: the gossip column, the home news or the letters page. Many papers provide a series of 'news in brief' paragraphs on the inside front pages, allowing readers to quickly grasp the essentials of the stories on offer that day. Page references indicate the more detailed articles within.

All these make good locations to try to place your material, as either a paid-for advertisement or a publicity feature. I confess that having scanned the paper, the first thing I read are the formal obituaries, and even then I begin with the final paragraph of each, to see how many partners and children people had before moving back, if I'm sufficiently interested, to read the rest. I thought there must be more people like me, and suggested to A&C Black that they advertise *Who's Who* (a natural title for people who like reading about the lives of others) on the personal pages, next to the personal obituary notices. It worked.

Mailshots are read in a particular way too. Chapter 5 on direct mail gives further information on this, but in general the letter gets read first, the headline, the signature and PS being the most highly noted parts. Look at the next one you receive and you will see how the senders have anticipated your reading habits.

HOW TO FIND A DESIGNER

If there is an in-house design department the choice of whom to use is largely made for you, although if there is a particular designer there whose work you like, try to steer it that person's way (which can be difficult if the studio manager has other ideas).

Finding freelance designers or local firms can involve more legwork, but in most towns where there is a demand for design you will find local services available. Ask your colleagues and printers that you use. Look in local trade and freelance directories. It is important to bear in mind the level of services you require. An individual freelance designer with his or her own desktop publishing facilities may be ideal for small jobs such as basic advertisements and flyers. For the creation of high-profile point-of-sale material or highly illustrated catalogues by a specific deadline you may need to commission a larger design group, to ensure that there will be additional staff to work on your job should a crisis strike.

You should certainly ask to see the portfolio of previous work of any designer you consider using. Look to see if the designer has done similar work to what you need. Why not ask in-house designers to show you their portfolios too, as a guide to the kind of projects they have worked on in the past?

Once you have found a couple of designers whose work you like and who respond well to a brief, hang on to them. While I would not recommend relying solely on one designer – you need to ensure you have other options – I would advise against spreading your work too widely. Give those who work for you a decent amount of business so that they have a real incentive to please you.

To get an idea of the prices designers charge, pass on printed copies of a couple of previous jobs and ask for an estimate of what they would charge for preparing something similar. Check their estimate against what you actually paid. If they are far too expensive I would tell them so, and use someone else rather than become a routine haggler. You may get a special price once but if you are consistently beating suppliers down below what they feel is a fair price you will earn resentment, and they will be less inclined to help you when you need a favour, for example a job that needs doing in a real hurry.

You may call in a new designer to discuss a potential project, but if you end up asking for their rough design ideas make it clear whether, if what is submitted is acceptable, they will get the job, or whether there are other candidates. Alternatively, agree a rejection fee of say 10 per cent of the fee. Most creative people understand that would-be clients like to brainstorm, and you have to spark – but taking someone's ideas without recompense arouses long-term resentment.

Time is likely to be an important factor. Ask for an estimate of how long the job is likely to take and when you can expect a first visual. Most freelances live with the difficulty of juggling a variety of different jobs (it is impossible to predict what will arrive when, and dangerous to say no).

HOW TO WORK EFFECTIVELY WITH A DESIGNER

Always remember when commissioning design that good designers will not only try to meet your project objectives but also take pride in what they do, so the more you can involve them and communicate what you are trying to achieve, the better.

The best design results are always obtained by clients who have a clear idea of what they want and can express it effectively, providing as much information as possible about the project at the beginning of the job. This is crucial. Designers are experts in finding visual solutions to problems, but you should be aware that once they have come up with one, it can be very difficult for them to see the project in another way. It follows that if you are specific about what you are trying to achieve at the outset, without being over-formulaic, you will harness the designer's talent in a more effective way. The other benefit of taking the time to explain properly what you want is that your bills will be lower. Thinking things through in order to explain them to a third party clarifies your own mind – and in the long run, the more you change your mind, the more the costs go up.

HOW TO BRIEF A DESIGNER

Writing a design brief is difficult. You need to provide a structure within which the designer's creative juices can start to flow, not a straitjacket to inhibit the good ideas which you alone would not think of. If you are too prescriptive, designers may respond with just what you ask for, denying you access to their professional expertise.

So while it is tempting, and saves time (in the short term), never just pass on the copy for a job and assume the designer knows as much as you do. It is your role to formally brief him or her. And even though you set up a meeting to discuss your plans with a designer, never rely on a word of mouth briefing alone as sufficient information. You both need something to refer to afterwards. After all, think how different people can report entirely different opinions on the same conversation – we tend to hear what we want to hear! And if with insufficient information, or simply the wrong take on what is needed, the designer does set off down a false path, it's not just time and money that are wasted – motivation is also substantially reduced.

A four-stage guide to briefing a designer

Describe the market you are talking to

Who are they, what kind of people, receiving what you send in what kind of circumstances? You can generalize to give a flavour of a market: for example, teachers tend to open their mail in the busy staff or faculty room. In general they have to consult each other before making a buying decision; they are natural collaborators.

If you can, pass on other information aimed at this market, such as copies of their professional journal, a website reference for a site much used by the market, or a feature from a newspaper that describes the market you are talking to.

Describe the product you are promoting

What benefits does it offer the market? How does it work (briefly) and what is its pedigree? How soon will the market notice a difference if they do buy what you offer?

Outline how you want the recipient to feel about your organization and the product or service you are selling

In marketing terms, this is 'positioning'. You are establishing a relationship between your product or service and the market you are talking to, and this is done through the image you present as well as the words you use. For example, do you want your market to see your offering as a prestige product that gives status, or as practical and good value for money?

Indicate what you want recipients to do as a result of receiving your information

Should they rush to fill in an order form or reach for the telephone to place an order, grasp the keypad to consult your website, or resolve to discuss a decision to buy with their lover or colleague?

Once you have established brief and succinct answers to these four questions in your head, put them in writing for the designer, either as an e-mail or on a single sheet of paper, no more. This is hard – it's much more difficult to write something short and succinct than to send people a copy of your marketing plan.

Supporting information needed by the designer

Once you have established the tone of what you want, the designer also needs some more specific information in order to do a good job.

Your house style

Many publishing houses today have prescribed design choices, such as which typeface or background colours to choose, and all have a logo. Others take this further and have drawn up standard borders for all sizes of advertisement in print and on screen. While such rules save time and ensure consistency, marketing attracts attention by looking interesting and often slightly unexpected, so if everything looks identical it may not get noticed. This is part of a wider debate. For now, your designer needs to know the rules, and with what rigour they are both implemented and policed.

The copy you are providing

Indicate how much copy there is, and which are the really important sections (you can indicate this in the text, but it is worth emphasizing too, by hand-writing on a printout). Copy passed on electronically must be perfect: all subsequent typographical changes will be charged to you.

What kind of promotional piece you have in mind

Try not to be closed to suggestions – the designer may come up with a better idea than you. If you have to stick to a prearranged format, include precise details (size and extent), and provide a sample of what you want if you have one.

What you are going to do with the material

If it is to be mailed, the overall size and weight must be considered in relation to postage bands. If the paper is to be very lightweight (to make posting as cheap as possible), the design will have to be planned accordingly to reduce the 'showthrough' of printing ink. Similarly, if you are planning a space advertisement in a magazine, as well as a sample of the magazine you need to state how the design should be provided: screen ruling (the number of dots per inch), size of the ad, the trimmed page size and bleed. If it is to be produced as film, your designer will need the appropriate film specifications (eg whether positive/negative, and emulsion up/emulsion down). These details will be given to you by the publication concerned. If you are booking the same advertisement into several publications, do not assume they all require it in the same format or size.

The budget you have for design

It is perhaps best to indicate the ballpark rather than the exact figure. Provide for a supporting contingency.

What supporting work is required

You must make it clear whether you want the designer to handle the production (eg print, packaging, loading on the website) for you as well, and if so the details of what you want and have a budget for.

The illustrations

You may need to commission special photographs (pack shots, point-of-sale shots, perhaps studio sets and so on). These can be arranged by the designer, or you may have your own (in-house) photographer to organize. Do bear in mind, however, that the arrangement, proportion and colour of the illustrations will be an important part of the design of the promotion piece, so if you plan to use existing illustrations your designer needs to know before starting work. The captions for illustrations provide an excellent spot for passing on key parts of your sales message. Reproducing covers also gives those reading your advertisements the chance to recognize your products in the shops.

When you want the finished job by

Never just say 'as soon as possible'. Look through your diary and note down a specific date for both parties to work towards. Doing this makes it clear you are well organized, and your job is consequently less likely to be left until last. Be sure to pass on any vital dates, such as the final acceptance date for delivery of loose inserts that you have booked with a magazine.

The designer's viewpoint

A designer comments:

> What kind of clients end up paying more than they should? Obviously this is a difficult thing to talk about – a client is a client after all – but in general problems often arise if there is no written brief. And then there are:
>
> ■ Clients who don't know what they want until they see it.

■ Clients who know exactly what they want but can't communicate it to the designer.

■ Clients who require visual after visual until we extract a brief from them, with both sides getting increasingly frustrated in the process.

■ Committees. Committees are often difficult to deal with. We may deal with one person within an organization but that person may need approval from several others who may not be in agreement with the requirement for the job (or even whether it needs doing at all), let alone how it is to be handled. The result is often the compilation of several design ideas with a dilution of the original concept, just to get the job out, with very little sense of satisfaction.

■ Clients who pass back lots of amendments individually rather than collating them and passing back one set. It is very time-consuming to do amendments, and it follows that the more sets arrive back, the higher the costs will be. Don't forget too that lots of sets of amendments can cause confusion and a greater risk that the job will have errors.

HOW A DESIGN JOB PROGRESSES

Definitions for commonly used terms and abbreviations are included in the glossary at the end of this book.

Should you ask for alternative designs for a single job? I tend not to. I prefer all the effort to be channelled into thinking of one presentational idea that really meets my brief, rather than two in which most of the design time has centred on making them different from each other. On the other hand, if you need designs to be approved by a meeting or outside body, more than one alternative may be advisable. Bear in mind that two or three choices presented to a meeting will nearly always result in a decision (whether a straight choice or combination of bits from different versions). This is a useful technique when dealing with difficult committees.

Using your brief on what kind of job it is, the designer will do a lot of thinking, make a few key decisions and then start work, providing you with a visual to show what the finished job will look like. This will display format and design layout, the colours, the position of headings and so on.

Once you have approved the overall concept the designer will proceed. If you subsequently decide to change the layout, the amount of copy or any other element of the design, the additional resulting costs will be your responsibility, although it is worth pointing out that on-screen editing means this is a lot less expensive today than it used to be.

You will then receive a proof of your job for you to check, and usually this will be on screen. Never rely on proofreading on screen, even if what you are checking is for a website. Print it out and check it carefully. Changes are expensive because they are time-consuming. To lay out a piece of text may take 10 minutes; to go back into it and locate precise errors in specific lines may take just as long.

You may have to circulate proofs in-house, and this may be a source of further expense. It is a common failing to be unable to take copy seriously until it has been laid out, and most people to whom you show the proof will feel they have not taken part (or 'managed' you) unless they correct something. How can you avoid the large correction bills that result from late changes?

How to avoid design costs going over budget

■ Establish who needs to see what and at what stage before you start work, so you don't end up circulating all the various stages of a job to everyone who could possibly be interested.

■ If you have to circulate a visual, make sure you attach a note of what you are trying to achieve and why, so that everyone understands how the piece has been put together (and you have a chance to influence how they view it). Ask all those to whom you circulate it to respond with their comments by a certain date. Never chase.

■ If several sets of corrections are expected back from your colleagues before a job can proceed, amalgamate them before you pass them back to the designer. If they cancel each other out, consider which route to take.

■ For jobs that have been changed heavily, circulate a note of the extra costs that resulted: this should get the message across!

■ People may write all over proofs but seldom seem to keep a copy of their changes.

Finally, here is one point of my own for your guidance when dealing with external suppliers. Do remember the power of saying thank you. So if you are pleased with a job, tell your suppliers. I suspect that many clients fail to do so because they assume that if customers show they are very satisfied, the bills will go up in future. In fact absolutely the opposite is the case. There is nothing more rewarding than providing a service that is appreciated, and if your working relationship is flourishing, your creative bills may well go down.

ADVICE ON HOW TO PROOFREAD TEXT

My main advice is, don't assume this is easy. It's a job that needs your full concentration, and there are courses (including by distance learning) available to teach you how best to do it.

I find it impossible to read for sense and to read for typographical errors at the same time. Try the following sequence:

- Always read from a printout, not on screen.
- Look at the headings and subheadings (it is very easy for mistakes here not to be noticed, especially if all the words are in capital letters).
- Read the whole text against what you provided (always keep a copy of what you gave the designer).
- Examine the individual words that make up the text, looking out for spelling mistakes and additional words (eg 'Paris in the the spring'), awkward word breaks, and words that are proper words but the wrong ones (eg not/now, it/if).
- Errors that are easy to miss include a narrow letter missing (eg 'signifcance') and an extra letter (eg 'billling' or 'acccountancy')
- Beware of skimming over long or familiar words; an error may be lurking there.
- Read for sense.
- Check the author's name. Twice.
- For direct marketing pieces, ring all the telephone numbers quoted and try sending an e-mail to the address given. Consult the website to make sure it is a valid address. Double check the postcode for return mail to be sure that it has not been changed.

When checking the final proof, look out for the following:

- If you have not seen the job since passing on your corrections, check that they have all been made.
- Check the position of headings.
- Where copy is split between columns (bottom of one/top of the next) check that the breaks are sensible. Try to avoid splitting dates, numbers, proper names and so on.

■ Are there any awkward spacings? Too much of a gap at the end of one page, too little space on another? Should elements be rearranged slightly to make the whole easier to read?
■ Circulate copies only to those who need to see them, making it clear they are for information rather than alteration!

If the design is for a printed item, once the proofs have been approved the designer will proceed to create finished artwork, which the printer will need in order to print. It follows that any late corrections, received once the artwork has been made, will be extremely expensive.

MANAGING WITHOUT A DESIGNER

It is not always necessary to use the services of a designer. For product information that stresses new information, hot-off-the-press or value for money, an overtly designed format could be entirely inappropriate. (The most obvious example is market research – the more you 'package' your promotional material and the report itself, the less it will sell, and the lower your price will have to be.)

If you decide to go ahead on your own, here are a few tips.

Draw attention to what is important

■ Assume that all your prospects have poor eyesight, and make your information easy to read. Cut down on special effects that jar and detract from the main message. Make it easy for readers to home in on the essential sales benefits of the product you are advertising.
■ Ensure the headings and subheadings are clear. Put a box around particularly important text or have it printed in a different typeface or colour. Do make sure however that the colour is really legible. Bright colours are difficult to read; most people find 'muddy' colours much easier on the eye.
■ Put the main heading at the top of the brochure or advertising space, not halfway through the body copy: as noted earlier, a headline in the middle of an advertisement encourages the reader to carry on reading halfway through the sales information!

Offer visual variety

■ Ensure the presentation is visually varied without being jarring. A good designer will use 'typographic colour' (special effects such as the emphasizing of subheadings, underlining, bold text etc) but without over-using it. A great mass of flat-looking text is suitable for the page of a novel but not for advertising copy.

Use of space

■ However much you feel you must say to promote your product, avoid over-filling the space. A format that looks confused or 'heavy work' will put the reader off. Use bullet points, vary your paragraph lengths and don't ask for text to be justified.
■ If your advertisement is appearing in a larger space (for example on a newspaper page), pictures work better on the outside edges of the space, rather than disappearing into the centre gutter. For both advertisements and feature articles, headlines on the right-hand side of the page tend to be more eye-catching than those on the left.
■ Readers do not have to absorb every word of what you say. Allow them to assimilate blocks of copy by scanning the headings. Make the words you use recognizable at a glance by setting in a 'serif' typeface (easier to read); limited use of italics can also be effective. Eye camera studies have shown that column widths in excess of 80 characters are more difficult to read.
■ When booking advertising space, routinely ask for a right-hand page rather than a left, and always for a space facing text rather than another advertisement. Most readers flick past double-page spreads of advertising. Tell the person handling the layout what you have booked, and provide him or her with a sample of the publication.
■ Find out what is going next to you, and in particular what is going beneath you. There is a natural tendency for the eye to move down the page; if there is a small feature (whether advertising or editorial) beneath the space you book, it may well draw attention away from your copy. If you are placing a direct response advertisement, put the coupon where it is easiest to cut out, and ensure that it does not back on to another such coupon.

How many colours to use

■ The costs of full-colour printing have fallen greatly in recent years, but if it is still beyond your budget, you don't need to pay for full-colour materials to make your promotions stand out. Consider the use of 'spot colour' in newspapers that are predominantly black and white. A good designer can make a two-colour job look extremely attractive, but it requires skill. You may also decide to use fewer colours to make your material look as if it has been cheaply produced, and is therefore more cost-effective. Political parties often produce their materials in just one or two colours to look more cost-conscious.

Design techniques to avoid

They make your text very difficult to read.

■ Don't use upper case (CAPITAL) letters too much. They are hard to read and prevent words from being recognized at a glance. For this reason don't put headlines in capitals.
■ Don't make the lettering too large. 50 cm is the normal reading distance for a magazine or newspaper; if your lettering is poster size it will be illegible.
■ Don't put extensive amounts of copy at an angle – it's very difficult to read. (On the other hand a 'flash' across the corner of an advert can be a very effective way of attracting attention.)
■ Don't reverse out too much text. It is very hard on the eyes (although for limited amounts of text this can be a very effective way of attracting attention).
■ Don't place text over an illustration unless the picture is truly 'faded back' behind the words. (Even then it doesn't always work.).

GETTING MATERIALS PRINTED

Most printers receive artwork from designers in digital format, the most common being a high-resolution PDF file. Commissioning printing and finishing may be the responsibility of a departmental print buyer or designer, or it may fall to you. Production of a reasonable job is likely to depend on three factors: your ability to match the job to the appropriate process, a supplier who can produce the goods on time, and a competitive price. Coming up with the right combination is more likely if you understand what is involved, although in addition to technical information, you also need to be able to ask specific management questions. For example, is the printer who is offering to do a job for you in fact planning to subcontract it to someone else?

There are a variety of different printing methods. None is superior to all the others; all have different benefits for different applications. The two most commonly used for jobs originating in the marketing department are lithography (litho) and screen printing, but you may also find letterpress, photogravure or flexography being used, according to the requirements of the job. Digital printing is getting better all the time, and offers the facility to introduce personalization and variable data into materials, which will become the norm in the future.

Finishing includes all the processes that turn the printed sheets into the finished product required, for example varnishing, embossing, laminating, collating, folding, binding, die-cutting, assembly and packing. It's unlikely that a single printing house will offer everything you need, so it's quite common for printers to subcontract on your behalf. If it is you that is doing the arranging, and print and finishing are being placed separately, it is vital to ensure the two suppliers communicate to ensure the right inks and materials are used.

The entire job, in all its specific detail, must be confirmed to the printer in writing. Nigel Dollin of John Dollin Printing Services Ltd comments:

> This is something that customers, for whatever reason, are reluctant to do and quite often will say 'as per our conversation' or 'as per estimate number'. It is wrong to assume that the supplier knows what you want as the only person who knows this is the person placing the order. Insist on receiving back a confirmation of the order from the supplier by post, as e-mails don't always arrive.

Finally, you must ensure that the printed materials arrive where needed, by the required date, by the most appropriate delivery method and in a satisfactory condition. Printers can handle the last two processes for you, but your own warehouse/office may have established contacts with carriers, especially to your regular customers, and therefore be able to offer a better service.

It's vital that file copies are delivered to you prior to the main consignment so that any problems can be dealt with before the bulk of your print run reaches its destination. Apart from allowing you to make your own check on quality, you will need them for your records and for any internal circulation necessary (getting stock back from the warehouse after delivery can take a disproportionate amount of effort!). Be sure to send copies immediately to those you are relying on to carry out whatever marketing initiatives you have set up. It's a particularly good idea to send copies to the firm's reps and your customer service staff: they will be dealing with the response!

How to request an estimate from a printer

Buy/subscribe to a guide to printing prices to use as a basic reference for what you should be paying for printing. Two or three quotations should precede any sizeable job. Ask for samples of the paper the printer will be using, and remember to ask about recycled and environmentally friendly materials (although they currently carry a small price premium, the more we use them, the cheaper they will become). The printer will need the following information from you in order to be able to estimate:

- a description of the component parts of the job;
- their size and shape;
- how many printing colours;
- how many different versions;
- the amount of repro work included, ie the size and number of illustrations and the amount of retouching to be done;
- the type of material you want to produce (eg brochure or letter, and if the whole package needs to be under a specific weight for mailing);
- how many copies;
- when the finished job is required by;
- where to deliver and what special packaging is needed;
- any additional requirements, eg coding order forms, numbering, collating, laminating, saddle stitching;
- the job reference number you would like to be used in any correspondence.

However specific your instructions, the resulting estimate will probably be marked subject to sight of artwork.

If you have a sample of the kind or quality of material you are seeking to produce, do pass it on. It will give the printer a clear idea of your expectations of quality, presentation and so on. Alternatively, ask to see printed samples of a similar kind of work that the firm has handled before. If the quantity required is likely to change (eg the export department has not yet let you know how many copies it needs), ask for a run on (r/o) price, say for 10,000 and 1,000 run on. Or ask for a series of quotes: 1,000, 2,000, 3,000 and 10,000. This saves you from continuously ringing the printer for further information.

Which estimate should you accept?

Price should not be the only consideration on which you award a particular project. You should also consider reliability, service and the likely quality of the finished product. Some publishing houses negotiate contract prices for jobs that occur frequently. (These need to be reviewed regularly to ensure competitive rates are being maintained.) Other houses cease to bother requesting quotations from habitual contacts. This is usually a mistake.

A good guide to working out whether a new firm is going to be good to deal with is to try to ask about its quality accreditation and how its working procedures operate. Does it have a complaints procedure? If asking questions like these arouses hostility, you may not be in the right hands. Remember to ask for the names of those you will need to be in touch with – just in case your key contact turns out to be on holiday when your job is going through.

If there are various elements to be printed at the same time, as part of the same job, it is always advisable to try to keep as much with one printer as possible, as this will reduce managerial input and help ensure uniform quality. If price makes you keen to look elsewhere, mention your desire to keep everything 'under one roof'. While I would not recommend relying exclusively on one printer, do not spread your work around so thinly that remembering what is where becomes a headache for you and a very small account for each supplier.

What to do when things go wrong

Output of a design to a cromalin digital proof (see the Glossary) before a file gets sent to print can forestall many problems. In general the higher the specification you choose for the digital proof (and hence the more it costs), the closer what you see will be to the finished job.

But what if you are just not happy with the final job? Your immediate concern should be the source of the mistake, and if it is the printer's, what the firm will do to put it right. If you think the material is usable, but below your (demonstrable) commercial standard, a discount should result; if it is not usable the printer should reprint at no cost to you. The two bargaining positions will be the printer's view of the job as 'commercially acceptable' (it will not want to reprint) and your concern for the reputation of your company (you will not want to send out substandard material even if it is costing you next to nothing). Be very wary of becoming known as a discount merchant and one who accepts poor quality or mistakes.

To avoid the situation arising in the future you need to decide whether the mistake was due to:

■ The printer's incompetence – if so, don't use the firm again.
■ Bad luck. If the firm agrees to put it right you can try it again, but watch out for possible cost recovery from it on the next job (charging you more than the going rate to make up for money lost last time).
■ The development of too casual a relationship between yourself and the printer, for example failure to put instructions in writing or to make specific requirements clear. You can remedy this.

You have one sympathetic ally in the company who will be able to advise: the production director. There may also be an advisory service run by a professional print buying association that you can consult.

Direct marketing

Direct marketing means selling or promoting straight to the customer, without the intervention of an intermediary such as a retailer, wholesaler or sales agent. This may take place through a variety of different media (eg mail, e-mail, telephone). What turns an advertising campaign into a direct marketing campaign is the appearance on the material of a mechanism for responding direct to the firm that placed it. Thus a poster in the street can be turned into a direct response advertisement with the addition of a telephone number or website address for the receipt of direct orders.

Direct marketing can be divided into two types, direct response and direct promotion. *Direct response* marketing invites a direct response back from the customer, as the name implies. For example e-mails or mailshots advertising particular titles might ask for orders to be returned to the publisher. *Direct promotion* marketing is more concerned with spreading information about products. The promotional message is still sent to the customer, but while the response may indeed be received straight back it may also be returned through retail outlets such as bookshops or websites, or result in orders placed with the firm's representatives. The mailing of seasonal catalogues to bookshops is an example of direct promotion.

Here the collected wisdom of the general public intrudes. Direct mail (or 'junk mail') goes straight in the bin: everyone knows that. Not true. Surveys of the treatment of direct marketing material have consistently shown, in various countries, that familiarity with direct marketing is growing. The majority of recipients find it useful, and either open what they receive or pass it on to someone who may be interested rather than throw it away.

In particular, in-bound telemarketing (allowing the customer to call and place an order) is growing hugely due to public demand. Customers find it convenient to do business this way, on the move and based on a voice instruction, without the need to write out a formal order. Response rates to direct mail are showing an impressive consistency, largely because of a huge increase in the amount of e-mails being sent. Hence a printed marketing package, from an organization that wants your business enough to formally solicit it, stands out as particularly effective.

Remember too that direct marketing is a very testable means of promotion. You can see within days (sometimes hours) of sending out your material whether or not it is working. You can test different offers and different formats to see which produce most orders. Promotions that you see being repeated are obviously drawing a healthy response. Direct marketing agencies are now challenging mainstream advertising agencies (which relied on space advertising), because their efforts are seen as provable and good value for money. And whereas at one time direct marketing was considered a specialized field for specific products, its use is growing among more general advertisers. Several large manufacturers and retailers are using the medium to promote the benefits of brand loyalty to their customers. Club cards operated by supermarkets are now a vast direct marketing exercise to support the brands to their core market, and find out more about their shopping habits and aspirations.

The second widely held belief is that direct marketing is a poor promotional medium because of the very low levels of response. It is common to hear of an 'industry average' response rate of 1–2 per cent, but no one is entirely sure where this figure came from! A recent survey in a UK trade magazine gave an average of 4.4 per cent for consumer and 1.8 per cent for business mailings. If you are mailing to a 'warm' list of previous customers you may well do far better. For consumer mailings, it was reported that 46 per cent of campaigns showed response rates above the 'average'. It is also common for there to be sharp differentials between the response from different lists sent the same mailing piece. Your best-performing list will typically outperform your worst by a factor of three to one.

Every direct marketer can probably come up with a horror story: loose inserts that failed to be inserted; mailings that reached their destination after the 'sell by' date on the offer had closed; leaflets printed upside down, without prices or with no room for the customer's address; e-mail campaigns that produced a very high 'non-deliverable' rate. Direct marketing demands immense precision, but a skilfully handled campaign can reward you with not only orders but also vital information about your customers.

THE ADVANTAGES OF DIRECT MARKETING

For the right product at the right price, direct marketing can be a very cost-effective form of promotion. Sometimes a single sale will pay for the entire campaign and make a healthy profit. Other advantages include the following.

Personal representation to your market

If it is done well, direct marketing to your customers is the nearest you get to the rep's visit: a personal communication about your product direct to the person most likely to buy it. At the time most convenient to the prospect, you have the person's sole attention, for as long as you are able to hold it.

If you compare the costs of sending a rep to each of the prospects you consider part of your potential market, direct marketing is a very cost-effective medium. There are no geographical limits to how far your message can travel. In inaccessible areas the value for money can be even greater, as it is difficult for customers to get to retail outlets, and they tend to rely heavily on the service offered by direct marketers.

High selectivity

Direct marketing is not a mass medium: it offers you the chance to make a specific sales pitch to a specific market. The increasing sophistication of data management systems means that you can pinpoint exactly who you want to contact with which message. For example, political parties are making extensive use of the medium's potential. They can target local groups with specific messages (eg policies on education for parents and plans for public transport for taxi drivers). Direct marketing makes such selectivity possible.

Perfect timing

Through direct marketing it is possible to time the arrival of your sales message very precisely, and to your greatest advantage. For example, back-to-school promotions can be timed to arrive just as the new term begins. There are other marketing media that permit this – you could book the front cover of an educational magazine to achieve the same function – but none permits this control over timing at such a low potential cost.

Following up your initial marketing campaign is easy

As the response comes back from direct marketing you gain new information about those who have ordered, and have the chance to make a fresh approach to those who have not. You improve your market and product knowledge by updating your database, and make it likely that future campaigns can be even more precisely targeted.

Good news for cashflow

Most direct marketing campaigns ask customers to send payment with their order, backing this up with a strong guarantee of satisfaction or a complete refund. While there is legislation covering the availability of the merchandise you offer for sale, direct marketing offers you the chance to test the popularity of particular products with specific market sectors before you commit yourself to expensive production costs and lengthy print runs.

Many publishers also find that the additional services offered to their customers (the chance to order an extra title, to benefit from a short-term special offer, or even the means of getting the material to the customer, such as 'courier delivery' or 'careful packing, mailing and insurance') offer a beneficial additional revenue stream.

Excellent support for other marketing methods

Direct marketing should not be seen in isolation. It can provide lots of market research to inform all your marketing activities, gain leads for your representatives, result in extra retail sales, direct customers to your website, encourage them to recommend you to their friends and colleagues, improve your company image and much more.

DIRECT MARKETING AND THE PUBLISHING INDUSTRY

The publishing industry adopted direct marketing early because it could never expect a physical bookshop to stock all its wares. It was particularly difficult to persuade booksellers to stock titles aimed at the professional markets, or those of very high price, because no retailer wanted to tie up large amounts of capital on titles for which there was an uncertain demand. Booksellers in any case found that titles promoted by publishers, direct to the end user, resulted in additional sales for them.

Today there are many retailer direct marketing operations, most notably Amazon, which can offer customers every single book in print. Other highly specialized booksellers have developed which run targeted direct selling operations, for example to industrial and governmental libraries, to individuals within the workplace, or to enthusiasts for a particular type of hard-to-find book. In many cases these booksellers win cooperation from publishers in the form of either extra discount or subsidy of mailing and promotion costs. It may well be worth exploring the possibilities for cooperative promotions, perhaps providing the direct seller with copies of your direct marketing materials overprinted with its own return address, or paying for inclusion in its promotions. In the United Kingdom, an interesting phenomenon is The Book People (www.thebookpeople.co.uk), which promotes titles within workplaces to non-regular book buyers. It takes huge discounts from publishers but reaches customers who would not otherwise be looking to buy books.

Direct marketing campaigns result in extra orders through the retail trade. Titles for which it would not be cost-effective to produce an individual campaign are included in thematic leaflets, catalogues or e-mails promoted to booksellers and libraries, and to professional end users themselves.

KINDS OF PUBLISHED PRODUCT FOR WHICH DIRECT MARKETING WORKS BEST

High price

As a rough guide, most direct marketing in the book trade is for high-price rather than mass-market titles. There can be exceptions. You might be promoting to gather new names for your database and therefore be well satisfied with a break-even response, and thus willing to offer books at lower prices, or you might be offering a wealth of low-price titles and incentivizing the customer to place a minimum order value (with free postage over a certain point).

Products for specific markets

It's hard to make direct marketing work for general interest titles – unless you are getting the customer to buy in bulk or offering an additional service unavailable from other ordering points.

Books for which the customer is unlikely to visit a bookshop

These are also books that a bookshop will be reluctant to stock, such as professional and high-price reference titles.

Products for which suitable lists of potential customers are available

If you are considering direct marketing, check on list availability early and make no assumptions. A list may exist but its owners may be unwilling to release it or be unable to do so because of the conditions under which the information is held (a particularly common issue with associations). If you are unable to obtain data from the most logical source, you may decide to build your own list, but the legal responsibilities and costs involved need to be considered carefully. Do you have further titles coming in this area (if not, there is a danger it will not get used again), and is it an effective investment for your future publishing programme? Are there ready-built lists in your area of publishing which you can rent? By doing so, you avoid the costs of research and maintenance, which should never be underestimated.

THE ESSENTIALS FOR A DIRECT MARKETING CAMPAIGN

A plan

All successful campaigns begin with a plan. What is your objective? Do you want a direct response or to spread information about your products? If the latter, will orders come back from other sources?

A list

You need to know whom you are trying to sell to and how best to access them. A good starting point is to ask yourself lots of questions about the market, to help you establish who they are, and how you might be able to track them down. For example:

- Where do they work?
- What organizations do they belong to?
- What are they interested in?
- How do they buy? How does the approval staircase work?
- What do you want them to do?

An offer

By this, I mean an understanding of what will motivate your target customer to buy/recommend/ask for your product. It may be just your product, or it may be the added value you are able to include (free carriage, strong guarantee, money-off for an order placed before a certain date, additional free gift).

A decision on the most appropriate format(s) for your marketing material

It does not have to be just one format. Direct marketing methods work well in combination: for example, a mailshot followed up by telemarketing, or a series of e-mails supported by radio advertising.

A decision on timing

You need to decide when the market is most likely to be receptive, and at what time you can best handle the response.

A copy platform

You need to think about how the words you use can persuade the market to take the next step. An outline of your overall strategy, with the impression you are trying to create, can grow into draft headlines and the basic message you plan to communicate.

Design services

Attractive and appropriate design makes your message appealing to the market. This means thinking about the look and feel of what you are planning. Your market will make instant decisions about what to do with your marketing piece, without rationalizing why.

A system of despatch

This determines how you get the message to the market. It needs planning rigorously, and with accurate time allocated to each stage of the process, working back from the date you want your material to reach the customer.

A method of monitoring success

You need a system that will monitor how effective your marketing has been and help you to take appropriate action. This needs to be based on the kind of information you want to capture and what use can be made of it in your future marketing and publishing decisions.

Fulfilment services

Before any promotional information goes out, fulfilment services need to be in place to support the marketing offers you have made. So the warehouse that will send out your products needs to have systems for locating, selecting and packaging items, and the customer information line you offer needs to be ready before you offer it to your buyers.

We shall now examine each of these areas in more detail:

A PLAN

You need to understand both what has been achieved so far, and what is expected of you in future. A good starting point is to find out what budget has been allocated. This will give you a strong sense of the organization's expectations – although this should not stop you trying to achieve more, or secure more funding, if you think that the opportunities available have been underestimated.

Start with a trawl for information.

■ What is the print run for the title to be marketed?
■ How many do you already have orders for?
■ From where?
■ How many are you trying to sell direct?
■ By when?
■ What other backlist titles can you sell on the back of this campaign?
■ What kind of people benefit from the product? Who/where are they?
■ Are they the same people who do the ordering (eg children's books are generally bought by adults)?
■ When is the best time to market?
■ Does the customer need to see the product before making a decision to buy (ie must it be available on approval or with a firm guarantee)?

■ What is new/excellent/noteworthy about the product?
■ What is the history of my company selling similar products direct in the past: are there list successes worth repeating, or failures worth avoiding?
■ Where is the product available from and by when?

One of the most important characteristics for direct marketers is that they are well organized. This is a medium that requires attention to detail more than huge dollops of creativity. Before any marketing activity is planned there are a variety of factors to be taken into consideration. You will find your objectives easier to achieve if these things are thought about before you begin planning your campaigns, rather than as you are doing them.

A LIST

I would to God thou and I knew where a commodity of good names were to be bought.

William Shakespeare (*Henry IV, part 1*, Act 1, Scene 2)

The list matters more than any other single component of a direct marketing campaign, because unless information is sent to the right people, it stands no chance of achieving a successful outcome. In general, publishers are much happier thinking about layout and design: whether the Pantone on the screen is an effective match for the company stationery, which of course matters not a jot to the customer. Too often the list is taken for granted or thought about last, because choosing lists does not feel creative. If you remember nothing more from this chapter, it should be 'List, list, list'.

Sources for lists

Within the confines of the relevant data protection legislation (discussed below), lists may be:

■ bought outright;
■ leased;
■ rented;
■ built;

■ exchanged;
■ negotiated.

Data protection

Today most countries have data protection legislation. Although the provisions vary from state to state, the principles behind them are constant. The legislation was originally designed to protect individuals from having incorrect information stored about them on computer file. In addition to all the other sorts of computerized information held, mailing lists have to be registered with a data protection authority and the uses to which the information may be put specified. Compilers of lists may only use the information for the purposes made clear to consumers at the time of compilation, and to which they have given their consent. Data protection is well monitored, customers are increasingly sure of their rights and the official bodies policing it are looking for test cases to show that the procedures that safeguard privacy are working. You have been warned.

The legislation has not been static and has since been extended. The most significant change has been a widening of the original definition of 'processing' of data to include any mention of an individual, whether at a work or business address. In some countries the definition of processing includes all handling of personal information; it also extends the provisions to manually held lists and to individuals at business addresses rather than solely at home addresses. Vastly more sensitive handling of all personal information is called for, notably relating to sexual orientation, religion and other personal details. Provisions about trading data with areas where there is a lesser standard of data protection have also been extended.

In addition to data protection, many countries also offer state-funded services that allow individuals to opt out from receiving direct marketing materials altogether, which cover individually addressed mail as well as unaddressed door-drops and telephone calls. The usual procedure is that a publicly funded database holds the names and records the interests of individuals who wish to receive nothing at all, and those who wish to receive more contact on specific subjects. This file is available to members of the service who can run it against lists they plan to mail, to both exclude and include individuals. The cost they pay for this varies according to the member's annual mailing volume.

For more information on data protection in general, consult your national data protection agency. The UK Information Commissioner's website is at www.ico.gov.uk. Computer filters are commercially available to reduce unwanted e-mails (spam) and viruses.

The main priorities when looking for lists

Precision is essential, and this can be difficult if you are not an expert in the subject area for which you are responsible. You may have a title that all chartered surveyors would consider an essential desktop reference. If you make the mistake of circulating quantity surveyors rather than chartered surveyors, a large percentage of your market will be missed. If you are circulating your information to international markets it may be even harder to be precise about job titles.

The basic choice is between compiled and response-driven lists. Compiled lists are established, often for purposes other than direct marketing, to give total coverage of a market. Response-driven lists are put together from the names of people who like to buy, or gain information, through direct marketing. So you might have a compiled list of all newly qualified doctors, established by the government, and a response-driven list of those who paid for a related professional membership online. There may well be overlap between these two approaches, but it will never be total. While compiled lists will give you access to more of the market, you will always get a better response to direct marketing campaigns from a response-driven list.

In general, you want to find the names of:

■ those who have bought through direct marketing before;
■ those who have bought or need a similar product;
■ those with similar lifestyle or values to these people.

The owner of a database of people who have bought a directly rival product would never release that list for use by a competitor, so you may be forced to think laterally. For example, those interested in buying travel books by direct marketing may have bought holidays online, or specific travel products such as lightweight clothing or suitcases.

Open your eyes to the possibilities of lists all around you. The first place you should look is among your own previous buyers or contacts. Most organizations have a variety of different contact lists, and not all of them are at the immediate disposal of the marketing department. For example, your accounts and human resources departments may both have lists that would be useful to you in a marketing context, and your company might also publish directories that can give you useful marketing leads.

From here you can branch out further. Associations whose membership is relevant to what you are selling are an obvious port of call. Begin by asking if you can put a loose insert into one of their mailings to members. If the answer is no but the association is particularly relevant, your firm might consider trying to become the society's official publisher and so gain access to names. If there is already an association journal, you could try an advertisement in it with an attractive offer, and so gain the names of those who respond. Does it run an annual conference or exhibition at which you can display your books? You could also ask your authors for contact details, or to suggest other associations to whose members information could be sent.

If you are unable to send mail personally addressed to an individual – perhaps if you are making an insertion in a society mailing – you need to think carefully about how to address your message. A job title may be a starting point, but these change or get amended according to politics and fashion (eg personnel managers became first Human Resources and then HR staff within a very short period). If you are not sure, ask advice from a member of the market. Getting it wrong before your message has even been opened is not a good start.

Dealing with list brokers

The most common source for lists is the professional list agencies which maintain data and then rent, lease or sometimes sell it to clients. They maintain the files, updating through programmes of de-duplication, list cleaning (they will ask you to return your 'gone-aways' for them to amend the list) and deleting those who do not want to be included, have moved or died. You choose the format in which the list is provided (it could be as a telephone list for telemarketing, a mailing list for postal use, or a list of e-mail addresses) and rent it for one-time use by a single mailer. If you mail the list again or include someone else's material with yours, you will be invoiced for a second list rental. List owners know if you use the list more than once because they all seed their lists with 'check addresses'. These masquerade as part of the list but are in fact the disguised addresses of company employees, which provide an ongoing check on who is using the list. Prosecutions do occur.

Leasing agreements entitle the user to use a list any number of times within a specific period. Selling a list to a client means that the client can use it in any way that is legally acceptable, and becomes responsible for its future upkeep.

Flick through a recent issue of a trade magazine (there are many direct marketing titles) and look in the back pages at the number of list rental and broking companies advertising. You can now start discovering the wide range of lists available, from new mothers to academics teaching at universities, from high earners to purchasers of specific shares. There are business and professional lists, and others of consumers' home addresses. Most countries have one or more professional organization(s) covering direct marketing, and they too should have a list of all registered list-broking firms.

The variety is not endless. Once you have asked a few brokers for details of the lists they can obtain, you will realize that there is an element of duplication in what they offer. Some firms have compiled and developed their own lists which they rent out to direct marketers; others rent out the data put together by retailers.

Prices for list rental are charged per thousand, depending on the amount it cost to compile the list, costs to maintain it and how valuable to other mailers it is likely to be. There may be extra charges for any selections you wish to make, such as geographical exclusions or mailing women only. There is usually a minimum charge (often the same as an order of 5,000–10,000 names). While no list brokers will guarantee a response, they should guarantee deliverability, within reasonable parameters (there will always be some changes in the list since it was last used). If you get a large quantity of items returned as undeliverable, within a specified period (that is, the list was used quickly and the returns also come quickly), you should be compensated with a refund. List brokers get a percentage of the rental as commission. You will have to submit a copy of your promotion piece (they may accept draft copy) in advance to ensure the list owner is happy for you to contact its customers.

These are some questions to ask a list broker about a list you are thinking of renting:

- When was it last mailed?
- For what kind of product?
- With what success?
- What other products have done well with this list?
- Who compiled it and how?
- Does it consist of people who have bought direct or subscribers? If the latter, how did they buy their subscriptions?

- How often is it updated (or cleaned)?
- In what format is it held?
- Can it be de-duplicated (de-duped) against your own list, so you don't contact anyone twice?
- What percentage are international names?
- Is it compliant with data protection and mailing preference legislation/ registration?
- What does the list owner credit for envelopes returned as undeliverable? (This usually applies only if over 5 per cent of the list is returned.)
- What is the time limit for such returns (normally three months from order date)?
- If you have your list de-duped against the one you are renting do you pay just for the new names ('net names') or for all those on the rented list, even those you already have? In the United States net name rental is standard; the practice is spreading.
- What percentage of the list are those who have just ordered?

If you take a look at the website of a broker you will find a data sheet on each of the lists it looks after. These will give you an idea of the sort of further questions you should be asking.

When dealing with list brokers you will find that there is an industry jargon to acquire. For example, 'nixies' are undeliverable items that are returned to the sender and need to be sent back to the list owner for updating/ crediting. Another frequently heard expressed is 'I gonned it', meaning 'I marked it "gone away" and returned it to the sender.' If you start reading the trade press you will soon pick up the lingo.

The arguments for renting lists rather than building your own

Computers are cheap, and it's simple to buy a database programme to hold names of those you want to contact. Why not build your own database?

- Data legislation. Do not underestimate its complexity and the regularity with which it changes. If the list is yours, you are responsible for ensuring your records are data legislation compliant.
- Whereas the hardware and software may be getting cheaper all the time, it's common to underestimate the overheads that come from maintaining data. The list holder needs to invest in sophisticated computer systems to store the information recorded. Staffing too is likely to be expensive.

Dealing with returns, re-keying order information and address changes is often a full-time job, two by the time you have allowed for holiday and sickness cover. If you rely on just one person knowing how to access information, you are very vulnerable!

■ Mailing lists go out of date very quickly. People in full-time employment change jobs at the rate of 20 per cent a year (in some fields/age brackets much more often), and around one in 10 homes changes hands every year.

■ If the market you want to mail is already covered by well-researched and efficiently managed mailing lists, it is cheaper to rent the names and addresses than start from scratch. Your time is arguably better spent negotiating special rates for frequent use of existing lists, your money on compiling specific market sector lists that do not already exist (you may then also be able to rent these to other users to subsidize your costs). Lists that are cheap to build, such as the addresses of schools and libraries, are also cheap to rent.

■ It is often easier to exercise control over a supplier than an in-house department. Firms that make their living selling lists have a strong incentive to provide a good service.

■ The best mailing lists are those that are used frequently, and rented-in lists will be used more often than your own. List rental companies can afford the complicated de-duplication procedures which save annoying potential customers with multiple copies of your mailings. They can also provide addresses in carrier-preferred order, which saves you money on delivery.

A compromise position is to use an external supplier to hold your lists for you, perhaps amalgamating your book-buyer names with those of similar companies' customers to produce a single and highly effective mailing list, which you can all then access.

Building your own database

If you decide to build your own list, the best place to start is by recording your own customers and past purchasers. There are many areas to be considered: the system on which to hold the names; who is going to update the list; how often you will use it; how it ties in with editorial plans for the development of your firm's publishing programme (there is no point in storing names for a particular subject area if no more related titles are coming).

The information you record will depend on the capacities of the system you choose and how much you need to access in the future. There are many database management software packages to help you set up and maintain your customer and mailing records.

The following list will provide ideas of the kind of information to record. Some facts are obtainable simply by making your order form a little more detailed, others require keying at the time of order processing or more detailed research.

- Mr/Mrs/Ms/Miss or professional title.
- Phone numbers (home and business, landline and mobile).
- E-mail addresses.
- Postal/zip code.
- What they bought.
- How much they spent.
- How they ordered.
- How they paid.
- If they did not pay or returned the item ordered.
- Total number of orders to date.
- Date of most recent order.
- Average value of order.
- Order history: date, titles, venue.
- How you found their name (recommendation, advertisement etc).
- Job function.
- Position.
- Size of company (employees).
- Type of company, by standard industrial classification.
- Turnover.
- Age (in bands).
- Other demographic information.
- Opt in/opt out. You must get the responder's consent if you have any plans to use the list in a non-obvious way (eg rent to a third party). 'Fair obtaining' is a requirement of data protection legislation.

Removal of duplicates from your own list

The same person orders twice from you. The first time he notes his address as:

Mr J Thompson
St Edmunds
Murray Road
Berkhamsted
Hertfordshire
HP4 1JD

The second time he notes it as:

John Thompson
7 Murray Road
Berkhamsted
Herts

Both are correct, but they are captured for your list as separate addresses. How do you avoid mailing him twice every time you circulate your list in future?

Ironically it costs more to de-duplicate than to send two copies of the promotion piece, but a de-duplicated list saves you money on postage and avoids annoying potential customers by sending them multiple copies of material. This looks highly inefficient and is environmentally unfriendly.

If you suspect that your in-house list contains a lot of duplicates it may pay to have them eliminated by a professional bureau. You provide a copy of the list (by e-mail or on CD ROM for larger lists), and the bureau runs a program that spots all the entries with the same postcode or a high percentage of similarity. It is important to point out that this is not an entirely scientific process. Most systems will yield a list of possible duplicates for manual checking, and the fastest way to end up with a final list is simply to remove all these possible duplicates (possibly removing valid ones at the same time). Whether or not it is important to deal with lists in any particular way, ensure that the data-processing team are well briefed to avoid queries and delays at a late stage.

Alternatively, many of the good quality de-dupe systems now run on the PC/Windows platform. These enable in-house users to de-dupe effectively, although it is probably a good plan to involve the in-house IT department. The software is not cheap, so for companies carrying out a small volume of mailings it may be just as easy to do it manually with imaginative use of a desktop database.

Ensure that all your response devices and order forms ask those ordering for their postal/zip code so that you can try to eliminate duplicates in future.

Merge and purge

For large-scale mailings you could use one of the many data agencies to 'merge' the mailing lists you want to try, 'purging' them of names that appear more than once (ie are on more than one list). The procedure works like this. You provide the agency with a copy of your own in-house list of buyers, and ask the list rental broker to supply each of the lists you wish to rent in the same format. The data agency runs each against the other and aims to produce a single complete list with no duplicates.

If you plan to run lists against each other on a large scale, it is worth trying to negotiate a 'net names' agreement. This means that your list costs will be closer to the number eventually mailed than the total of names run against each other. (Such deals are usually restricted to a minimum percentage of the total.) These arrangements must be agreed before you start processing, but a good list broker should be able to help.

Avoid the trap of de-duping the cheapest list first, in the hope of removing more names from the most expensive list. This may lead to the worst-quality list forming the bulk of the mailing. Ensure that you obtain a signed data-processing report from the mailing house or agency handling the output of names. This must be passed back to the list broker for your net names credit. If you are mailing from the same lists on a regular basis, you may be able to agree a predetermined percentage of additional names. This can save problems later if your total mailing quantity comes below that expected because of a large number of duplicates.

If you are de-duplicating lists and being rigorous about response tracking (discussed later), ensure that responses are accounted for against all the lists the names came from. If this is not attended to, and there is a large overlap between the lists, you risk the chance of not being able to identify your best list.

Don't be disappointed if a high overlap factor between the lists you choose gives you a much smaller mailing total than you had originally planned. The more overlap the better, as it shows your selection is on target.

List analysis

Regular direct marketers want to know more about their customers. There are two main reasons for this. First, they need to meet their customers' needs better (sell more to them now and develop new things to sell to them in the future). Second, they need to find more of them.

The combination of market research techniques and the increasing sophistication of hardware and software has made possible the development of highly sophisticated information services for mailing list analysis. There are two main options.

Analysis of geodemographic criteria

As a basis for the classification, geodemographic analysis uses electoral roll and census information, overlaying with financial, household and age data to produce effective postcode analysis. It is ideal for segmenting the mass market.

Analysis by lifestyle criteria

This offers a more detailed and personal approach, ideal for pinpointing specific niche markets. A huge number of individuals are sent questionnaires at their home address. Any individual's response may contain up to 700 different variables, on age, income, spending habits and so on.

Publishers can use the services of organizations involved in these areas in two main ways. It is possible to have your existing lists (for example of customers, past customers and key prospects) analysed, to make your search for more of the same easier. A minimum quantity for a statistically viable sample would start at around 10,000 names. Alternatively, armed with a detailed profile of what kind of people buy your products you can pull a very specifically tailored list of prospects from the huge databases such companies hold. On consumer surveys, it is possible to sponsor questions or buy responses to a particular question.

This type of analysis is only good for consumer or residential data. For commercial organizations, firms offering this type of resource will carry out a similar exercise using business variables such as SIC (standard industrial classification), number of employees and so on. Alternatively, you can locate good-quality lists and match against them.

If you cannot afford market analysis of this sophistication, start lateral thinking: what kind of person needs your firm's product, and what else he or she might buy. It was such a thought process that led a major news magazine to try mailing previous buyers of high-quality shirts and accessories, with very successful results.

For information on firms offering different list-handling services, contact your national professional direct marketing association or look for advertisements in the back of trade magazines.

AN OFFER

Consumers today are used to getting added value in every purchase, through price promotion, or perhaps the aura of exclusivity that early ownership brings. How effectively you communicate the benefits of purchase to your market will have a big effect on how willing they are to order.

Thinking of an offer to consumers is an important stage in a direct marketing campaign, because often focusing on how to attract attention generates excitement and enthusiasm. And once you have thought of a benefit to offer, it helps you write the copy.

An offer may be value-added, providing:

▪ an additional title to those who respond;
▪ free postage and packing;
▪ a discount for orders received by a particular date.

Or it can involve a feature of your service:

▪ access to a new product;
▪ a fulsome guarantee of satisfaction;
▪ the solution to a long-standing problem.

Another very good tactic is to make a choice of offers, so the recipient gets involved in deciding which one to take, and moves further along the route to purchase or response. One final point on offers: in general try to offer added value rather than discounts. The perceived benefit of giving an additional book for orders over a certain price point may be greater to the customer than the actual cost to you. Offering a discount has a direct impact on your overall profitability, and may create expectations of something similar in the future.

THE MOST APPROPRIATE FORMAT(S) FOR YOUR MARKETING MATERIAL

You have a wide variety of different methods for reaching your customers by direct marketing. These include:

- snail mail;
- e-mail;
- telephone (both incoming and outgoing calls);
- website;
- door-drop;
- 'off the page' advertising (space advertising in a magazine or newspaper with the response 'off' the page back to the organization that placed it);
- poster sites (eg in the street or transport advertising such as in bus shelters, train stations and beside escalators);
- television and radio advertising;
- text message;
- catalogues;
- parties;
- clubs (some with rules, offering special arrangements to members, others just called 'club' to promote identity);
- conferences;
- 'reader get reader' promotions: incentives to individuals to recruit other potentially interested parties.

Think carefully before deciding on your format. Do you want to copy your competitors or do something different? Your selection should be based on the type of customers you are talking to and the product you are promoting. For example, a high-price item may need expensive marketing materials; a low-cost product may be best promoted through e-mails or text messages.

If you are relying on external suppliers, get at least two estimates for any sizeable job, and get them in writing. Include all the extras that you require, such as the coding of your response device or the delivery of printed material to your mailing house, which could be some distance away.

For circulation via the web, the costs of the hardware and the cost of the designer (if using outhouse staff) can be estimated, but don't forget to factor in the amount of your/the organization's time it will take (which will of course impact on how soon you are ready to mail out). Dr Dominic Steinitz has this formula for working out how long any online project will take:

make your first estimate, multiply it by two and then add a unit. Thus if you think it will take, say, two hours it will take you four days. If you estimate three weeks it could be six months, and so on. In my experience this is very accurate.

A DECISION ON TIMING

You need to think about when your potential customers are most likely to be responsive to your marketing approach, as well as when you can best handle the work involved. The first consideration should be your own starting point. The market's rhythms and sensitivities are of key importance, but you obviously then need to think about scheduling the work when it can best be fitted in. There is no point in trying to get all your campaigns out in the same month!

How to plan a schedule for direct marketing

Work backwards from the date you want your message to arrive with your prospects. If you are going to complicate your approach by including a 'sell by' date, or the market has a key deadline looming (eg the end of the school term), you must be very accurate. It is easy to allow slippage but it can be fatal to a campaign's success.

For a mailing, the schedule could look like this:

Response device in the mail	1 week
Time prospect needs to consider the offer and respond	5 weeks
Best time to arrive	1 September
Rebate sort and second-class post	1 week
Stuffing the mailshot	1 week
Printing	2 weeks
Circulation of final proofs, passing for press, ordering lists	1 week
Design and layout, corrections	2 weeks
Copy approved and passed to designer, visual prepared and circulated	2 weeks
Finalizing copy	1 week
Copy presented, discussed and circulated	1 week
Time for writing copy	2 weeks

Drawing up schedule, briefing suppliers, requesting
estimates, sourcing lists, setting up monitoring procedures
for mailing response   2 weeks

Working back and allowing a little extra time, you should start thinking
about the mailing at least three months before you want it to arrive. Note
that although your list research needs to be one of the first things you do,
to establish the size and shape of the market, the actual ordering of the lists
should be one of the very last things you do, to ensure they are as up-to-date
as possible.

A few other hints on timing

■ Try to plan ahead. The problem in most publishing marketing departments
is the sheer volume of work. Books tend to slip beyond their estimated
publishing dates, and there are natural convergences of season, such as
publishing for the new financial or academic year. You may think you will
have time to finalize marketing plans and order list estimates while proofs
are circulating, but the more planning you can do ahead of schedule, the
better. Bear in mind that too much time can be as bad as too little: it offers
everyone the chance to change their mind.
■ Try to limit input. Try to establish before anything is written or designed
who needs to see what: the copy, the visual, the list selection and so
on. Keep the list as small as possible, but remember that senior managers often take a particular interest in direct marketing plans (their
success/failure is provable – and quotable – unlike the majority of more
amorphous marketing techniques).
■ Keep rigorous control of costs. Keep track of your costs by starting a
methodical system, using an electronic or manual spreadsheet. At the
top of the sheet note the title's budget. Divide this between the various
items you need: design, copy, printing, mailing costs and so on. Next to
these figures note the amounts you have been quoted and the suppliers
to whom you award the contracts. You then have everything to hand for
quick expenditure decisions, and a ready means of checking invoices as
they come in.

A COPY PLATFORM

Direct marketing is above all a writer's medium. Whether you have to write the copy yourself, or commission it from freelances, it really matters. There is no eye contact, no body language to coerce the recipient into purchase; the words have to do it all. If you have additional funds, you are far better spending your budget on effective copy than expensive illustrations or photography for your mailing piece. If you have to do it yourself, begin by thinking rather than writing. If you think as you write you will find it takes longer, and is more muddled.

If you are commissioning the words from a freelance copywriter, you will need to provide information on the product benefits to the anticipated audience. (This is best done by giving answers to all the basic research questions listed on page 15.) Can your copywriter also have access to all the various in-house forms and so gain an idea of the evolution of the project (on a confidential basis, of course)? Don't forget to pass on all the background information that you take for granted, such as details of rival products. An effective copywriter will write for a specific format (he or she may well suggest an alternative to your original idea) and provide you with a rough layout indicating what goes where for the designer.

Information to put in a direct marketing piece

The best way to learn about how to put together a direct marketing piece is to become a direct marketing addict. It always worries me when people are dismissive of the medium in general and yet seeking to use it in a professional capacity. You can't expect to benefit from direct marketing if you don't feel it has any value in your own life. Get yourself on as many mailing lists as possible, and study what you are sent. To get started, buy by direct marketing or send some money to a charity and see how you are contacted afterwards. Examine the loose inserts that fall out of magazines when you open them. Look through newspapers and notice which headlines on direct response advertisements attract your attention, and ask yourself why.

Through this process you will start to notice that most direct marketing consists of four components (even if they are part of the same physical thing). In direct mail, for example, there is almost always:

■ an outer envelope to get the information to the recipient – usually with a message on it;
■ an accompanying letter, to introduce the contents of the package, the product being sold and the offer;
■ a brochure or leaflet, to explain in further detail;
■ a reply device or order form.

In some mailshots these components may be amalgamated, for example into a long sales letter that has an ordering coupon along the bottom. Similarly, in an off-the-page advertisement, all the component parts must necessarily be part of a single space. An e-mail or telemarketing call will be structured in a similar way. But even the simplest direct marketing format will combine the features of the four items listed above:

■ a headline with an offer or key benefit;
■ an introduction;
■ an explanation;
■ a means of ordering.

HOW TO MAKE EACH COMPONENT PART AS EFFECTIVE AS POSSIBLE

Your task in putting together a direct marketing campaign is to ensure your package is compelling to read and motivates an order. All the advice in Chapter 3 on techniques for preparing successful copy applies here too, but the following hints which are specific to direct marketing will also be helpful. Although they are based on a physical mailing, the principles discussed can be extended to other marketing formats.

The envelope

The aim here is to ensure the package gets opened. The envelope must give the return address for undeliverable items – and if you are paying to have it overprinted with this, you may as well include a sales message too.

It is sometimes claimed that for direct mail going to people at work the outer envelope is less important because the post is often opened by a secretary or assistant. Even so, many people flick through their in-tray first, and something that looks different may be pulled out and opened, or if the envelope is sufficiently interesting to the secretary, it may get passed on with the contents. Bear in mind what else the reader will be receiving at the same time (how much, how interesting?) and the time of day it will be opened. Most working people open mail sent to their home address in the evening. Some suggestions:

■ Provide a 'teaser': start a sentence that sounds interesting, but don't finish…
■ Say something controversial (but not so alienating that people are repelled).
■ Print on both sides of the envelope, so whichever way up it lands there is something to look at.
■ Make the envelope an unusual shape.
■ Add a quick checklist on the back for recipients to either request more information or have themselves deleted from your list.

The return address can be either your company or your mailing house, which can then batch up returns and send them on at regular intervals.

The accompanying letter

The sales letter is the one essential component for a direct marketing package. Time and again research has proved that packages with a letter pull more response than those without. Sometimes you can dispense with the brochure altogether, just send an effective letter and a suitable means of ordering.

Why is this? A letter is a highly personal form of communication. Watch how you react to the next mailing piece you receive. If the sender is not immediately apparent, you look for explanation. The almost universal reaction is to extract the letter, turn it over and look for the signature and company name at the foot of the second page.

■ Your copy will work best if it is personal. Picture an individual recipient. What does he/she look like; what does he/she wear/read/watch on television/do at the weekends?
■ Make your tone conversational and personal, not stilted. Be reasonable and logical. Don't overclaim: it sounds ridiculous and discredits your sales message. If you can, make your copy topical and newsy, fascinating to read. Check for readability by reading the text aloud.

■ Keep your sentences short so the copy reads well. For the same reason, avoid very long paragraphs (around six lines is fine). Don't use too many adjectives or complicated verbs; they slow down the reader.

■ Start with a headline stating the main benefit: what the product will do for the recipient, how much time/effort/money he or she will save by buying.

■ Begin the main text with a short sentence to attract attention, or a question (which doesn't invite a quick 'no' and the wastebin).

■ Introduce the offer, and explain the benefits, rather than features. Repeat the message (in different words) to be sure your key points come across – not everyone will read from start to finish.

■ Use bullet points for the main selling points; these can always be expanded in the main brochure. Numbering the selling points can be effective, but don't give too many (four is plenty).

■ Underline key benefits for extra emphasis. Blue underlining apparently improves the response still more (although do not over-use this technique). You can also use the second colour for your signature at the bottom of the letter.

■ Provide enough information for the reader to make an immediate decision to buy. Describe in clear detail how to order.

■ Mention all the other items in the mailing. Provide a short cut to the order form for those who have already made up their minds to buy and do not need to read the brochure.

■ The final paragraph too needs to be strong, to urge a positive reaction to the product and your offer, and to provide the motivation to fill in the order form straight away.

■ Another very important part of the letter is the PS (apparently the second most widely read part of the letter after the headline). Think of a really important reason for buying and put it there.

■ Don't make assumptions or use jargon, even when mailing past customers. You will almost certainly get it wrong and may sound patronizing.

■ Business-to-business mail is often addressed to a job title rather than a named individual. Past customers in the post might have moved on, and the mailshot should make sense to the new incumbent.

■ Long copy usually outsells short copy provided it is being read by the right person (ie the right list has been chosen), and is relevant and interesting. However, if your letter is designed to create leads for the sales force, don't make it so long and detailed that the recipient has no need to see a rep. A two-page A4 letter (the standard length) should break at the page end in mid-sentence on something interesting. Never say that someone will follow up the letter with a phone call: it's a real turn-off.

■ Layout is important: make it look like a letter. Resist the temptation to try out layout gimmicks. Don't get it typeset in anything other than a plausible computer face. If you want to look really hard-up, choose a typewriter font such as Courier. Ensure your finished copy looks varied. Make the paragraphs different lengths, give subheadings, allow plenty of space to attract the reader's eye.

The addressee

Direct mailers spend a great deal of time agonizing over this. Database management makes a range of personalized mailshots possible, but if price rules this out can you make a specific greeting to the job title you are mailing? For example, 'Dear Senior Partner' is better than 'Dear Sir/Madam'. You may find it is too expensive and labour-intensive to produce a different header for each batch of letters you send out, in which case 'Dear Reader' is probably your best option. Think about what greetings you find patronizing: 'Dear Decision Maker' may fall into this category. Try testing to see whether increasing the precision of the greeting improves the response.

The signatory

This should be the person the recipient would expect to sign. This is not typically the chairman of a multinational or managing director of a publishing house, although that person's name might go on an optional extra item in the mailing. In academic and educational publishing it's sometimes thought letters signed by the relevant editor are met with more respect. Don't be afraid to adapt your job title if it's not appropriate. For example, I've found arts academics responded poorly to 'Product manager' on my business card at a conference. Science academics might have been less concerned; teachers of business studies might have viewed it positively.

One final point. A letter is a very personal communication. Although you should to try avoid offending sensitivities, don't worry unduly if you get a few angry letters protesting about the content. One copywriter told me that if you don't get a couple of cross letters per campaign, no one is reading your material. If you get them, notice your response (you probably feel rather uncomfortable). That's part of the power of direct marketing.

The brochure

The brochure too explains the product benefits. The sales points will be those covered in the letter, but explained in different words and ways so that the information seems fresh and interesting.

■ You have more room in the brochure to explain your product and answer questions that, were recipients examining the item in a bookshop, they could answer for themselves.
■ Give precise and believable information, not vague puffery.
■ Again, stress the benefits to the recipient, not the key features from an internal perspective.

Checklist for writing brochure copy

When writing copy for direct mail brochures I have a standard list of questions I seek to answer. Often this information goes in a box in the brochure.

■ What are the key benefits of the product to the market?
■ Who is the product for? You can give a list of professions or job titles.
■ How can it be used? Give examples applying to the recipient's everyday work.
■ Who is the author? What are his or her qualifications, experience, appointments and previous publications relevant to the book, national and international? If possible, include an author photograph captioned with the name. Remember that a well-known name is not the same as a well-known face, but if the author is extremely recognizable, use the caption to link his or her name to the product. Captions get read before body copy.
■ What interesting facts are included? General, interesting information in a brochure tends to get read.
■ What is the scope, ie breadth of coverage?
■ What are the main contents or main revised sections for a new edition?
■ What does it replace?
■ Who has reviewed the title and in what?
■ Has anyone the market respects said anything interesting about the book (ie can you provide testimonials)? If not, might someone be persuaded to do so?

■ What does it look like? A photograph of the book cover is useful. If it is not yet available, get your designer to make up a dummy. This is interesting to direct mail purchasers just as it is to browsers in bookshops. If the title is expensive and has an impressive format or long extent, ensure the book is shot from the side, spine upright to show the value for money it represents.

■ A photograph is particularly important for high-price publications such as multi-volume reference sets, where prestige of ownership is one benefit you are selling. Show the books beautifully lit in the best possible surroundings. If the book is one of a (collectable) series of titles, show some companion volumes.

■ What is in it? Offer a substitute for the bookshop browser's flick through. Choose pages to reproduce that show the book to its best advantage. Use arrows with captions to make sales points. If you reproduce illustrations from the book, they too must have captions.

■ When is the title due to be published? What are the publication details? Give the extent, number of illustrations, number of entries, date available and so on.

■ Who else should see the information when the recipient has finished with it? When mailing institutions, try printing 'route instructions' on the top of the brochure to suggest that it be forwarded to the librarian, the head of department and so on.

■ A high-price product might be better justified by describing it as not a book, but a volume, indispensable reference, source, file or library. All sound more expensive!

The reply vehicle

This is your point of sale. It must:

■ stand out in the package;
■ be easy to use;
■ invite response.

Remember the overall level of response will always be in inverse proportion to the level of commitment required, so you must make ordering as trouble-free for the customer as possible. If you can supply goods on approval, do so. If not, ensure there is a complete guarantee of satisfaction, such as a money-back offer, restated on the order form. If you cannot accept large orders from institutions without a credit check, explain how this helps protect them as well as you.

Format of the reply vehicle

What you enclose in your mailing will depend on the kind of response you are soliciting (how much information you need before taking the sales process any further) and the budget available. Cost will probably be an important consideration. In general, separate order forms attract a higher response than integral ones that have to be detached from the brochure or letter. Of the latter, perforated forms tend to do better than ones that require a pair of scissors, but again the extra finishing costs more. If you cannot afford perforations, show a pair of scissors and print a dotted line where the cut should be made. Be wary of approving order forms that require recipients to destroy the reference material. If it is an expensively produced brochure they may well pay you the costly compliment of putting the form to one side to be photocopied later, leaving them with their information intact, but if they fail to get round to it, leaving you with lost sales. If you have no alternative to putting the order form in the brochure, don't put the product information on the back of it. Most people like to keep a record of what they have ordered until it arrives.

In a brochure with an integral order form, probably the first thing to be laid out should be the coupon. Never cramp the coupon to make room for all your brochure copy; cut the copy instead! For similar reasons, never produce a cleverly shaped coupon which is time-consuming to clip, or one that is in an awkward place to cut out. The bottom right-hand corner of an odd-numbered page is best.

Some order forms are complete sheets of paper with arrows marking where they can be folded to turn them into mailable items ('self-mailers'). Others leave it to responders to provide the envelope, perhaps offering a freepost address so they don't have to pay for the stamp.

If you provide a reply envelope, ensure the order form fits into it. For one of my early business mailings the cut-out form was slightly larger than the envelope. I assumed people would fold it to fit, but many trimmed it so it fitted the envelope exactly. They cut off the codes on the bottom which showed from which list the order had come! The cheapest format for separate order forms is probably a reply postcard with blank spaces for the customer to complete on one side and a freepost address back to the publisher on the other, but if you ask for complex or personal information you must send an envelope as well.

Always try to fill out your own order form before finalizing the layout. You will then see how easy it is to fit the information in the space you provide.

Information gathering

An order form is your chance to compile accurate information about your customers in the hope that you can sell to them again. What kind of space should you provide for your customers to fill in?

Bear in mind that the more information you require, the more space will be needed, and that asking for too much information may offend recipients (who can spot an attempt to load them on to a database) or dissuade them from completing the form. A box (often far too small) for each separate letter of the name and address can be annoying: it's better to provide blank lines and mark underneath the vital information you need (first and second names, county, postal/zip code etc). Ask for block capitals, which most people will write 'joined up'.

Keeping a standard order form

If you produce direct mail regularly it is useful to keep a standard order form on your computer. Find out from your customer services department the firm's trading terms and conditions: approval periods, how you accept payment, which credit cards and so on. Do you require a customer signature? Do you need to print a disclaimer, eg 'prices subject to change without notice' or 'subject to fluctuating exchange rates'?

Other tips for making order forms work harder

- Don't call it an order form (that much is obvious). Instead try 'special opportunity', 'your chance to order' or 'how to get your hands on ...'.
- The less small print, the better. 'Offer subject to our standard terms and conditions, available on request' covers most eventualities.
- Free draws for swift responders attract replies. If you try this on a regular mailing to the same list, be sure to announce who won: it boosts credibility

and creates a club atmosphere. Try a pre-publication offer or, for projects that are even further from completion, a 'pioneer supporter' price: this can work particularly well for expensive multi-volume sets that take years to come to fruition, and helps to subside your development costs.

■ Involve the reader on the order form. Some mailing pieces ask the recipient to stick peel-off labels or yes/no stickers on the form, increasing customer participation.

■ Repeat the offer and the name and address of the publisher on the order form. If it gets detached from the main part of the information package, people will still have the details they need to order.

■ Offer the option of a standing order for titles that are part of a series or year-books. To libraries this may be a welcome chance to obtain important information reliably and without hassle. Stress that an invoice will be sent each year before the book is despatched, so it is possible to decline a particular issue.

■ For titles that are being price promoted, put the discounted and non-discounted prices side by side, with a line through the latter to show that a bargain is available (attracts attention).

■ Ensure it is easy to extract.

■ Make it really clear what to do with it, to the level of spoon-feeding.

■ This is a good place to restate the guarantee.

■ How much commitment do you require? If not much, make a benefit of it.

■ List the various ways you accept payment. Choice involves readers in selecting and moves them towards purchase.

■ Ask the designer for symbols to show how you receive orders rather than words (eg a sketch of a telephone and computer). These are easier to spot in a hurry.

■ Ask for all contact details to be printed LARGE.

■ Offer recipients something else in case they don't want the main offer.

■ Can you ask them to recommend a friend who might also like information?

Other items you could consider including in your mailings

■ A postcard with the address, writ large, of your website.

■ An extra order form. Once customers have ordered they will have the opportunity to buy again. Code it so you can see the response it generates.

■ A checklist of all the related titles you publish.

■ A 'recommendation to purchase' form for recipients working in institutions (academic and business) to pass to the information manager or librarian. Most new academic and company library purchases are the result of recommendations by the other staff.

■ Another letter, perhaps a 'lift letter' from a satisfied customer or a (famous) admirer of the product, or a 'publisher's letter', say from your firm's managing director or the book's editor. Such a letter need not come from someone famous, just someone plausible. For example, when mailing schools the ideal candidate is a head teacher or subject adviser. Charities use this technique in fund-raising mailing pieces, for example, enclosing letters from field workers describing the value of their work.

■ A sheet of quotations from published reviews of the title you are promoting.

■ A news sheet on an existing product. Even best-selling titles can become boring to the market. How about a news sheet describing developments being made by the editorial team, or how the material is being used by some buyers? It's all good stuff for improving customers' perception of your product and hence their loyalty.

■ Instead of offering a discount or stressing value on the order form, try a 'money-off coupon' for customers to enclose with their order. Again, it involves readers and adds value to the package. Put 'offer limited to one voucher per household' on the coupon and you further increase its apparent value.

■ A reply envelope for the return of the order form.

■ A quiz sheet or competition giving further product details.

■ Information from another company which sells non-competing products to the same market, and subsidizes your marketing costs (provided your list can be used in this way).

■ Forthcoming related product information.

DESIGN SERVICES

People read direct marketing material in a different way from the rest of their messages. They remain fully aware they have a choice whether or not to read it. To start with, their reading habit is seldom linear (moving logically through the content); rather they dart around, allowing their eye to be grabbed as it will. Your design layout should anticipate this and provide lots of interesting snippets to dwell upon.

Provide a complete brief on what you are trying to achieve and the ideas you have had so far before the designer starts work. (For further advice on dealing with designers see Chapter 4.)

A SYSTEM OF DESPATCH

Whether you are using an external supplier, colleagues in another department, or your firm's warehouse, do give them plenty of notice of your schedule. It's far better to sort problems out early than to end up grovelling on bended knee to get your marketing material out.

Whether the service is in-house or out-of-house will be dictated by what is already in place, and what level of service you require in future. Mailing houses and bureaux can handle the despatch of bulk mailings, and have specialized equipment to handle the insertion of complicated combinations. Machine insertion (as opposed to manual) means the costs go down. Remember too that they are experts and see many more campaigns (and hence many more mistakes) than you could ever do. Learn from them. Discussing your proposed marketing materials with a mailing house before they are printed may save you money. For example, folding a rectangular leaflet on the short side rather than the long may result in it being hand- rather than machine-stuffed (more expensive), but will probably make little difference to the overall impact. If you provide the mailing house with details of the format and paper weight of all your planned items, it will be able to work out the overall weight and hence mailing cost, and perhaps suggest amendments that would reduce the financial outlay. (Using a cheaper envelope could bring you within a lower weight band for mailing and save money.)

Put all your instructions in writing, making it absolutely clear what goes where. In the case of a mailing piece, make up a sample and send it to those handling despatch. Try to anticipate potential problems. For example what should the mailing house do if it runs out of stock of any of the components? A letter or order form can be photocopied, but what about the brochure? Will the size of mailing entitle you to a discount on postage if it is presented in postal/zip code order? Can the mailing house organize the discounts for you? Do you need a freepost licence? Sort out all these details now rather than hold up the printing of your material while you wait for a licence number.

MAILING COSTS

The biggest cost of a direct mailing will usually be postage. There are a variety of different discount schemes available from both national carriers and a range of different consolidation services. Bear in mind that if you provide your mail in postal or zip code order (which is how most mailing lists are provided anyway) you might receive a discount on the delivery cost.

You may also want to discuss 'freepost' and business reply services. Allowing customers to reply for nothing may attract more business, but it may also draw 'loony mail'. It is not unknown for recipients to attach bricks to reply envelopes (which the postal service then delivers and charges you for) or to use your reply envelope to enclose a blank order form. Whatever method you choose, there will be precise requirements, usually including the positioning and reproduction of a bar code on your mail. You will need to follow the instructions carefully, and the carrier will need to see proofs of the response device before it allows you to proceed. You must decide whether the size of the mailing and the possible response make this extra effort worthwhile. A visible barcode also makes your promotional material look less individual. International postage reply services enable customers anywhere in the world to reply to you without cost to themselves. Some firms have reply envelopes produced in very large quantities, so the smaller totals needed for individual mailings can be drawn out of stock as needed.

You can also pay to have a postage paid impression (ppi) printed on the despatch envelopes (at the same time as your message or slogan) so items do not have to be individually franked (and can be mailed out more speedily). Stock of ppi envelopes can be kept for future mailings. You pay the carrier for what you despatch at the going rate. The right to produce a ppi is subject to account approval with the carrier, and there are usually minimum quantities. This is a service your mailing house can arrange for you.

A METHOD OF MONITORING SUCCESS

You need a system that will monitor how effective your marketing has been and help you to take appropriate action. This needs to be based on the kind of information you want to capture and the uses to be made of it in your future marketing and publishing decisions.

Trial mailings

Direct marketing is a very testable medium, as we are continually reminded. With telemarketing and e-mail you have feedback within hours on whether your product is likely to be a success; with direct mail within days. All large-scale mailers test the market before they commit themselves to extensive campaigns, by mailing a selection of addresses from all the lists they are considering.

List rental companies can produce a trial list for you with an 'nth' selection from each possible list: perhaps every fifth or tenth name. It is best if they 'dump' the entire list to computer file before the selection is made, otherwise there need be only one change to the master list between your trial and your actual mailing, and the 'nth' selection will be thrown out, so you end up mailing some people twice. For a substantial mailing (200,000 plus) most mailers carry out a test of at least 10 per cent.

These are suggestions for publishers whose budgets are not extensive enough to permit large-scale test mailings.

■ Compare like with almost like. What is the track record of your company's promotion of related products to similar markets? Does this give you any useful hints on the selection of lists? You will see that accurate monitoring of your mailing results is crucial if you are to learn for the future.

■ Try testing at the time of mailing. Send two different sales letters to two halves of the same mailing list, or try different subsidiary titles on the order form to see which produces the most orders. Code the coupons and watch the results.

■ Don't over-complicate your job! If you don't want to end up being confused by your testing, and wasting money on pointless research, test only variables that can dramatically alter the results: product(s) offered, price, offer, time close and so on.

■ Set up the management system first; involve and interest those doing it.

■ Code the lists you use, making different offers.

■ Change the cheap elements in your direct marketing packages.

HOW TO WORK OUT WHETHER YOUR DIRECT MARKETING IS SUCCESSFUL

One of the advantages of selling direct is that you can measure your results against costs, and so prove whether or not your marketing strategy is achieving satisfactory targets. The degree of accuracy possible depends on the kind of products you are promoting.

If a substantial proportion of the orders resulting from your mailings will come through the book trade rather than direct (eg when approaching the schools market), the best way to see your results is to examine sales figures before and after a promotion, and compare the total with the original estimates of market size and possible penetration (usually made when a title is commissioned). Other firms count inspection copy requests after mailings to estimate success, or compare year-on-year sales figures.

On the other hand, if you are promoting to business or industrial markets you may expect 70 per cent plus of your mailing response to come back direct. Although publishers are still not in a position to isolate and identify all the orders that result from a specific mailing, you must try to establish the cost-effectiveness of each campaign.

To measure results against costs effectively you have to calculate the response rate of your mailing.

$$\text{Response rate} = \frac{\text{number of replies}}{\text{number mailed}} \times 100$$

No guarantees of what to expect can be made, and your criteria of what is successful will depend on the selling price of your product and how many you have to sell to make a profit. If it is high-priced you could make money even with a very low response rate.

More important than the response rate is the cost per order, ie how much it is costing you to secure orders.

$$\text{Cost per order} = \frac{\text{costs of each mailshot} \times \text{number mailed}}{\text{number of orders received}}$$

Your costs of mailing will include all the various elements of the campaign: list rental, printing and design costs, copywriting if you have to pay for it, despatch and postage. A quick comparison of your cost per order and the selling price of the product will show whether your mailing is heading for profit or loss.

For more specific information on profitability you need to establish the contribution per sale for each title sold. To calculate this as well as production costs for the titles promoted you need to know your company's policy on the allocation of overhead and other costs: your department's share of everything from bad debts and warehousing to staff costs and photocopying. A quick way of doing this is to establish a production and overhead cost for the main item you are selling (say 50 per cent of the sales price of the key title featured). This enables you to calculate the break-even response rate: the minimum quantity of products your campaign must shift before it starts to justify the costs of the promotion and make money. The equation for working this out is as follows:

$$\frac{\text{cost of each mailshot} \times \text{number mailed}}{\text{cost of production for main title}}$$

(This formula is used as the basis for the break-even response rates in the example that follows.)

The equations get more complicated if a variety of lists is used for which rental values vary substantially (and so marketing costs differ for each list), or your order form features a variety of products. If responders order more than one product your total costs will be a smaller proportion of total revenues generated, and the economics of the whole mailing are improved.

Your calculations will need to be recorded in a mailing analysis form which can be circulated to your colleagues. This is best done in tabular form. Figure 5.1 gives you an idea of how it can be laid out.

One final word of warning. Avoid including on your mailing analysis reports titles that receive a mixture of direct mail and general promotion through the trade. Many of your direct response orders will come back through bookshops, and your cost per order will look unreasonably high as a result. For this type of title it is better to concentrate on sales totals and compare them with previous years or similar titles.

FULFILMENT SERVICES

These need to be in place to support the marketing offers you have made, so customers who have ordered receive good and prompt service. Before your material goes out, the warehouse that will send out the products needs systems for locating, selecting and packaging items, and the customer information line you offer needs to be ready.

The fulfilment service needs to know all the things you know, but will not know them unless you tell them. For example:

Graham and Green monthly mailing report to 31 March 2007

Mailing and title	Code	Date mailed	Quantity mailed	Units main title	Units secondary title	Secondary units value	Total order value	% response	Cost per order
Mailing 99 – 4; NBL Financial Directory (price £95.00), 2 Secondary titles (prices £110 and £46.50)									
NBL own list	01	January	4,000	172	14	778	17,118.00	4.65	6.04
Directory entrants	02	January	10,000	91	–	–	8,654.00	0.91	30.88
G&G financial bookbuyers	03	January	1,500	68	4	266.50	6,460.00	4.80	5.85
List swap (another publisher)	04	January	1,500	30	2	220.00	3,070.00	2.13	13.17
List swap (another publisher)	05	January	2,300	18	2	156.50	1,966.50	0.86	32.31
List swap (another publisher)	06	January	5,000	42	–	–	3,990.00	0.84	33.45
List swap (another publisher)	07	January	4,300	22	3	139.50	2,229.50	0.58	48.33
Subscribers to Business Journal	08	January	3,500	27	4	186.00	2,751.00	0.88	31.72
Daily Tribune Business Information Subscribers	09	January	2,500	8	5	232.50	992.50	0.52	54.04
Total			34,600	478	34	1,979.00	47,231.50	1.48	18.99
Cost of mailing = £281.00 per 1000									
Break-even for 34,600 = 205									
Inserts:									
1.	10	December	5,000	20	3	33.00	2,230.00	0.46	24.60
2.	11	December	12,000	5	3	266.50	741.50	0.07	169.76
3.	12	January	10,000	18	5	232.50	1,942.50	0.23	49.20
Total			27,000	43	11	532.00	4,914.00	0.20	56.59
Cost of insert = £113.17 per 1000									
Break-even for 27,000 = 64									
Total sales to date:									
returns				677	58				
				5					

Notes

1. The publishing house's own list pulls best, followed by that of the company that provided the data for the book, which was provided as part of the agreement to publish.
2. Swaps with other publishers meet with varying success, but lists of known direct mail responders do better than subscriber lists.
3. Loose inserts tend to produce lower response rates than individual mailings, but this need not mean they should be avoided; they cost much less to arrange.

Figure 5.1   Sample mailing analysis form

■ what the offer is (deadline and policy on late arrivals);
■ how much is being charged for carriage;
■ what guarantees are provided and what the policy is on returns;
■ the format of the promotion piece and the mailing date;
■ when orders are likely to arrive.

Bear in mind that the more you involve staff, the more enthusiastic they are likely to be, particularly if they are geographically distant from the main offices. Sweepstakes to predict the size of the response or the timing of the first order often go down well.

CODING YOUR ORDER FORM

Ordering devices need to be coded so than when orders start to come back you can see which mailing lists have produced them. The cheapest way to do this is to run a felt-tip pen down the side of a wedge of leaflets and record which colour went to which list. A step up from this is the more reliable 'scratch coding'. A different code is assigned to each list (eg A, B, C, D, E, if there are five lists used), and all five codes appear on the initial printing plate. Once the quantity for the fifth list (E) has been produced the printing machine is temporarily halted, the last digit of the code gets wiped off the black plate and the quantity for 'D' is printed, and so on. Scratch coding will increase the costs over a straightforward run for your printed materials but is much cheaper than the printer producing split runs for individual codes. Ask how many 'up' the printer is producing at one time: this gives you the number of mailing pieces on the plate at the same time and the number of changes that must be made each time the machine is halted.

Your order forms can be coded with much more sophistication: in specific places, with more detailed codes and reference words, even with sequential numbers, as needs dictate. But bear in mind that with each additional specification the costs are likely to go up.

A key part of establishing codes for order forms is ensuring that they are captured when orders are processed, and this is more difficult than may at first appear. For telephone orders, customer service staff are usually time-target driven, so their efficiency rating is based on how many calls they answer within a specific period, and they may resent having to ask an additional question about the code on the material. You will need to provide guidance on what they should say to customers. It should be phrased to suggest that giving the information benefits the customer, rather than your organization. For example, 'Can you give me the long number at the top right hand of your order form so I can be sure we have all your details if we need to get back to you?' sounds much friendlier than 'What's your customer number?'

You need to ensure customer services staff understand that capturing additional information increases the relationship between the customer and the organization, and this makes everyone's long-term future more secure. Initiatives to reward performance, such as chocolates or gift vouchers, can encourage the staff to oblige, and once they get used to asking for the information it will become routine.

POSTAGE AND PACKING

This is a standard customer charge for most direct marketing, and your customers will not be surprised to see it (although that may not stop them resenting it, or seeking to avoid paying). Postage and packing can become one of your marketing variables, to be experimented with in the hope of making your material more attractive. Don't assume you must offer the same conditions as have always appeared (although any changes must always be agreed with customer services staff before your material goes out).

Can you describe the item more seductively? Visit the people who pack up your parcels, watch what they do and consider how the service can be made to sound as if it offers additional value to the customer. 'Careful postage and packaging' sounds nicer than 'p&p'. 'Courier despatch' sounds faster than 'delivery'. Signing for a delivery can be annoying because customers have to be present to receive it, but it protects both parties' interests should the parcel go astray. Describe the precious commodity they have ordered as such and you increase both its value and the pleasure with which it will be received.

Think too about relating the additional cost for carriage to the cost of going to place the order in person: the petrol, the search for a parking space, the hassle, the time, the threat of a parking ticket. Order online or by phone, and you can be doing something else within minutes.

If you are a small business and cannot afford to offer free carriage, explain why. For example:

Why do we charge for postage?
We seek to keep our overheads as low as possible, and to offer our customers the best possible value for money. At the same time, we

are a small business and costs that we cannot control eat into the sustainability of what we do in the future. We are always pleased to see customers who want to collect their goods from our offices, but for those of you who are not able to travel, rest assured that the postage charge we make covers the cost of getting your goods to you in a condition we consider vital to ensure their protection, nothing more.

Can you experiment to make the structure of your additional charges cleaner and clearer? In general, the briefer the explanation, the better. Postage costs to you are fixed according to the carrier's weight scales, but packaging is at your firm's discretion. 'Postage and packing' together can be levied as you decide best, as either a fixed total or a percentage of the amount spent. (Bear in mind that most people cannot work out a percentage other than 10 per cent in their head, and will resent being asked, or even not bother to order if asked, to calculate postage costs.) Consider too that people often think postage costs more than it actually does, and books are heavy items. Some firms make quite a lot of money from carriage. Alternatively, try an offer with free postage and packing, maybe over a certain order value. This may well push up the overall response rate enough to justify the extra costs incurred. If you are doing this, write 'FREE' in the subtotal box on your order form to make the point more clearly.

If you ask customers to work out the p&p payable and add it to the total value of the goods ordered, but receive cheques for less than the sum due, it is probably deliberate. Bank the money; it is not worth rejecting the order to obtain the extra 10 per cent.

WHAT TO DO WITH THE RETURNS

All direct marketing campaigns produce returns, because the messages go to individuals who are essentially unpredictable. However well the list is kept, people on it will have moved, changed jobs or died. The important thing is to ensure the changes that produced the returns are noted.

Envelopes returned as undeliverable might come to your firm or the mailing house, depending on the return address provided. If they come to the mailing house, ask it to batch them up and send them back to you at regular intervals. Extract the contents, write the code from the order form on the envelope to show which list it came from, then delete the same code from the order form. You then have leaflets ready for re-use (exhibitions, insertions in other company post and so on) and envelopes ready to go back to the list owner. You should get a credit if the returns total more than 5 per cent of the list you rented, otherwise you will simply have contributed to cleaning the list. Don't forget a credit on list rental is a small element of your actual costs in mailing the addresses provided; some firms may be willing to compensate further.

Gone-aways on e-mail lists come back quicker and need to be noted on the master list. Pay particular care to institutional e-mails: rather than indicating that the individual has gone away, the returned e-mail might draw attention to a wider change of address format that needs investigating.

WHICH DIRECT MARKETING FORMAT TO CHOOSE

Although we have focused above on hard-copy envelope mailings, the principles are the same for any format, from simple postcards to multi-component mailings. You will invariably have less space than you would ideally like to explain product benefits, and you always need to attract recipients' attention quickly and to direct them to the ordering mechanism.

Printed direct marketing

When the internet started to explode, and more and more organizations came to use websites and e-mail, many assumed it would be the end of direct mail. Not so. It's true that mailings are getting increasingly specialized. As direct marketing becomes more efficient, and data handling more precise, mailers can store and access information to make really effective promotions. And the huge increase in e-mail means that many people delete 'junk mail' without reading it carefully, if at all. An effective printed piece grabs people's attention as it is physically in front of them.

Use hard-copy mail when:

■ You can be really precise about whom you want to get to.
■ The physical format of the mailing will impress your market.
■ The product or service needs to be discussed before a commitment is made. This is more easily done with a printed format in front of people than a screen reference.
■ The product you are promoting is impressive, and carries a status and weight that is best relayed through print.

■ The product or service is best promoted without an implication that targeting has been used, and a personally addressed e-mail would be threatening or unpleasant.

Catalogues

See page 30. Catalogues used in direct marketing need to make lots of references to how to order (don't just put an order form at the end or in the middle, and leave your customers to work it out for themselves).

Card decks

These are bunches of cards, mailed like a pack of playing cards. Each card advertises a different product and bears an order form and reply-paid address on the reverse. They are popular as the individuals receiving them find the shape appealing (many end up in wallets or pockets), and often pass on cards they know to be of interest to colleagues. Publishers have experimented with including deck-sized mini catalogues within the pack, which provide handy reference to everything they produce.

L-shaped cards

These are much used as loose inserts in consumer magazines. The main part of the copy is on the larger upright part of the 'L'; the 'foot' detaches, usually along a perforated strip, to form a reply card. They can be cost-effective to produce, particularly if two Ls can be laid out as a jigsaw fit on the printing plate, making maximum use of the card. They work best for creating interest, eg stimulating requests for a catalogue or 'invoice me' type orders. Note that unless they have the confidentiality provided by a reply envelope, recipients will not be willing to give information such as a credit card number.

Roll fold sheets

This is a single sheet of paper, printed on two sides, with arrows and dotted lines indicating where the customer should fold and tuck the flaps in. This turns it into a reply device for which no envelope is needed. They are ideal for mailings where you want to imply value for money, or for information-seeking exercises where the details being sought are not personal or confidential.

'Bang tail' mailshots or one-piece mailers

This is the most sophisticated sort of self-mailer. A long strip of paper folded several times, the outer end is stuck down to form an item suitable for mailing. When the mailing piece is opened and the information revealed, the other end of the sheet has been gummed to form a ready-made reply envelope, which the recipient has only to detach to use. Thus all the component parts of the mailing piece are combined in one convenient and attractive format. These mailing pieces are expensive to produce, given the origami standard of folding and finishing required, and provide much less space for explanation than a traditional multi-component mailing package. They tend to work well for products that are already familiar to the audience being addressed. For a further cost they can be fully personalized.

For other ideas on direct mail formats consult your letterbox, trade magazines, printers and designers involved in the medium, or visit the annual direct marketing trade fairs.

TELEMARKETING

The popularity of telemarketing is growing fast, for both creating sales and following up on other direct marketing initiatives. Selling over the phone is the natural extension of the personal contact for which direct mail strives, but by talking directly to the market much more comprehensive feedback can be obtained. Telemarketing is increasingly used for the promotion of goods to consumers.

It can be difficult to estimate the extent of telemarketing. Many firms offer a telephone number for the receipt of orders ('in-bound' telemarketing) and involve their customer services staff in making 'out-bound' calls, but never calculate the costs of operating the systems independently. They get lost in overall company overheads. Out-bound work carried out by telemarketing bureaux can of course be estimated, and current feedback shows that more is spent on telemarketing in some markets than on direct mail. It is also growing quickly, although it is difficult to be clear how much of the spend goes through bureaux.

The advantages of telemarketing

■ A highly effective means of selling; it produces orders.
■ It usually results in faster sales than other methods of marketing, which is better for company cashflow.
■ You get immediate feedback on whatever you are promoting. Through first-hand contact with your market your company gains valuable and current sales information. Every call is an opportunity for research.
■ It can lead to improved customer relations. Telemarketing reinforces the reputation of your company for service. You gain by talking directly to your customers: everyone likes to be listened to, and although poorly handled cold calls can be irritating at home, they are generally acceptable at work if well handled.
■ Recording market reactions to your product and company offers you long-term leads as well as initial sales opportunities.
■ It is very cost-effective. It is true that the cost per contact made is high in comparison with direct mail, so a mailing can cover more of the market for less money. But with telemarketing every contact yields information (compare this with a mailshot yielding a 2 per cent response; 98 per cent of those contacted provide you with no feedback on why they did not order). You therefore waste no further money on contacting those not interested in your products. Responses are measurable on an hourly basis. You need to commit yourself only to a test marketing, and can decide to expand or cut back your efforts depending on the results.
■ By using a telemarketing agency you can carry the number of staff working on your account without being responsible for the expensive fixed costs of staff hiring or training.

How to go about telemarketing

The introduction of telemarketing within your company will be most effective if the principles involved are adopted by the company as a whole rather than seen as the particular practices of a single department. This means making it clear that telephone orders are welcome rather than a nuisance, and encouraging the telephonist to return to those 'on hold' rather than leaving them to make their own decision whether to hang up. To assess the situation, try ringing your own switchboard from home to find out what scope there is for improvement!

Second, telemarketing should not be seen as a separate marketing technique, but integrated into all your other marketing activities. Telemarketing can be used to follow up mailing pieces, make appointments for reps or invite customers to preview evenings for your forthcoming list. The research you gain as a result should be central to how you plan to promote in the future.

Whom to ring

Another acronym for you. The prospect you are searching for is the MAN: the person with the Money and the Authority to purchase, who has the Need. The starting point should be your own list of past customers. Provided they were satisfied with what they bought, those who have purchased from you in the past are the prospects most likely to order from you in the future. If you make a few adaptations to your direct mail order forms you can start building your own permitted (data protection applies here too) telemarketing lists for future campaigns. You should obviously ask for the telephone number (office and home), but other small additions will help you to build a database of future contacts. For example, before 'Name' write Mr/Mrs/Miss/Ms/title and record what comes back.

Firms that rent mailing lists are increasingly offering telemarketing lists too for an extra charge. Some job titles are much harder to reach than others. If you have selected managing directors you may find you only reach two every hour. Training and personnel managers are notoriously difficult to find: they are always running courses or interviewing. Marketing and financial managers are generally available. If you find a personal assistant persistently blocking access to a particular manager, try ringing back during the lunch hour or after 5.00 pm. You can usually get through then.

If you are planning to mail a rented list then follow up with a telephone campaign, find out if there is a reduced list rental for the second copy of the list. It will not be offered unless you ask.

Examples of telemarketing usage

Market research

Telemarketing is an effective way to test customer reaction to new products and ideas; to identify new market sectors and measure market attitudes; to find out who within an organization should be targeted with sales information and how large their budget is; and to test a price, offer or incentive.

As part of a direct marketing campaign

Telemarketing is an excellent way to update mailing lists, to qualify (establish real interest from) sales leads generated, to follow up a mailing piece and thus increase the response rate, and to carry out post-campaign research and analysis. The results of a telemarketing campaign can be set up as a database for future mailing of a market about which the company already knows a great deal.

To generate sales opportunities for reps

Telemarketing can be used to canvass sales leads and set appointments. This reduces the need for cold calls, establishes the prospect's interest in the company's products before the call is made and improves the effectiveness of the sales team.

To build customer relations

Telemarketing is a very good way to handle potential or actual problems such as customer enquiries or complaints, and to reactivate old contacts.

Who should do the ringing?

Successful telemarketing is a skill. It requires a combination of product knowledge and an ability to communicate on the telephone. The caller has to build a relationship with the prospect, while noting information passed on (whether directly or indirectly), preparing the next question and keeping the conversation going. In searching for the right people to do the ringing, you have four basic options:

■ Ring the contacts yourself.
■ Employ someone to do it in-house.
■ Pay an agency to do it for you.
■ Pay someone to do it for you freelance, at home or from your office.

Whereas you may have all the requisite product knowledge, creating the time and the inclination to carry out telemarketing in-house can be very difficult. To find a freelance or employee, you could advertise in the local paper. Provide a telephone number for those interested to ring you for more information, so you will hear them in action. Bureaux look for staff in the same way: the telephone manner should be confident and friendly and the voice clear.

Remember, if you use salespeople in-house you must provide the administrative back-up they need. Each call they make may require some follow-up: a confirmation of order, or a letter to accompany a brochure that was requested. These are hot leads and must be dealt with straight away; they must never be allowed to sit at the bottom of an overworked (and probably resentful) administration assistant's in-tray for three or four days.

A dedicated telemarketing agency probably offers the best way to test the water. Having briefed them on your product, market and competitors, you benefit from their expertise on how best to target and time the approach. They are responsible for training the people who will work on your account, in both product knowledge and selling skills. Most agencies offer a basic package including the creation of a 'framework for calls' (never a 'script') based on a thorough understanding of product benefits, an initial number of telephone contracts and a report on the results. After this the client may decide to abort the campaign, make changes or carry on as is.

Employing a freelance to work for you at home is possibly the least satisfactory option. Those making the calls benefit from the competitive and supportive atmosphere of a telesales office, and it is difficult to keep morale up at home. Faced with a difficult question an operative in an office can seek advice immediately; with rudeness he or she can complain to colleagues rather than the walls. The actual time spent by those making calls from home can also be difficult to monitor.

Most telemarketing staff are paid according to the number of calls made and the time taken, with an incentive bonus scheme based on commission.

Planning a telemarketing campaign

Give detailed consideration to the objectives of the campaign, and how far they are measurable by telemarketing. Establish a framework for calls. It should act as a basis for questions rather than a script to be read. For this you need to consider which of the selling benefits are most relevant to the target market, whether a special offer is appropriate, how customers can pay, what further information is available should a prospect ask for more details, and how the information obtained should be recorded for future use. If the product being sold is complicated it should be demonstrated to the people making the calls; if it is portable there should be one in the telesales office.

Figure 5.2 is an example of the kind of information-seeking ('open-ended') questions a telesales person should ask. The product in this example is *The Truck Driver's Handbook*, an annual publication featuring the key safety and legal requirements for those driving lorries within Europe. An individual copy is £20, a pack of 10 costs £175.00. The list is the publisher's own list of previous purchasers of bulk copies.

To the switchboard:
Good am/pm, this is Ann Scott ringing from Overdrive Publishers. May I please speak to Mr/Ms (previous contact)?
Could you tell me what department that is please? Note (1). What job title? Note (1).
Could you put me through please?
If the contact has left, ask who has replaced, note the new name, initials and spelling and then ask to be put through.

To the contact:
Good am/pm, this is Ann Scott ringing from Overdrive Publishers. Do you have a couple of minutes to speak to me now? Note (2).
We publish *The Truck Driver's Handbook*, of which you bought x copies last year. I presume that was for use by your drivers with some copies for head office?
If yes ask: How many drivers do you have now? Note.
If no ask: Who uses it? Note.
The reason for my call is that the 2008 edition will be available in two months' time. Do you know how many you will need this year? If you order now we can ensure copies are with your staff as soon as they are available.
Listen to how many required. Note.
Is that enough for all your staff who need access to the book? If you order over x quantity we are able to offer you a discount, and we will also cover the express delivery costs of getting the books to your offices.
Explain discount structure.

The close:
So how many would you like to order? Note (3).
Thank you very much. Our customer services department will invoice you for the books within the next few days.

Figure 5.2   Sample telesales guidance

Check the address of company, postcode etc, confirm spelling of name and any others terms you are unsure of.

Finally:
This is just one of a series of business handbooks that we publish. Would you like me to enclose a copy of our most recent catalogue with the invoice? Note (4).
Thank you and goodbye.

Notes

1. Gather all the information you can.
2. Depending on the level of contact you are calling it is important to establish permission for the call to proceed. As there are few things more annoying than having your train of thought (or a meeting) interrupted by an unexpected and irrelevant call, be courteous. If you are polite enough to establish that it is an inconvenient time to call and you suggest that you ring back later, you will usually be offered a call back time.
3. This is called an assumptive close, a method of closing (or clinching) the sale. For this positive approach to be used the caller has to be sure the prospect wishes to order. Other possible techniques are the alternative close:

> So would you like one pack at £175 or 10 packs at £750? (Either answer is a yes.)

or the incentive close:

> So if I take your order for the copies you need now you will save a further 5 per cent. How many would you like to order on this basis?

This can be used whether or not you have made a sale.

4. Always agree with the caller then go on to explain your point of view.

Figure 5.2 *Continued*

As well as the framework for the call, you need to provide your telesales people with the relevant information to deal with possible objections or questions. This is probably best stored on a series of screen prompts or cards that the person making the call can refer to quickly without being 'thrown'. For this product they might include:

It's too expensive.
Yes, £20 may sound a lot, but this is information your staff need access to every working day; details that they are legally required to know and comply with, wherever they are. (Note: never knock the competition. It debases the whole tone of your conversation and makes prospects sound stupid if they are already committed to the other option mentioned. Instead, if the competition is brought up by the prospect, make a positive comparison with your product by stating its benefits.)

Don't forget that if you buy 10 you get a substantial discount, and if you were to order more copies the unit price could go down still further.

We did buy copies last year, but won't be doing so this year. It is company policy to buy copies only once every two years.
That is a way to keep costs down, but your staff will be referring to out-of-date information. Each year around 40 per cent of the information included in the book changes, so by the end of two years they will be substantially out of date. And this is information they are legally required to know and comply with, wherever they are.

Don't forget there is a generous discount structure for customers buying bulk copies for their staff, so you could perhaps afford to buy copies every year. Explain the discount structure.

We will get copies for the drivers but will make do with a couple of copies for head office this year; our staff can share.
Yes, of course that is a way of keeping costs down, but in our experience we find those who regularly use the book need it on their desks, every day, to refer to when they are on the phone, or for instant access to information. You risk wasting expensive employee time as your staff hunt for the shared copy every time they need it.

It goes out of date so quickly.
Of course the information in the edition does go out of date during the next year, but then it is accepted as the bible of the industry; it is what everyone else is using. And we offer an advice line all year round to those who buy on standing order from us.

We use online services.

Online services are very valuable but we find they simply do not provide information as quickly as flicking through a desk copy or keeping a copy in the driver's cab at all times. (Note: you should be armed with any statistics you may need to refer to before any calls are made: for example the cost of online services; how long it takes to get information on screen compared with accessing information in a reference book. In this case it would be useful to make a few calls to people who regularly use the book before ringing any prospects.)

And of course, the costs of online services are substantially higher. (Note: if you don't know, never bluff. Say you will ring back and give the information the prospect asked for later.)

Don't forget that for those companies buying 10 or more copies on standing order we offer an advice line on current legislation all year round.

We let our drivers buy their own copies.

Asking drivers to buy their own keeps your costs down, but when they are driving for your company, don't forget the legal responsibility is yours. Your firm must ensure each driver understands and adheres to local laws.

How to keep track of calls

Information from the questions answered should be recorded on a ready-made telesales contact sheet. Notes should be made as the call proceeds or immediately afterwards. Once a few calls have been made all will blur into one another and the caller will not be able to remember who said what.

DIRECT MARKETING BY E-MAIL

E-mail provides us with a particularly valuable direct marketing tool. It is quicker for the recipient than reading a physical mailing piece, and non-intrusive (unlike telemarketing). It also offers much lower costs of delivery than other direct marketing methods, with often much higher responses.

You should aim both to increase sales via e-mail promotions to your customers, and to develop mailing lists through the collection of names and e-mail addresses (within the provisions of data protection legislation). E-mail also provides a very valuable method of market research via direct customer contact and sophisticated statistics reporting.

An effective e-mail should be targeted to the appropriate audience, be short and entice a reply. The goal should be to start a relationship with recipients and encourage them to request more information. Think what you have to offer the recipient: a sample chapter, author information, press release, a visit to the website and so on. E-mail can also be used to send press releases, highlight forthcoming events and distribute flyers and leaflets.

It is advisable to use a multi-e-mailing facility software package such as Campaign or MailKing, and a contact database as a storage solution for collecting e-mails and maintaining lists. This allows you to mail lots of people individually at the same time (without the entire circulation list appearing at the top of the message).

Here are some further hints for producing effective e-mails:

■ To successfully convey your brand without a logo, use a simple header at the start of your e-mail (your name and the company name rather than anything 'clever').

■ Keep the subject line short (no more than 55 characters) but interesting.

■ Use BCC (blind carbon copy) for multiple mailings. Choose the 'address' field and then put yourself in the 'To' field. Use BCC or individual addressing depending on the number of e-mails being sent. If you use 'CC' then everyone who receives your mail also gets a copy of your customer list – not a good idea.

■ Keep the body copy short, inviting and certainly no more than a screenful. Avoid using attachments.

■ The look of the message is determined by the user's software, so it is difficult to predict how it will be received. Problems occur with spelling, truncated messages, and non-standard characters such as quote marks, bullet points, apostrophes, asterisks and underscoring. It is advisable to use a line length of no more than 50 characters so the whole width of the message is visible on screen at the same time. Use underscores or asterisks to convey emphasis, as using capital letters is regarded as shouting.

■ Signatures need to be standardized company-wide, and include all contact details and your URL. (For business e-mail, it's usually a legal requirement to include standard information on the sender, in the same way that a letterhead offers information on the sender.) Beneath these details you can add a tag line featuring news or a headline. These need to be changed from time to time to avoid boredom.

■ Many companies now add a disclaimer to the end of all external e-mails. This can be reassuring to individuals who are often more protective of their e-mail address than their terrestrial one. You can cover who the message is meant for and the use to which you plan to put the data, such as 'We will keep your details on file to keep you up to date with our publishing programme but will never pass your e-mail address on to a third party.' Provide the chance to 'unsubscribe' for those who wish to do so.

Where to find your audience of e-mail users

First, send press releases with your URL to your media list. Some information requests will come back via e-mail. You should also place alert/announcement e-mails in appropriate internet discussion groups and forums. You can locate appropriate groups/lists through your authors, editors, search engines, service providers and super-sites, such as:

■ www.JISC.ac.uk
■ www.lizst.com
■ www.listtool.com
■ www.usenet-addresses.mit.edu
■ www.lsoft.com

Before you start posting messages, it is a good idea to do some market research. Study group/list guidelines, legal messages and existing e-mails to understand the audience for each channel. Check the relevance of the announcement and the style of message to be used. Bear in mind that the majority of groups and forums are now moderated, so it is a good idea to find out who does this or who cultivated the audiences, and develop a good working relationship with them.

DIRECT MARKETING BY FAX

Fax machines may now be old technology but there are still a lot of them in the marketplace. What is more, placing orders by fax appeals because it means the printed order can be sent as an image, and then filed. There's no hunting back through the e-mail 'out' or 'deleted' box to find a copy of an order placed.

Sending marketing material by fax means that recipients have to pay for its receipt, and the message being sent blocks incoming calls. As a result sending direct marketing material by fax is now illegal in several US states.

But where an established trading relationship between two companies exists, sending information by fax is an excellent way of communicating – for example to inform a client company about last-minute availability of something they had requested.

A FINAL CHECKLIST FOR ALL FORMS OF DIRECT MARKETING

- Is the copy really strong on product benefits and reasons to buy?
- Would I buy from me? Is the copy strong enough?
- If you are writing about something you do not understand, has the copy been checked by an expert such as the editor or the author?
- Have you called the book by the same title each time?
- Have you used the title too often (boring)?
- Is it clear what the price is and how much should be added for postage and packing etc?
- Is it clear how to order and by when?
- Are the publisher's name, address, telephone, e-mail, website and fax numbers on all the elements in the package?
- Are the contact details really large enough to find and read in a rush?
- What does the customer do if he or she is unclear about some aspect of your product? Are you offering a telephone number for enquiries? Is it working (try it now)?
- Have you included an option for capturing non-buying prospects?
- Triple-check the final proofs for press for consistency, grammatical errors etc. Publishers are expected to get these things right! Last-minute changes are very expensive.
- How is your marketing piece to be followed up: by your reps, by remailing, with telemarketing etc?
- If you offer a slot for those who do not want to order now saying 'Please send me further information on ...' have you sorted out what you are going to send?
- Have you told everyone who needs to know, from customer services to those who may answer your phone?
- Is your address on the outer envelope so that undelivered shots can be returned?

This is the longest chapter in the book, which shows how much there is to say about direct marketing. Good luck.

6

Using the internet to sell

There is little point in starting this chapter with statistics about how the internet has grown; they would be out of date before the book had reached the publishers, let alone made it onto the printing press. Perhaps more interesting for publishers is to note how they have been affected by the rise of the internet, how the industry's usage of it as a marketing medium has changed, and how they can best benefit from it in future.

THE RISE OF INTERNET SALES

Books are one of the most commonly bought (legal) products over the web (along with CDs, clothes and flights). It's not hard to see why. One of the main characteristics of products bought this way has to be their certifiable brandedness; consumers cannot see or touch what they are buying so they have to be sure that the item they are buying is what it says it is. Consumers like to cross-refer to check they are getting the cheapest price – and they can only do that effectively if they are sure they are checking exactly the same item on each site. Then once the decision to purchase has been made, the consumer must have confidence that the retailer will deliver. In the same way that the Virgin Atlantic flight from London Heathrow to Miami International is a standard item, whose price can be cross-checked on a variety of different travel websites, or on the airline's own, books are strongly branded items. Barring outright fraud, there is only one product that is 'the new John Grisham', although the number of outlets for obtaining it may be numerous.

This has a huge advantage for publishers in that all their products are now continually in stock and permanently available via internet bookselling facilities, whether their own or other people's, even if the quoted delivery times are long (perhaps allowing for print on demand). No book need ever be out of print again. The internet also offers publishers a very long 'tail' on traditional sales patterns: long after conventional bookshops have stopped stocking older titles, books can still be available online. This can yield substantial extra sales.

Internet bookshops are able to offer unlimited shelf space and consequently a much larger number of titles (average about 1.5 million) than even the largest physical bookshop (average 150,000). They can also do, all the time, what no physical bookshop can possibly achieve with similar consistency: organize, recommend and cross-refer according to the tastes of the individual customer, with the added benefit of being open for business 24 hours a day, every day of the year. The returns rate from internet bookshops is also very low (less than 4 per cent). Sales are dominated by backlist titles, including reprints of out-of-print and difficult to obtain material, and hence are very high in the academic sector.

But this increased availability is accompanied by a range of issues that publishers must also deal with. Marketing theorists have long emphasized the need to manage a push–pull process to make the relationship with retailers as effective and profitable as possible.

> *Push*: through promoting to intermediaries who are then expected to promote the item to the final consumers.
> *Pull*: develop strong demand amongst final buyers who exert pressure on intermediaries to obtain what they want.

Thus publishers must *push* stock out to shops, by persuading retailers to take sufficient to meet expected consumer demand, and then encourage consumers to *pull* that stock off the shelves by going into shops and requesting the titles they have heard about. Up to now this has been managed through providing the right kind of information, disseminated over extended, and familiar, lead times. Information is sent to booksellers so they understand the significance of the product that is coming, what the publisher will be doing to support it and how great the demand created will be; to consumers through the media and other established information channels, so they desire the product and know where to source it. This process has been going on for so long that it is highly automated.

With online sales, the same overall strategy is required, but the processes through which this is achieved are slightly different. The publisher's challenge is first to treat online book retailers like any other account: keep in touch with them and try to ensure they are supporting the firm's publishing through ordering enough stock to meet demand. But to create the corresponding pull from online customers publishers have to provide information about their products via the wide variety of information sources that online customers find useful. This is something that many publishers, with full-time jobs and reliance on traditional book marketing and delivery mechanisms, find difficult. Guidance on how to do this will follow.

Second, the discounts demanded by internet book retailers are big; greater than those sought by physical bookshops, while their own marketing costs have usually remained constant. The publisher may thus be paying high marketing costs to inform the market of their product and then giving away big discounts to internet retailers who scoop up the order. In this way even targeted marketing campaigns for specialist product can result in an online purchase, with the publisher paying twice!

The third issue is that customers shopping for books online have to know what they are looking for; browsing mechanisms are getting more sophisticated all the time, but at the moment cross-selling opportunities offered by internet booksellers are to their advantage (selling more books, increasing the value of the customer's order) rather than the publisher's (selling more titles from the same house).

HOW INTERNET USAGE BY PUBLISHERS HAS CHANGED

The first publisher websites were copy-heavy and not at all interactive. Publishers simply loaded catalogue copy onto their sites and expected users to seek from them the kind of specific detail they were used to finding in the other information vehicles they were used to receiving, such as leaflets and seasonal lists.

Today there is a much wider understanding that online customers are time-pressured, of short attention span, searching for convenience, and want to interact with those whose sites they visit rather than simply seeking to absorb information. Habits acquired through social networking on the internet (for example on MySpace and Facebook) influence how customers use publishers' websites: they want to take part, not just read what is there. Publishers need to think about how they can perhaps use social networking to their advantage and help to market suitable books.

Whereas customers reading a catalogue may flick on a few pages if they are not interested, bore website browsers and they respond by quitting the site – and quickly. Publishers' sites are consequently becoming more inter-active, and the copy is being loaded in a more customer-friendly fashion, with more space (aids legibility; always a problem on screen which is tiring for the eyes), and more 'added-value' information in click-through boxes. But the pace of this development is highly variable: many publishers simply do not realize the power of the internet, and continue to view it as 'add on' rather than 'core' marketing.

Publishers are however in a better position than other types of producer. When the website explosion started, and firms realized they needed web-sites, most turned to one of the many newly created specialist web marketing agencies that began to appear. These agencies were new, but crucially being independent of the traditional advertising agencies that had serviced the promotional needs of these firms in the past, were now competing for the same marketing spend. Clients often found themselves at the mercy of two groups of creatives, who both wanted a lion's share of the marketing budget, and were in competition with each other rather than jointly committed to promoting the brand. Often the online communication message bore no relationship with that being sold offline. Lower marketing budgets in publishing at least meant that rather than seeking to involve external agencies, website solutions were often developed in-house, and so long-term integration as part of the organization's overall marketing strategy was less problematic.

Today publishers need to see online marketing as part of their overall marketing effort, reinforcing and providing a supporting message, not something that is thought of afterwards. Not having a website is not an option: it's an essential, not a luxury.

HOW TO IMPROVE THE EFFECTIVENESS OF ONLINE MARKETING

Look at – and use – lots of websites

It always worries me when publishers seek to direct market their customers but confess a disdain for the medium in general (eg 'I never buy online/read my junk mail/can tolerate telemarketing'). You are unlikely to be able to get onto the wavelength of the potential customer if you do not see how you respond to marketing messages sent in the same way.

If you are seeking to promote your titles through the internet you need to understand how it feels and how the system works. Recent research revealed that most internet users keep track of about 8–10 sites on a regular basis, and that once we have decided a particular site no longer appeals, we are unforgiving. This rings entirely true with me: there are sites I used to check on a regular basis, but once I made an (often subconscious) decision to stop looking, I never revisited them. I simply found somewhere else to go instead.

Similarly, you must pay attention to all the little details that keep people on a site (often referred to as its level of 'stickiness'), such as:

■ Pop-ups that indicate how long you will have to wait. A 30-second wait may not sound much, but if a site fails to tell you how long you will be kept, and that while you are waiting the computer is really doing something for you, the impatient customer is likely to be off and looking somewhere else.
■ The site's ease of navigability. Is there a prompt that tells you where you are at all times? Can you always get back to the home page in just one click?
■ Can you find an instruction that says 'Contact us'? I find this is one of the first things I look for, and if it is not there, assume the site will be an effort to grapple with – and often give up.

Madeleine Parkyn, a former senior manager in publishing and now a web-weaver who has designed websites for Orion and Virago, asserts that paying attention to good usability is the key to creating successful websites:

> If people can't understand something, they simply won't engage with it. All of us, when we are able to, avoid things which make our lives more difficult. Someone visiting a website might be able to get what they want from it, eventually, and they will persevere if it is the only place they can get that information; but ideally you want to help them to get what they want with the minimum time and effort – then, having had a good experience, they will keep coming back. For a website to provide a good experience for its users, it has to be fast loading, designed in a way that is appropriate to its content and intuitive to use.

The usability of a website can be tested and improved during its development. Very useful insights can come from observing how even a small number of people from the intended user group inter-act with the website.

Understand the internet customer

Internet shoppers are usually looking for one of two things (and sometimes both). They are seeking information or/and entertainment.

If it's information they are after, they want it quickly. What's the price? What's the availability? How long do I have before I need to make a deci-sion? What can I find to say at my book group this evening that gives a different slant on the author and why he or she wrote this book? When it comes to choosing sites for entertainment people are engrossed for as long as they are interested – and time can flash by while this goes on. But once the first enthusiasm wanes, if no new attractions or information are added, or the features grow stale, they are quickly bored and move on to something else.

Buying or browsing online also offers the consumer a very real sense of personal empowerment. Completion can come remarkably quickly. It's possible to progress from information trawl to purchase in a very short period of time; this sense of self-determination feels efficient and quickly becomes addictive.

Disintermediarization (see the Glossary) is the common result. In this case it takes the form of an interruption in the former process of buying things: few who have bought airline tickets online go back to buying them through third parties. In part the trend results from consumers' determination to get better value for money for themselves, and there is also a significant new type of direct buying, from customers who want to ensure more money goes to the producer rather than a middle person. Both can also be seen as proof of the emergence of vastly more aware consumers, who are prepared to source and investigate the origin of goods they want rather than simply accept a third party's self-interested edit of what is available.

Penetrate information sources used by internet browsers

Publishers have up to now tended to view the internet as a means of providing information about their products and ordering mechanisms if the consumer decides to proceed. But this simplistic view vastly underestimates the medium's role as a means of communication, and hence the extent to which they need to penetrate the various communication channels that feed demand.

The internet is fast becoming a social and viral network through which ideas, trends and information are exchanged. Jokes, anecdotes – and other people's e-mails – move quickly round the world, with added comment; our social life takes place both off and online. People 'Google' their new acquaintances to find out more about them.

At the same time, with daily life becoming more and more automated, and everything available online, individual customers are looking for relationships with their preferred brands; to find out more about them. And if they are offered what they like, they will enthuse about them to other people they know like to buy and communicate in this way. This means it is essential for marketers to get involved and keep up to date with how information is being exchanged, and to seek to offer the kind of relationship that their customers are willing to both get involved with and talk up to other people.

Have a good website – and that means update it often

An effective website is a conversation with viewers; it feels personal. Thus while the same organizational personality is promoted, the things it says need to change – in the same way that friendships are between individuals, but if the person you are meeting with always said the same things, or wore exactly the same outfit, the relationship could quickly feel staid. Organizational commitment to having a website means that there must be equal commitment to keeping it up to date.

The other important factor is that maintaining a website should be seen as an integral part of marketing in this way, not an add-on. Thus rather than repeating the same information that is featured in your catalogue or blurbs, offer added-value, quirky information that readers can feel they have exclusive access to. This is particularly important for publishers, whose sites are often used by journalists, or those with a particular interest in specific authors (eg those hosting reading circles or teaching a book in schools), who are looking for additional interesting material. If they get the feeling that you provide the kind of details they like and that give them additional and interesting things to say, they will return.

Website marketing also offers smaller publishing houses a huge advantage: you can present the image you want your potential customers to see, even if the reality is that you only have a tiny staff. In a world of creeping blandness and huge organizations which seek to dominate every aspect of our needs (but at the same time limit our choice to what they have chosen to stock), this is the place to talk about your commitment to what you do, your previous job paths (and why what you do now is much more satisfying), and to treat your potential customer to a snapshot of your vision. This is interesting information, and may motivate the start of a relationship with you – and even persuade your customers to buy directly from you rather than through a internet retailing superstore.

Reassure the browser that the buying mechanisms work

Branded security mechanisms to make your customers feel comfortable about buying directly from you are vital. If you do not provide them, customers have an easy alternative in the large online book retailing mechanisms that already exist, so you risk creating demand without sharing in the profits of fulfilling the order. Alternatively you can create a link with and kickback from with the large sites, so every order placed via your site earns you a small rebate. Better than nothing.

HOW TO SET UP A WEBSITE

I shall not offer detailed advice on how to do this, because there are many other sources of expertise. I will confine myself to the basics (sufficient for you to ask the right questions). But before we proceed to the basics, there are a few key questions for the organization to think about.

What is it for?

A clear policy statement now will save time later on. The website should be a communications channel with specific aims in mind, not a repository for information no one is sure where to put.

So is it for general company information, product and service inform-ation, customer support and feedback or online transactions? Or all of these things? Bear in mind that if you are going to be accepting money online, the development time for your website must be multiplied by a factor of at least four. It's self-evident that the less interactive your website, the easier it is to get it up and running. If you are going from a standing start (ie you have never had one before) this may be your cheapest option. You also need to decide how much money you want to spend on your website. This will dictate the level of sophistication.

Who should be in charge of the website?

I would argue it should be part of the marketing department, as it is a crucial channel of communication that should be part of the wide range of strategies and tactics used to market and communicate. If it is under the orbit of the IT department there will be a tendency to think about functionality (what it can or can't do) rather than what it needs to do in order to be most effective. You would not allow a printer to say what should go inside a book, and for the same reason your IT department should not be in charge of website content or usability. Its role is to provide what the marketing department deems necessary.

How often is it to be updated and by whom?

Site maintenance is very important. Decide now who is to be responsible for maintaining content, developing and updating your website. The person selected should have an overview of the entire company's priorities and customers. The updating bit is crucial – it offers your customers a very bad impression if they take the trouble to visit your website and then find out that the information is stale or out of date.

This need not entail major changes but it does require alertness. Make sure that somebody is responsible for checking the website content regularly, to remove out-of-date news, or even simply change the copy from future to past tense. One way to ensure that the information on your website is up to date is to generate your pages from your company database so that changes in your product profiles, price or availability can be updated automatically.

Who needs to be asked for content?

Anyone concerned with the development or wider sale of your products. So encourage your colleagues in- and out-of-house, your authors and your sales team to feed back interesting anecdotes, press features and customer reactions that offer potential for inclusion.

Your authors are an obvious starting point. Some are vastly more websavvy than their publishers; many have grown used to feedback from their readers in this way. You may want to set up a standardized page for each author you represent, and make a link to their own site (the organizational policy on whether or not to do this usually depends on who else publishes them). For less technically adept authors, you may like to create a website that feels specific to them and their writing but is in fact part of your house site (eg www.jacquelinewilson.co.uk is part of the Random House UK site).

THE BASICS: WHAT TO DO FIRST

To get access to the internet you can either use a server belonging to a commercial service provider (an Internet Service Provider or ISP) or install your own. Intense competition between providers is bringing about a rapid fall in subscription prices and the amount of bandwidth you can buy for your spend.

When deciding whether to go it alone or use an ISP, you need to think about how big your site is going to be, what kind of support levels you need (how much do you know now about setting up a website?), how quickly you will need to change your information on it and what the charges will be for doing so (beware very high update charges, the most essential point about a website is that it should be updated often).

Most ISPs start you off with a certain amount of space on their server and will increase it in additional blocks. Look at the support levels they offer – ideally this should be 24 hours a day, 7 days a week. How flexible are they? Can they allow you to handle credit card transactions and capture customer details? If you want to link your database to your website it may be worth considering a leased line. This is much more expensive, and will most probably entail an upgrade of your computer system, but will give you greater control and flexibility in the long run.

What domain name

When choosing a domain name keep it short, memorable and unlikely to be misspelt. Registration costs are not high, and it is worth registering alternatives (eg for an Australian company both .com and .co.au). As well as your main website address you might want to register imprint names, brands (eg for popular series) and potential misspellings. Potential customers who do not know your precise address will look for you through a search engine, and this may bring a completely different firm with a similar name to their attention (and lead them off in a completely different direction). You can search and register names with:

■ http://www.internic.com
■ http://www.nominet.co.uk
■ http://www.whois.co.uk

Bear in mind that you may have to think of an alternative name to your first choice, which may already have been taken by another organization. Most publishers have been forced to add 'books' or 'publishing' to their firm's address because someone else had already taken their most obvious domain name, thus the Orion Publishing Group's website is www.orionbooks.uk.

Try to think how people will find you – web surfers are usually wanting to get quick access to the information, not to play clever games; anticipating what you might have chosen as a domain name. When publishers first launched websites many chose interesting names: the first UK HarperCollins website was www.fireandwater.co.uk, a reference to its logo which features flames and waves, but significantly it has now morphed into www.harpercollins. co.uk. If web browsers do not find what they need in a hurry, they move on (and don't come back).

PLANNING AND DESIGNING YOUR WEBSITE

Exploiting the opportunities presented by the internet raises the same difficulties as a bookshop presents: you have to get people to visit your site and, once there, you have to get them to buy. You can be situated in a prime site at great expense (within the electronic shopping malls) or in the back street of a small market town (on your own pages with a little-known server). You can pay thousands to have your shop fitted out stylishly (getting a web consultant to create your pages for you with bespoke software for interactive communication and secure transactions) or you can fit your shop out yourself on a budget, having planned what you want and using a local carpenter. (The building of web pages is much easier than people think, and if you already have a suitable computer, you can be up and running quite cheaply with an e-mail address and enough server space for a web page or two.)

If you decide to use an external web design company, you will need to evaluate its experience and decide whether it is relevant to your own requirements. The typical costs for design and supply of five pages of graphics can be judged from the small ads in magazines appealing to potential customers, and they seem to be falling all the time (although commissioning decisions based on price are seldom satisfactory in the longer term).

Here are some useful questions to ask of potential web designers:

- How much experience have you got in web design and production?
- When did you create your first website?
- Can I have a look at examples of sites you have created? Can I have access (you may need a temporary password) so I can visit them and see how they work?
- What is the price range of the sites you have created?
- How do you charge? By the hour, the page or by the project?
- Could you talk me through the process of creating a site? Then ask yourself whether you feel they have covered everything and whether they explain things in a way you can understand. What are the approval procedures?
- How long does it take to create a website? (Beware over-optimistic, short estimations.)
- Can I meet the people who will actually do the work? If not, why not?
- Can I take over the maintenance of my site? Will you train me to manage and update the site?
- Can I get in touch with any of your previous clients? This is to find out what the designers were like to work with, and if their clients are still working with them. Would they use this web company again? Were the web designers flexible to work with and did they listen to the client?
- Did they stick to the budget and deliver on time?

Before assuming that low budgets mean you must set up your site by DIY, you need to consider what else you would not be doing while you were learning how to make a website, and also bear in mind that this option means you will lose out on the expertise that people working with the web all the time acquire, about the technicalities and the culture of the web, what works well and what doesn't. Beware of reinventing the wheel.

THE COST TO SET UP A WEBSITE

Typically the costs for enrolling with an ISP are a set-up charge and then a running charge every month. If you have access to the web through a service provider, you'll probably get a mail account automatically (perhaps for an additional monthly fee), but some providers allow more than one per user, which can be useful in larger companies to 'pre-sort' incoming mail.

As to whether to do it all yourself, website shops are appearing on the high street, and these firms will take your information and lay it out for you. Art and design students often take modules in website design as part of their course and so can be persuaded to lay out sites for you at a lower initial cost – because their experience and overheads are lower – but you need to think about what will happen when the information needs updating. Will you still be able to find them, and will the costs rise disproportionately?

If you decide to get someone else to set up your site, costs can vary markedly according to the level of skill and experience available, how much suppliers want the work (in the early stage of their career, designers may be very keen on building a portfolio of working examples) and how difficult they estimate the client will be to work with. Clients who don't explain what they are trying to achieve, keep changing their mind, and then don't expect to see the increased time reflected in an increased bill, are particularly hard work – and may be charged more. In general, costs rise according to the size of the business doing the commissioning.

You also need to consider the ongoing costs of running a website: the commitment of staff time, the need for an annual budget to cover the cost of keeping the content up to date and new feature developments. Don't forget this. Keeping a website fresh and up to date once the novelty has worn off is hard work.

Whomever you use, even though you draft the text yourself, check it carefully again once it has been loaded onto pages. Sometimes the process of setting up pages means that parts of what you supplied are retyped, and what is uploaded may not be the same as your original copy. Do not assume everyone is reading your material on a large screen (many will be using portables) or that everyone has broadband (usage is growing, but it's by no means universal).

Sean McManus is the author of *Small Business Websites That Work* and the e-book *Journalism Careers – Your questions answered.* (His websites are at www.sean.co.uk and www.journalismcareers.com.) He comments:

> Whatever option you eventually select for the creation of your website, be sure to check out how it looks on the web and from someone else's computer, and from several other browsers (including Firefox, Opera and Safari alongside the market leader Internet Explorer).
>
> The skill in web design is to make something that works on a wide range of computer and browser types and adapts gracefully to what's available. Even if a user is using an ancient browser that is text-only and doesn't even handle pictures, the site should be usable. Publishers have a responsibility to ensure that their content is accessible to people using assistive devices, such as Braille readers and screen readers that read websites aloud. There might be a legal requirement (under disability discrimination legislation), and there's certainly a moral imperative.

SEARCH ENGINE OPTIMIZATION

The vocabulary you use on your website matters hugely. It is vital that your website uses the right kind of words, keywords that will drive people to your site. Use relevant keywords and descriptions in the meta tags, titles and text of each page. Headings in the copy are picked up by search engines as being more important than the body text, so if the right words are used here, they will help the search engine find your website when someone enters keywords relevant to you and your work, and your eventual ranking may be higher. So a story that is described as being 'set in the time of Jane Austen' will get more highly rated than one that is described as set 'in the early years of the 19th century'.

This has to be achieved without overdoing it, because then search engines will think you are trying to trick them by manipulating your ranking, and you risk being banned. This is such an important aspect of website set-up and maintenance that there are companies that specialize in doing just this.

TESTING AND LAUNCHING THE SITE

Testing is essential prior to launch and every time changes are made to the site. You will usually be able to work on an administrative site and view changes on a pre-live website. Be particularly careful about your editorial standards: poor grammar or spelling mistakes look very sloppy from a publishing house. Do ensure the site is easy to navigate. Jarring colours, too many images, an over-wide text measure, reversed-out copy and too many words all distract from the pleasure of viewing a site, and remember that most people browsing the web are looking for a pleasant experience; it's not compulsory reading.

Once the site is launched you need to concentrate on marketing your site and attracting the relevant audience. Thorough analysis of traffic through your site will allow you to develop the future content and structure and address any complaints, problems or suggestions you receive.

MARKETING YOUR WEBSITE

Offline

- Consider producing postcards, sticky labels for your stationery, or mugs with the address on them. Mouse mats are a touch passé.
- Print your URL (Uniform Resource Locator, or the web page address) on all your promotional material, stationery, business cards, invoices etc.
- Try to achieve editorial coverage for your website.
- Give people reasons to visit your website by listing the benefits of doing so, for example by offering exclusive author interviews, pre-publication extracts, competitions and sample copies. Simply announcing that you have a website has long since ceased to be news.

Online

- Allow visitors to tell other people about the website by including a 'tell a friend' button, which will e-mail a link to and an extract from the page to the friend's e-mail.
- Registration. You need to list your URL and keywords in all the appropriate internet directories, catalogues and search engines in order to

increase both your website ranking and the traffic going to your website. This can be done through either individual registration and submission or professional web marketing products and services. Some of these are free; others have to be paid for.

■ Host a forum so users can chat to each other.

■ Use your e-mail signature (the block of copy your word processing package can add automatically to the end of all your e-mails) to advertise your website and your latest book.

■ Display blurb and jacket for all major titles. You could allow visitors to vote on alternatives you are considering for a well-loved author.

■ Feature major titles permanently, but update regularly by adding in new reviews/press snippets/comments from readers.

■ Run special promotions such as competitions and special offers for bulk orders/orders by a specific deadline.

■ Feature your press releases.

■ Provide articles on authors or audio interviews with them – in particular, reading circles love 'added-value' information that they can pass on to promote good discussion.

■ Have a guest contributor (for a limited period) who answers questions sent in by visitors.

■ Provide sample chapters.

■ Give useful URLs.

■ Actively solicit links from other websites, especially your authors' websites.

■ Give details on forthcoming conferences.

■ Feature articles (or links) in the press that endorse the area in which you are publishing.

■ Get people to sign up for a newsletter from you (and then remember to produce one!).

■ Provide information on how to submit new product ideas. Many readers of blogs harbour the long-term ambition to be published in a more permanent format, and suggesting how they can submit an idea for publication is motivating and boosts the fledgling relationship between you.

Above all, be sure that company information (ethos, how you started etc), promotional copy, contact details and so on are all kept up to date.

E-MAILS

These provide a cheap, instantaneous and unobtrusive method of contacting a vast number of people personally. Because they are cheap and quick to write, many people assume they are easy. Not so. A recent book described them as the 'hardest written medium of all'. The biggest risk is that without facial signals or tone of voice to interpret and explain your works, you will be misunderstood. Authors David Shipley and Will Schwalbe (2007) comment, 'E-mails encourage the lesser angels of our nature', making us angrier, less sympathetic and more easily wounded than usual because we are unable to monitor the reactions of the person with whom we are communicating.' The authors' two top tips are 'think before you send' and 'send an e-mail you would like to receive'.

You can experiment with a variety of different messages, from sending out your press releases to announcing new acquisitions or providing regular feedback for your authors. It's an immediate medium that feels personal, so be careful that the impression you give is the one you mean to. Never send your first outline, always stick it in the 'draft' box and reread later. All business e-mails must carry information on the organization they came from, just as a company letterhead would provide information on the sender of a letter. For information on how to direct market by e-mail, see Chapter 5.

ONLINE ADVERTISING

This offers great potential for targeting the precise online audience you want to attract. For example, you can try banner advertising (thin boxes with a message that flash at the reader) on selected websites or against certain keywords on search engines, where 1,000 banners are available at a very reasonable cost.

BLOGS

A blog is a user-generated website where entries are made in journal style and displayed in reverse chronological order. The term 'blog' is derived from web log, but the word is also used as a verb, meaning to maintain or add content to a blog. This is an area of huge – and recent – growth: in November 2006 the blog search engine Technorati was tracking nearly 60 million blogs. Blogs are popular because they are individualistic, and this is the age of the opinion rather than the moderated consensus. Readers also like the opportunity to leave comments in an interactive form, so they are taking part rather than just reading what someone else has to say.

If your publishing firm includes a blog on your website, it should be from an individual rather than the organization as a whole; it should feel informal and like a conversation, not a stilted extract from the annual company report. A small organization, with a strong ethos, is in an ideal position to expand on its aims and objectives through a blog.

There are many good blogs about books. Their scope is very wide and covers all areas of publishers' markets from the highly technical and academic to the mass market. These sites are perhaps of most interest to publishers when they overlap with specific interest products they have produced, and are accessed by users with similar passions. This is an excellent opportunity to spread information to a market that you know is likely to be interested – and furthermore can link you with other enthusiasts at the press of a button.

Publishers often question how they can influence such bloggers to write about *their* books. Mark Thwaite, managing editor of The Book Depository (www.readysteadybook.com) says in his blog:

> My response is clear: these are the wrong questions!
>
> The blogosphere is a conversation. And the first thing publishers need to do is to join that conversation, not seek to dominate it. How do they do that? Well, they get a blog and they start blogging! But I'd recommend that they don't simply use the blog as a publicity blog (ie as an online catalogue or as a transparent marketing mechanism).
>
> To get the most out of their blog, publishers need it to be a genuine part of the wider conversation about books that is the blogosphere, but one that just happens to be hailing from a place that also happens to publish books. Publishers often forget that, as publishers, they create the products (books!) that we bibliophiles love and the process of that production – why they chose a particular title, why they believe in the book and its author, what gap in the market they perceive this book to be filling – are fascinating to a certain group of book lovers. If they add this kind of insider information… to the blogosphere they will be bringing something new and exciting to the conversation; if they also show an interest in what others in the blogospheric conversation are saying, by showing a knowledge of

the 'sphere, linking to interesting posts and commenting on them, they'll be welcomed as friends. If they simply seek to influence and dominate they'll be ignored as the overbearing bores they will have proved themselves to be.

Incidentally, this is an excellent marketing strategy for approaching all specific markets: talk about what *they* find interesting. For example, production people are fascinated by new developments in online delivery and alternative locations for printing; librarians like to hear about how publishers have considered archival permanence in the decisions they made about format. In short, find the right group of people, talk about things that fascinate you both, and they will spread the word to others they know who will find it equally compelling. Enthusiasm is catching.

LEGAL RESTRICTIONS

Nicola Solomon (2007), an expert in the law relating to publishing, comments as follows:

> Be aware that the internet is not a law free zone and you should be as careful about the legalities of how you present information on the web as much as in more traditional formats.
>
> Defamation. You have freedom as to what to write in a blog but not if it is defamatory of another living person. Therefore ensure what you say is true, accurate and can be backed up by facts.
>
> Check your blog does not include anyone else's work. Ensure that you have copyright clearance for use of any photos or illustrations. It is easy to cut and paste images from Google images but even if there are no copyright notices on them, re-use will normally be an infringement of copyright for which you could be sued.
>
> Be careful when using photographs of others. If you took the photos then you will own the copyright but the law of privacy may mean that you are not able to publish them on the web without the subject's consent.
>
> Make sure your work is accurate; if following your advice could be risky include an appropriate disclaimer: you don't want to be sued if your recipe for your favourite dish causes an outbreak of food poisoning.

Think about what use others can make of your work. Would you be upset if they re-used it? If so, include appropriate copyright notices and terms of use. If you don't know how to draft these consider using a creative commons license http://creativecommons.org/worldwide/uk with which you can keep your copyright but allow people to copy and distribute your work on conditions which you can choose from a simple checklist given on the website. For example, you could allow your work to be used only non-commercially and amended so long as you are given a credit.

7

'Free' advertising

Publishers of books and journals are lucky in that they have access to a wealth of free promotional space, in all kinds of media. Free feature and review opportunities are available to no other manufacturers on such an extensive scale.

News coverage or a feature in an influential newspaper can help your message reach a much wider audience. Presented as editorial material (rather than as an advertisement), you have the chance to inform public opinion and reorientate popular debate, or simply to spread information by word of mouth.

Similarly, getting authors on to talk shows can make a tremendous difference to their public image. When media coverage is harnessed (as it always should be) to information on title availability, you should achieve the real aim: larger sales.

Features and reviews of books in the media are one of the most influential ways of shaping reading habits. They are important to almost every kind of reader, from academics noting reviews in a journal they respect to general readers in a bookshop, turning to the back cover of a paperback to see which newspapers or columnists have endorsed it. For some books it is not even important that the coverage is favourable; getting a book banned can do tremendous things for its sales potential. To quote Brendan Behan, 'There's no such thing as bad publicity.'

Getting this kind of coverage is often known as 'free advertising', although done well, it takes an immense amount of time and effort. This chapter is devoted to telling you how to go about it.

PEOPLE WHO LIAISE WITH THE MEDIA

The large general publishing houses usually have a team of specialist press officers or publicists which liaises with the media on behalf of a variety of lists. In smaller houses, this is a job that falls to the marketing department.

WHAT YOU NEED TO SUCCEED IN DEALING WITH THE MEDIA

■ Determination.
■ Persuasiveness.
■ Knowledge of and belief in your products.
■ Imagination.
■ A voice and personality that comes over well on the telephone.
■ A good memory.
■ Persistence.

WHEN TO START PURSUING COVERAGE

The best time for thinking about media coverage is early in a title's development. Author tours, radio and television appearances, competitions, entry for literary prizes and so on are best thought about well in advance as they take a lot of planning. If you are liaising with authors you will have their long-term commitments to consider too; the author publicity form should have alerted them to what kind of involvement may be needed. Of course having written a book does not make you a fluent speaker, but today most authors understand that helping with publicity is vital in getting their title better known.

Planning press coverage is easiest if you have an existing network of media contacts with whom you are in touch on a regular basis. It is a good idea to make a list of all the journals and programmes likely to be significant to your list, and to find out the name of the features or news editor. Ring up and introduce yourself, confirm that they are the right person to send information to, and check the address and spelling of their name. Ask if you can take the most important contacts out to lunch: it will be easier selling ideas if your face is already known.

Don't just pursue contacts in the media that you read or watch yourself. Try to get into the habit of buying a variety of different papers to see the kind of opportunities for coverage that they offer; watch and listen to broadcast programmes of all kinds. For example, mass-market newspapers have more regular book buyers among their readers than the 'quality' press, simply because their circulations are bigger. Similarly, remember to send copies of your press information to the news agencies – they may feed it to many different regional papers. The local papers or radio station in an author's home town will almost certainly want to do a feature too.

Then, armed with a list of contacts, work at feeding the right people with the right information at the right time and in the way that they are most likely to use.

RECORDING THE NAMES OF YOUR CONTACTS

A campaign for coverage usually starts with the sending of a press release to a mailing list of journalists, then this is followed by telephone calls to secure definite features. The press release will probably go out as an e-mail attachment, but you will need printed copies to go out with review copies and to hand out as and when you meet relevant people. Never assume that just because you have sent a journalist a piece of information once, he or she will either remember or hang on to it. Journalists are inundated and as it is you who want something from them (coverage), the onus is on you to give them what they need in order to be able to write about your title – even if you have sent it to them before.

Whatever system you decide on for the management of your lists (in-house or out-of-house) do keep a basic point of reference on your desk, or PC, ready to refer to at all times. Be very methodical about recording ideas that particular contacts have responded well or badly to in the past, their particular interests, days off, the best times to contact and so on.

If you are starting from scratch, a good way to build up press information is to subscribe to the services of a media agency. For an annual subscription you will receive access to a website that lists all the press names you might need. You can then get in touch whenever you want to send out a press release.

HOW TO WRITE AN EFFECTIVE PRESS RELEASE

If you are charged with preparing a press release, what should it say? The most important point is that a press release should contain news. It is far more likely to be the news value or topicality of the subject matter in what you send that appeals to the journalist, than the fact that another book has been written. As for how to spot what news is, here are some of the maxims of the late John Junor, famous journalist and newspaper editor:

■ An ounce of emotion is worth a ton of fact.
■ Everybody is interested in sex and money.
■ When in search of a subject, turn to the royal family.

Make it enticing but short. You are trying to assail the overworked and overwhelmed journalist with the news or feature value of your particular story. Make it pithy and interesting. Remember that thousands of press releases land on most editors' desks every day. It should make the recipient want to know more, but provide sufficient coherent information for inclusion should he or she decide to use it straight away.

Don't devalue the impact of your press releases by producing them too often or sending them to the wrong homes. If you send information 'just in case', journalists will almost certainly take a similarly marginal view. The danger is that they may then devalue what you send in future.

The first couple of paragraphs of the release should tell the basic story (who, what, where, why and when). Sub-editors, especially those on regional papers or local radio, may have gaps to fill and be looking for copy. If your information is succinct and sufficiently interesting it may get used whole (in which case it will be cut from the bottom upwards). Follow the initial explanation with an expansion of your arguments, illustrating with examples from what you are promoting. Tell enough of the story to make the journalist want to know more, but not so much that there is no angle left to discover.

Supporting quotes

All journalists want quotes to support the story they write, so if you provide them that's very helpful, enabling them to reinforce their argument without having to go to the trouble themselves of looking for further endorsement (useful if they are in a hurry). What they don't want is to feel that every

PRESS RELEASE

The global history of advertising – according to the people who helped make it.

Please don't release before publication date on 26th July 2007

'Immensely readable.' Sir Martin Sorrell, CEO, WPP

'A great story: full of character, fun and life.' Kevin Roberts, CEO Worldwide, Saatchi & Saatchi

'A must for anyone interested in the history of advertising.' Sir Alan Parker

The book includes brand new interviews with, among many others, Jean-Marie Dru (President and CEO, TBWA), John Hegarty (Chairman and Creative Director, BBH), Maurice Levy (President, Publicis Group), George Lois (Madison Avenue art director), Keith Reinhard (Chairman Emeritus of DDB Worldwide) and Kevin Roberts (CEO Worldwide, Saatchi & Saatchi).

ADLAND, published by Kogan Page on 26th July, § Æ Ø £ †   ° § ≠ ÆØ. ù ™ ™¶   Ø ™
ú ü ± † ≠ Ø § Æ§ © ¢   ° ≠ ™® ú © § © Ø † ≠ © ú Ø § ™© ú ß   ´ † ≠ Æ´ † û Ø § ± †
ú ü ± † ≠ Ø § Æ§ © ¢   ß ú © ú Æû ú ´ †   ° Æ ™© † §© Æ ≠ ¥ ≠ §©¢ ™§ ©Æ † § © ≥ Ø ß †'
Ø £ †   † © ü   ™°   Ø ≠ ú ü § Ø § ™© ú ß   è ë   ± § † ≤ § © ¢   £ ú ù § Ø Æh

Ö ™ ∞ ≠ © ú ß § ÆØ   à ú ≠ ¶   è ∞ © ¢ ú Ø †   Ø ≠ ú ® ´ Æ   à ú ü § Æ ™© { ± † © ∞ †
ú © ü   ~ ú ± § ü   ä ¢ § ß ± ¥ f   ú © ü   ¢ † Ø Æ § © Æ§ ü †   ¢ § ú © Ø   è ™¶ ¥ "
≤ § Ø £   Ø £ †   ß † ú ú § © ¢   © ú ® † Æ ú§ © gØ § Ø Ø † ©   üÆ ∞ Æ§ § † Æ ÆŁÆ   ™ꞁ
£ ™ Ø Æ£ ™Ø   û ≠ † ú Ø § ±† ú Æ § §≠Ø† ™ ß ¶ ™¶ ≠ ÆØ ™ £ ≤ ú ™≠ ¶   § © à ú © £ ú Ø Ø ı
k s r j Æy   É ™≤   £ ú Æ   ú ü ± † ≠ Ø § Æ§ © ß Ø Ø à ≠ ™© ¥ Ø ≠ § ™≤ Ø § ü Ø Ø¥£ † ™
û £ ú © ¢ †   Ø £ †   ° ú û †   ™°   Ø £ ¥Æ§ §© ü ÆÆØ ± ¥ ± † †} Ø® † è ä § ¢ § Ø ¶ ¶'
ú ¢ † © û ¥   ™°   Ø £ †   ° ∞ Ø ∞ ≠ †   ß ™ ™¶   ß § ¶ † y

ADLAND ú © Æ≤ † ≠ Æ   Ø £ † Æ†   ¨ ∞ † ÆØ § ™© Æ   ú Æ   Ø £ †   ú ∞ Ø £ ™≠   Ø í,
à § ß ú © ú © ü   ™© Ø ™   Ø ™   Ø £ †   † ® † ≠ ™Ś § © ¢   ⊕™≠ ⊕£ Ø Ø Æ® ≠ ™ § ü © ©Æ
¢ ß ™ù ú ß   £ § Æ ÆØ ™≠ ¥ ¥
™°   ú ü ± † ≠ Ø § Æ§ © ¢ h

About the author

Mark Tungate § Æ ú | ≠ § Ø § Æ£   · ™∞ É ¶ ú § §ÆÆØ £ ¢ ú Æ₺ Ø£ §ꞏÆ£ȅûꞏfashionû ≠ Ŝ
Brands: Branding Style from Armani to Zara† ú ß Æ ™   ´ ∞ ù § § Æ£ † ü   ù ¥   Ü ™¢ ú © ©
û ™≠ ≠ ≠ † Æ´   ™© ü † © Ø   ° ™≠   Ø £ †   *Campaign* Ø§§©ÆÆ§ ©≠¢ ≠ §§©©†ú Æ ÆØ ≠∤ † ▪¶"
À ≠ † © ú £   ® ú ≠ ¶ † † Ø *Strategies* ù ú É § Æ§ © ™¶≠ ≠ ¶   £ ú *The Times* † © ä † *Telegraph*
© † ≤ Æ´ ú ´ † ≠ Æh   É †   ú ß Æ Æ™   û ™®™§ §§§© §© ™¶ § ú Æ¢ ¥ ± § Æ§ ™ ††   Ø ≠ ™¥ © ™©£
b í Çé â hû ™® c h   É †   ≤ ≠ § Ø † Æ   ™°Æ Æ´ †ß ú® † Æⁱ™¶ Ø ™¶™™™¶ ¶¶≠ û ™£ £ †™¶ ∞∞∞ ú ß ™
ú ü ± † ≠ Ø § Æ§ © ¢ h   Ñ © À ≠ ú © § ™™ † † † £Æ ßÆ Æ àè ä ™ÆÆ ≠™¥ Æ≠ û Ø Ø ™©† ™© ™ù

> For further information, to request a review copy, or to interview the author:
> Please contact: A N Other email: another@kogan-page.co.uk

£18.99 • Hardback • 272 Pages • 234×156mm
ISBN 10: 0749448377 ..ISBN 13: 9780749448370

Figure 7.1 Sample press release

angle of the story you are offering has already been explored. So if you include quotes:

- give the name of the source but not the medium in which it appeared;
- don't provide too many;
- an interesting quote from the author can be effective, prompting the journalist to suggest an interview.

If you are absolutely sure where you want your information to appear, tailor your approach to individual media. Ring and discuss the prospect of a special and exclusive feature with your editorial contact, offering the publication sole access if he or she moves quickly. Such a call may also establish how a particular journal wants information presented, and suggest the angle from which your title will be looked at. The easier it is for a paper's staff to assimilate your material into their format, the more likely it is to be used.

The layout

Remember that, as with any other written format, long blocks of justified copy put the reader off. Illustrations, particularly cartoons, attract attention. Provide clear information about what the recipients should do next: whom they should ring to arrange interviews, how to obtain a review copy and so on. Do make sure there are enough contact details in case they want to know more. Journalists quite often work on stories late at night, so offering a single contact name, and during office hours, may not be enough. Give at least two names, and the relevant mobile numbers. Ensure that you add to your press release all the essential information you would wish to see included should it get used whole: publication date, price, availability and so on. And before you send anything out, add additional information journalists may find useful (not just what is on your press release) to your website.

Adding an embargo date to the bottom of your release means every journalist has the same chance to prepare the story before publication; no one should print the information before that date and 'scoop' their rivals (very important if you have sold the serial rights!). The release risks being ignored for precisely the same reasons.

It always pays to follow up a press release with an e-mail or phone call to those journalists you particularly wish to take up the story. Whether or not you get coverage is often due to not just the interesting nature of the story you present but the surrounding package of ideas you offer. You are trying to tempt journalists to cover your story to the exclusion of all the others they have competing for their attention, so do be imaginative! For example, could you offer a specific journalist an interview in an interesting place (with afternoon tea or cocktails?) or a tour around a building/along a beach important to the story? Many authors do not want to be interviewed in their own homes (too revealing!), so offering a third-party venue might suit all parties.

Suggest ideas that sound appealing – locations, people, vehicles – perhaps in unusual combinations. Features do not have to be written by the paper in question. If you can arrange for an author to write an article for a particular magazine, he or she may receive a fee and the book a valuable push (publication details should be mentioned at the end of the piece). Similarly, can you persuade the educational press to accept an article by a teacher on how your new reading scheme works in practice, or one by a mother for the parenting press on how her son has at last learnt to read using it? Often the personal stamp on this kind of feature gives it more authority and makes it more interesting to readers, who in these two examples would consist mostly of other teachers and other mothers.

In addition to getting editorial coverage, there are also lots of opportunities for getting images used. And don't forget that the trade press in particular likes to receive relevant pictures.

Top ten tips for getting images into the trade press

■ Make the images interesting. Four people lined up with drinks in their hands is not interesting. Editors of the trade press do not want their pages to look like wallpaper!

■ Send them in at the right time. The main seasons for launching books are when, surprise surprise, most images get sent to the trade press. So be imaginative about when you send them in. In January, Easter and the summer holidays journalists are often actively searching for images, so you stand a good chance of being included if you approach then.

■ Send the image in the right format. About 70 per cent of the images received cannot be used because the resolution is too low. Use at least 300 dpi.

- Close-ups are more interesting than long shots, unless the building is particularly significant (if so, say why!).
- Say who is in the image – and be specific. Don't assume the magazine knows who the marketing director is, however well known he or she is within your company. Ensure all names are spelt right – if it is wrong, it's the journalist who gets the blame!
- Submit a caption too. The publication may or may not use it, but it gives a starting point on how to write about the image sent. Avoid in-jokes that only you understand.
- Be exclusive. Don't send the same image to competitors without telling a publication (in which case it won't include it!). If you are sending it just to one publication, say it is exclusive, and it is much more likely to be featured.
- The trade press likes images that reflect the whole trade, so if you can line up your author with a bookseller, or member of the publisher's staff, that is great. They like to reflect all jobs, so don't assume an image has to be of the great and good within your organization – it's good to have pictures of the more junior staff too!
- They would love more images of promotional highlights, 'screen grabs' or stills from television advertising or features. This is an excellent way to extend the coverage you have already paid for – but not often thought of by publicists.
- By all means let them know an image is coming, or check to see they have got it, but don't keep ringing up. Email is quick and efficient, and journalists like to think they are quick at replying. The high quality of the images you send should speak for themselves.

Provided by Joel Rickett of *The Bookseller*.

THE BEST TIME TO CONTACT JOURNALISTS

The best time seems to be after about 10.30 am until about 12.45 pm, then from about 2.45 pm until 4.30 pm. It isn't that those are the only times they work, just that those times provide the best opportunities of catching them at their desks and willing to talk to you.

AUTHOR INTERVIEWS

As well as considering setting up interviews in newspapers and magazines, ask yourself whether your author would come over well on radio, television or perhaps through hosting a forum on a website. Are there specific programmes that would be interested in recording his or her point of view? Local radio stations offer lots of opportunities for coverage. If the author is unavailable, could you do the interview yourself? Alternatively, offer a different author from your list for interview and you may still secure coverage for your house's titles ('switch selling').

If you set up interviews, be meticulous in confirming all the details to everyone concerned, even if you are planning to accompany the author. Write down the name of the programme and interviewer, and where the author should be and when. Brief the author on the programme's reaction to the press release you sent. This may give hints of the type of question to be asked. When it's all over, and if it went well, consider sending a postcard of thanks to the relevant journalist/producer, or even a small memento (you have a warehouse full of suitable items). You may want to be in touch again.

Speaking effectively on radio and television

How you or your author prepare for a presentation on the air will depend on the attitude of the interviewer: whether it is likely to be 'hard' (typical for prime-time current affairs slots) or 'soft' (like the majority of local radio interviewers). Think carefully about your aim(s) when accepting an interview.

Points to get across?

Politicians react to a hard interviewer by 'springboarding', using each question as a possible launch pad for conveying what they have decided they want to say, the essential points they wish to get over. ('I'm glad you asked me that, but of course we must not lose sight of the really important issue which is… .') The 'hard' interviewer resists tangents and puts forward difficult questions that demand real answers, not waffle. A 'soft' interviewer, on the other hand, will allow the interviewee to shape the discussion, guiding or prompting with questions to ensure an interesting programme, or to change the subject (about 4 minutes per topic is considered sufficient to satisfy the attention span of the audience for popular radio).

If you are doing the interview yourself, immerse yourself in all the information you can find and practise answering questions in your head on the way there. Don't over-rehearse; you will sound wooden and unconvincing. If it helps, take along a postcard with three or four prompt words to remind you of the key points you want to get across, and perhaps a couple of important statistics that you want to refer to, but certainly no more than that. (Lots of notes will confuse you and produce 'rustle' – and many presenters will not allow them onto the set/into the studio.) In any case, talking from memory enables you to concentrate fully on the questions being asked. Talking of key statistics, remember that figures are hard to absorb at first hearing. Don't use too many. Alternatively, can you restate them as fractions? Whatever you do, don't read out prepared statements; not only does this sound very impersonal, if it is information in your press release the interviewer will probably have used it to introduce you.

Live interviews need not be daunting. The knowledge that it is for real (not for editing later) can help you to marshal your thoughts. It is easy to forget how many million listeners there are when you are actually talking to just one.

SELLING IDEAS BY PHONE

How successful you are in setting up the kind of coverage suggested in this chapter will depend on the kind of books you look after and the way you target and present information on them. But equally important will be your own personal contribution: how persuasive you are when talking to journalists on the telephone. Here is some basic advice on how to sell ideas over the phone.

Prepare yourself

Try to find somewhere quiet to do your ringing. Even if this proves impossible, still put yourself in the right frame of mind. Concentrate on the job in hand and work out what you are going to say so that you are coherent but not word-perfect.

After a few phone calls you will find a pattern to the calls emerges, and that this affects your presentation. Ring the really big prospects third or fourth, once you have ironed out your presentational style but before you start to sound too smooth. Don't make too many phone calls on the trot; you may begin to get casual.

How to start and what to say

Once you have said who you are and why you are calling, start by asking if now is a convenient time to talk. If it is not you will almost always be offered a time to call back and speak to your contact directly. The journalist you call may be in the middle of writing something, and just launching into what you want to talk about, whether or not he or she is willing to listen to it, can be irritating.

Involve the person you are speaking to. Ask basic questions. If the paper has covered the author before, jog the journalist's memory about the story that appeared last time, and say how this one differs. If you are talking about a well-known author provide some little-known details to perk up interest. Talk about basic trends in society that your product highlights.

Ensure you are being listened to by putting your points clearly and asking for a response (using open-ended questions). Don't talk too fast or be afraid to hesitate. If you listen to some of the best radio interviewers you will hear how they repeatedly rephrase their questions, and use 'um' and 'ah' to ease the impact of hard-hitting ones. It is all designed to involve interviewees, and coax them into answering responsively. Think of yourself in the same position: you are trying to persuade the journalist to take interest, but with no eye contact or body language at your disposal, your voice has to do it all.

Try not to be too complicated. Use words that are readily understood and that you won't stumble over. At the same time, don't overwhelm the listener with information. A brief description of the story on offer followed by two or three good reasons why the journal you are ringing should cover it is plenty. Suggest the kind of feature you think would work best: an author interview, a visit to a school to see a major new scheme in progress or a new angle on an existing news story which information in your book provides.

Be methodical

Write down who said what immediately (you may think you will remember but after an hour of phoning you won't be sure which call was which). If you are following up a press release be sure to have by your side copies of whatever it was you sent; many of those you call will say they have either not received or can no longer find it. Send it again. Do this straight away so that the new copy of your release is received while your conversation is still in their minds.

If the correspondent you want to speak to is not available, by all means leave your name. But if an assistant offers to return your call, don't expect it will happen; it practically never will. You are the salesperson and the journalist will expect you to ring back with your story.

If an interview or visit is promised, confirm everything by e-mail, ringing the contact numbers you were given (just to make sure they are correct) the day before to make a final check on the arrangements. Make friends with the secretary/production assistant who is more likely to spot double bookings.

Track the coverage you get. Scan the papers you circulated for what subsequently appears, or employ an agency to do this for you. Stick a copy of each item of coverage in the title file so it can be incorporated in publicity or used on the jacket of a new edition.

Let others know what you have set up

Don't forget to let your reps know about forthcoming coverage; anything that is likely to increase demand can encourage booksellers to take more stock. Let the trade press know. Tell your colleagues: it's motivating to know that a house's authors are in the media, and they may get the chance to talk it up further.

Don't give up

Getting a journalist to come along to hear at first hand the story you are pushing is not the end of the matter: you then have to hope that the promised feature appears. Someone may well turn up from the right paper and make notes, but this only serves to increase your anxiety as the days go by before the story finally appears in print.

Is there anything more frustrating than your carefully nurtured feature being squeezed out at the last minute by something much more up to date, with the added annoyance of having to start all over again with a now rather dated story? Or offering a scoop, only to have it turned down at the eleventh hour when it is too late to fix up an alternative?

In conclusion, it may be disheartening when no one wants to cover the story that you have convinced yourself is a winner. It is worth remembering that you would have scant respect for a newspaper that printed everything it was offered. In dealing with the press, a very large part of your success will depend on the skills you develop in matching your expectations to journalists' ability to deliver. Like so many other parts of marketing, it can be both utterly frustrating and absolutely exhilarating.

ENSURING PRESS COVERAGE FOR VERY SPECIALIZED PRODUCTS

If you are responsible for promoting a list of academic or highly specialized books, the kinds of coverage for which you should be striving are reviews and specific features, perhaps backed up where appropriate by news items in the right journals. Achieving general 'publicity' is often a waste of time better spent elsewhere – although having said that, even academics are becoming more aware of the benefits of press coverage, and universities that employ them are increasingly keen on newsworthy research projects.

Target the right person. Find out the name of the gardening and bridge correspondents, as well as the literary editor. Similarly, you can get worthwhile coverage for high-level topics by developing good relations with particular correspondents on papers in which you wish to be featured, especially if you feed them stories on an exclusive basis. Very specialized titles too can provide the subject matter for interesting features with a little imagination. For example, when Macmillan published *Faraday Rediscovered*, a collection of papers on different aspects of the physicist's immense importance to the history of science, one of the book's two editors was working at the Royal Institution where Faraday's laboratory was still preserved. We held a launch party-cum-demonstration, and invited all present to watch him demonstrate two of Faraday's major discoveries. It was a novel way of engaging press attention.

BOOK REVIEWS

The theory is as follows. New and revised books are reviewed in the media, and the reviews are read/heard by the market, who are consequently motivated to buy. Such coverage is highly influential in all markets as it offers objective analysis of the product.

You will be required to put together a review list for almost every title you publish, and the prospect sounds enticingly simple. Be warned: achieving review coverage is not as simple as it sounds.

Building up and maintaining intelligent relationships with review editors requires immense attention to detail and a great deal of time. And the sheer volume of books being sent for review in the small media space and time available means securing coverage can be very hard work. Book pages are frequently a casualty when a paper's editor wants to save space for a more pressing news item. It also often takes a long time to see results. National quotidiens may be able to offer a relatively quick turnaround from receipt of book to appearance of review, but in academic journals it can take months, during which the author too is impatiently waiting to see the title featured.

The role of the literary editor

Most magazines and newspapers have a literary editor who organizes the coverage of books. It is to this person that you will probably be sending review copies of titles you are working on. Accept right now that literary editors are a crucial allies. It is their job to find interesting copy on books; it follows that they are the only people you can truly count on to be interested in your products.

They may also open the gates to other people within the magazine, and get personal satisfaction from seeing book features on pages other than the literary section. Paula Johnson, until recently literary editor of the *Mail on Sunday*, told me that every Friday she would put together a list of book-based snippets, and forward topics that were capable of exploitation by other journalists on the paper – perhaps the news editors or the gardening correspondent. To this list she would append photocopies of all the relevant press releases sent in by publishing houses. So even if you do decide to send your review copy and press release to the news or sports desk, it is almost always worth sending one to the literary editor too.

Particular hints when putting together press releases for literary editors

■ Do you really need a press release? Would a phone call to a key contact work best, if you want to make an exclusive offer? If you do decide to send one, consider how the press release will fit in within your company's PR as a whole; will it detract or add impact?

■ Bear in mind the environment in which your material will be received. A literary editor on a prestigious newspaper will get 40 to 70 book packages a week, into an office already overflowing with other titles, press releases and people. Titles are shelved by the month in which they are scheduled for publication, but additional piles of books soon build up wherever there is floor space. It follows that information that is clearly laid out and quick to digest is best.

■ Put the press releases inside the book you are sending so they don't get separated on opening.

■ If you use quotes keep them crisp, short and relevant. A long list of quotes looks boring and implies that every angle has already been thought of.

■ Cover the basics: date of publication, author information, publisher and contact details (phone, fax and e-mail). Ensure the date includes year of publication in case the book gets put to one side for use later. Correct information saves the journalist time and makes it more likely that your material will be used.

■ Get the name of the literary editor you are sending it to right.

■ It's absolutely unforgivable to send a literary editor material with grammatical errors in it.

■ Be sure to mark paperback originals as such; they will be given special treatment as they have not been reviewed as hardbacks. If you fail to make this clear they are likely to appear in the 'new in paperback' feature with much less space accorded.

■ Don't put copy that is on the book jacket in the press release that accompanies it. Literary editors consider this boring and an insult to their intelligence.

■ What you send may well end up being e-mailed to other people, and even in what is meant to be a paper-free age, it's a good idea to ensure that your press release is photocopiable.

■ Think carefully before sending free gifts. Literary editors tend to feel very strongly about making their own mind up and are inclined to take a dim view of 'bribes' or facetious additional enclosures. The book should stand on its own merit; it follows that anything additional should be tasteful and pertinent.

■ Find out when the 'copy day' is (ie when material is sent to press) and target material accordingly (to arrive just before it, when prices will be at their lowest). For example, for a Sunday paper, Friday is a very good day for material to arrive.

■ As with all promotional formats, the conventional can bore, whereas the attitudinal sound-bite or quirky approach may attract attention.

■ If you have a really important project or piece of news (eg new author taken on, existing author chosen as a judge for a major literary prize), ring your contacts and let them know. This may spark them into asking your author to write or review something, giving valuable pre-publicity.
■ Don't ring and remind literary editors if they haven't yet covered a book – most hate it! Instead, consider sending an e-mail or well-written note with details of really key titles not yet covered, hoping that they will not be forgotten.

In-house review lists

Many marketing departments already have an established review list, probably printed. It may be a fairly extensive document divided into different subject areas or perhaps consist of a series of different sheets, each one listing specialized media in specific areas. The fact that this list is readily available should make you suspicious. Magazines change their readership and formats extremely quickly these days: new ones are launched, old ones go out of business. A ready form means it has been around for a long time and probably no one has got around to updating it. Use such a form as the basis for your review list and you will end up opting for journal and magazine titles because they sound right: about as sensible as voting for people because their names are nice.

Find out whether anyone bothers to update the address list when magazines and newspapers move or die. This is even more unlikely if several departments are using the same system, as everyone will assume it is someone else's responsibility. And things do change. A media agency reckoned that each month there are over 2,000 changes to its contacts directory. Worst of all, ticking a list and sending it off for central despatch deprives you of the chance to add a personal message, and unless your mailing list is very up to date, address it to the relevant review editors by name.

How to compile your review list

Keep an ongoing reference point for review editors you have worked with in the past and those who represent journals that are important to you. Keep it on your desk at all times and update it as you go along.

Search the book's title file for suggestions of where to send review copies; locate the author's publicity form; have a think. Look through media directories. Use your common sense: ask any friends you have who work or are interested in the relevant area which journals and magazines they read. Ask the title's editor.

If this throws up some important journals where you have no contact, that's excellent. Ring up and find out who the review editor is. Introduce yourself. Mention the book in question and ask if the publication would be interested. Better still, if it is a journal likely to be useful to your area of responsibility in the future, suggest you meet up. You can use the opportunity to guide the review editor through your company's publishing programme for the next six months, and perhaps offer page proofs of forthcoming titles before other journals as a 'scoop'. Ask about the reviewing policy (time taken, where to send, the kind of books they like to see, etc). Note it all down.

Then, prompted by the information you have secured, remain in touch. Tell review editors about the books you want to send; suggest how they could feature them; gently remind them they have not yet reviewed what you last sent. Such contacts often enable you to speed up coverage: can the book be sent directly to the reviewer, to the editor at home or to a new feature writer?

When not to give books away

If you have a limited number of copies available for review (and, if the print run is low, giving away five more than you need can make the whole project uneconomic), send out a press release to the journals you think may feature the title and ask the various review editors to contact you if they would like a copy.

Similarly, bear in mind that today it isn't just the marketing department and magazine staff who know the meaning of the term 'review copy': you will receive many requests for free copies of the titles you are responsible for promoting. Don't erode your basic market.

What to send out with review copies

It is essential that review copies do not go out unannounced. It is surprising how many publishers forget to enclose a 'review slip' giving title and author details, ISBN and publication date and recommended price (which is not always shown on the jacket). Provide a name, address and telephone number from where more information can be obtained and to where copies of any review should be sent.

In addition, send any other information you think may secure the interest of review editors: a press release, a copy of the book's promotional leaflet if you have it already, a photograph of the author (not for use – there should be a version available digitally if they want it – just to whet their appetite and make them think the author looks interesting) or copy of an illustration from the book, and a handwritten note from you saying why you think coverage of this title will appeal to their readership. In fact, send anything that might encourage them to select for review the title that you sent, in preference to all the others received the same morning.

Sending out very expensive/desirable books for review

What happens to all these books once they have been considered for review? In general those doing the reviewing regard the books as a perk. They are usually sold on to specialist bookshops; the prices paid depend on how recent they are. A difficulty arises here for the publisher of very desirable or expensive books: are requests for review copies really genuine or a 'nice little earner' for the review editor? Send out a large pile of books to a comprehensive list and you will still get calls from editors on the list to say that they have not yet received their copy.

One solution adopted by a fine art publisher was to send out review copies by special delivery/taxi and ask for a receipt from each magazine before handing the book over. Publishers of very expensive works such as encyclopaedias may hold a viewing day for journalists to attend in a hotel, or send out review copies with an invoice which they cancel once the set is returned. Alternatively, they may offer to sell the work at a trade discount to the reviewer.

FREE COPIES FOR MINIMAL COVERAGE

The recommended reading lists produced by academics and teachers feature only the briefest of book details (author and title, and if you are lucky, the name of the publisher) but inclusion is vital. Most educational publishers offer 'inspection copies' for this market, sending unconditional free copies to particularly influential figures. See Chapter 11 for further information.

THE RELATIONSHIP BETWEEN EDITORIAL AND ADVERTISING ON MAGAZINES

The relationship between editorial and advertising is a tricky one; you are getting involved in the internal politics of other companies. If you try to point out that a connection between editorial and advertising sales exists you will be met by a haughty indifference (from editorial) or a jocular denial (from advertising). Nevertheless in most cases the one pays for the other and it is common practice for the advertising department to sell space around forthcoming editorial features.

If your advertising budget makes you a major supporter of a magazine, you have a right to have your books looked at seriously by it. Undoubtedly the best way is to avoid the issue arising in the first place by making friends with the review editor and keeping in touch about anything you send in. No contact followed by an accusation of no coverage is a bad way to begin.

Organizing advertising and promotions

There used to be a sharp distinction in marketing terminology between advertising that was paid for and promotions that were negotiated to be mutually beneficial to participating parties. These were commonly referred to as 'above the line' marketing (eg space advertising in the press or through the broadcast media, which is directly paid for) and 'below the line' marketing (eg promotions offering free gifts or discounts for bulk purchase, and other marketing in which the cost is less apparent).

Today the understanding is very different; things are not nearly so clear-cut. There has been an explosion of opportunities for marketing and the emergence of a wide variety of selling vehicles. For example, there is now a huge range of new marketing media such as websites, new magazines, commercial radio and television stations. There has also been a complete revaluation of the role of promotions. Once seen as downmarket activities that might engage the consumer's passing interest, but didn't support or build the brand in the longer term, they have today become much more mainstream activities. Promotions are advertised in the press; firms placing space advertisements use the opportunity to make special offers directly to their market. Significantly, there are now marketing service companies offering 'through the line' services.

Publishers too have been affected by the changes. Traditionally, the book trade spent little on advertising (which was seen as too expensive) other than in the pages of trade magazines. It did not take part in many promotions because of legislative and territorial restrictions covering resale price maintenance. But as the trade has opened up, and books have had to compete more effectively with other products for the same business budget or 'leisure spend', the techniques employed to sell them have had to become more professional and mainstream.

Publishers are also increasingly concentrating more of their marketing spend on fewer titles, and affording some high-profile advertising is part of the enhanced marketing effort that is possible through spending the budget in a more concentrated manner. Today it is commonplace to see books advertised on the sides of buses, on the subway (in the cars, on the platforms and beside the escalators) as well as on 'adshels' (poster sites protected by perspex covers on bus shelters or on pavement sites). At the same time, books are now commonly the subject of promotional campaigns. For example, promotions have featured books on sides of breakfast cereal packets, available free to those who collect coupons through newspapers or at supermarket checkouts; special book and toy packs have been produced as incentives for certain stores, and books are regularly the subject of editorial 'features' and 'reader offers' that magazines and newspapers consider likely to appeal to their readership, and promote loyal purchase/subscription.

This chapter looks at both paid-for advertising and promotions in further detail. These two areas are deliberately linked. Straightforward space or broadcast advertising on its own is not a particularly effective method of persuading people to buy books. It is very difficult to isolate the sales that result, and for academic and specialized titles, advertising can be particularly hard to justify. What is more, there are often cheaper or more accountable ways of reaching the same market than simply taking space in a publication (loose inserts, bind-in cards, test mailing a small section of the subscriber list and so on).

Publishers are increasingly finding that it is much more effective to link space advertising into a promotional campaign. For example, they might take the message that is being put over in the ad and reinforce its understanding as part of a competition, or offer readers a special price that is redeemable through a cooperating bookshop, with all parties sharing the advertising cost.

What is more, books offer advantages to those planning promotions over other types of product. They tend to be permanent: they are more likely to be held onto rather than thrown away. Even tatty books tend to be kept. Thus if an advertiser's name is on the front of a promotional book, it has a long life in the market's mind as well as home or place of work. They are also seen as aspirational and/or educational. Significantly, supermarkets have persuaded lots of groups of people who do not have children to collect the coupons that offer free books to schools on behalf of other people.

WHERE TO ADVERTISE

Trade advertising

Mass-market publishers announce high-profile advertising campaigns to the trade as part of their new title information. Look through a recent edition of any trade publication and see how the copy for major new titles stresses how much is being spent on space advertising. The publisher's aim is to isolate a main title in booksellers' minds, in the hope that they will respond by stocking in quantities appropriate to the promotion budget. It should be pointed out that not all the activities announced actually happen.

Advertising to the end user

Deciding where to advertise is a matter of successfully identifying first the market for a particular product, then the media that the market reads/listens to and respects. Which websites do your market regularly consult (recent research indicated that most people who use the web have 8–10 sites they check regularly, not more)? Which magazines do your target market read? Which radio programmes do they listen to? Look at the author's publicity form for suggestions; talk to editorial and marketing staff; use your imagination. Make a shortlist, and look up the relevant timings and advertising rates. If they are roughly within your budget, ring the advertising manager for each publication and ask for a sample copy as well as details of the audience profile. (All media that quote a circulation figure must be able to prove where it came from, and the demographic breakdown is useful ammunition when you start to be pestered for a booking.)

COST

Your first reaction should be that advertising is not cheap. While you should never accept that the first rate you are quoted will be the total you eventually pay (see Chapter 10 on negotiating), the cost of advertising does not end with buying the space/time. For example, for a space ad, the associated costs include:

- the writing of the message (your time or freelance help);
- the design and layout of the advertisement;
- photography;
- providing final artwork.

For a broadcast ad you have to pay for studio time and most likely for the actors. Many marketing plans include the 'setting up of an accompanying website' but the costs of this are usually much greater than are apparent at first sight.

Some regular advertisers book space through a media buying agent who handles bookings for a variety of clients. Because they are booking time and space on a large scale such agents get much greater discounts than are available to individual publishing companies. The arrangement between agent and client is usually based on splitting the discount/commission the agent receives (on a prearranged basis), so it can end up costing clients nothing to use the agent's services.

STUDY THE MEDIA

If you have decided to advertise in a particular publication or on a particular radio or television station, get to know the audience by studying what they see/hear. Copy works best when it is personal, so when you start writing you should be aiming your message at one typical individual. Can you picture him or her? If you can't, your copy is unlikely to be convincing.

For example, in a magazine or journal, look at the job advertisements – they should tell you clearly who is reading the magazine. Read the letters page; look at the editorial; examine the spaces taken by other advertisers. You want your advertisement to be sympathetic to the style and format of the magazine and yet sufficiently distinctive to attract attention. If you are taking a series of advertisements ask if you can be added to the free circulation list, to which advertising sales reps usually have the power to add names.

Where to appear

When you read magazines look out for those advertisements you notice and observe their position. In most publications you can specify a definite position; in more specialized media or in return for discounted advertising rates you may only be able to express a preference. 'Run of paper' (ie at the discretion of the person handling the page make-up) may be the cheapest option.

Certain pages may be more expensive than others: a news page will generally cost more than a book review page. It may pay to take the more expensive slot if in return you reach people interested in the subject matter who do not read book reviews. Consider specifying a position next to a regular feature: the crossword, winning lottery numbers or a cartoon.

The range of prices available to those booking broadcast media slots varies enormously depending on audience figures at specific times of the day.

WHAT TO SAY

How much you write is likely to depend on four factors:

■ how much there is to say about the product;
■ how much the market needs to know before deciding to buy;
■ how much time and inclination the market has to read;
■ what you want the market to do as a result of reading your ad (order direct or rush to the nearest bookshop).

In advertising a new general fiction title to the trade it may be sufficient to include publication and promotion information in an eye-catching format; conveying the atmosphere of the book and your promotional theme through arresting design or illustration. Bear in mind that the fact the product is a book and that it comes from your publishing house may be the least interesting things you can tell the market. Most publishers greatly over-estimate the extent to which readers either know – or want to know – who is publishing a particular title! Author reputation (or notoriety) and subject matter will almost certainly be much more significant.

If you are writing to the trade to remind them that your new novel is top of the best seller lists, don't make the mistake of assuming everyone is convinced of its saleability. Provide all the information the bookseller needs before making a decision to restock: the sales patterns of the author's previous books, details of promotional highlights to come that will further support demand, proof that strong sales will be a continuing trend (the number of people who regularly watch a related programme/buy a similar magazine can be effective).

For books that have a more exact application, for example academic and business titles, additional information will be required. You will almost certainly find you have less space than you need, so make the best use of it. Emphasize all the key benefits to the market, and be clear and specific. Get on with your sales message straight away and don't waste space on general statements. Omit words you don't need. For example instead of 'This book provides... ' start with 'Provides...', which has much more impact.

If the title is expensive, make sure you stress the guarantee of customer satisfaction. (A good way of offering further reassurance is to quote a satisfied customer or enthusiast for the product.)

Limited space is the more usual problem, but if your market has the time and opportunity to read long copy, do provide it. For example, on the underground in London, it has been estimated that 85 per cent of travellers do not carry anything to read, or cannot get access to their reading material because the trains are so crowded. Given the choice, wouldn't you rather stand opposite an advert that provided you with plenty to read?

A checklist of information to consider including

You won't have room for all of this, and depending on the type of title being promoted, will have to make decisions about what information will most likely persuade the market to respond. Some of the information – such as the kind of book – you may be able to convey more accurately through design than words. For example, your layout and the colours chosen should make it clear whether it is mass-market fiction or a title for the business community. Considering putting in:

■ an eye-catching headline (not just the title);
■ publication details: title, author, extent, price, ISBN, publication date;
■ key market benefits;
■ briefly what the book is about, the theme or flavour it offers;
■ contents;
■ the offer if there is one;

- who else thinks it's good (third-party opinion is much more persuasive to the market than the publisher's view);
- statement on value for money;
- the author and his/her qualifications to write this title (eg the author of last year's hottest seller; of the standard work on the subject, or a leading name in the area);
- why the product is different; in what (new) way it meets market needs and future requirements (concentrate on this rather than knocking your competitors);
- new features/highlights if a new edition;
- format (without using industry jargon eg 'hardback' not 'hb');
- related titles you publish (relevant new and backlist; part of a series or house reputation);
- relevant testimonials or review quotes;
- information on how to order (if it is available on free inspection say how and where from);
- a guarantee of satisfaction.

For ideas on how to present the copy see Chapters 2 and 3; for information on how to ensure eye-catching design and legibility see Chapter 4.

How to order

Any form of marketing material should entice readers to buy the product or service described. When planning an advertising campaign the marketing manager has to decide the most efficient and most likely way of getting the customer to respond.

In the case of high-profile advertising, for which a trade sale is likely, it is vital that the trade knows in enough time to have the books in store when customers ask for them. Make it clear how the product is available, providing a website address or phone number for enquiries – and making sure relevant information is on your website, or passed on to those likely to take any resulting calls, before the campaign goes out. If your product has a very high selling price, indicate how to progress to the next stage in the buying process (for example a catalogue or prospectus containing further information), but always also provide the opportunity to purchase straight away.

The despatch of an inspection copy precedes most large-scale adoptions of academic and educational texts, so provide a coupon for that purpose or information on how to obtain one. Don't just give an address and leave it to readers to write in – most won't bother. Always provide website addresses and phone numbers for direct ordering, and ensure they are large enough to read without spectacles. (Phone numbers should be bigger than the rest of the type so they can be found in a hurry.) Don't confuse the customer: just one telephone number is enough, so don't give alternatives. Those wanting a more general customer services number can either ring this number and ask for it or consult your website. For further ideas on how to make your ordering mechanisms easy to spot and respond to, see Chapter 4.

When you use the broadcast media, you can explain simple products and urge viewers/listeners to buy them. If you feel the product needs a longer explanation than time permits, give a phone number or website address: 'To hear more see www.../ring...'. (Not both – you are trying to embed a single number in your market's mind, and if you provide too many digits you will confuse them. Many of your listeners will be doing something else, like cooking or driving whilst they are listening.)

SPACE ADVERTISING FOR SPECIALIST PUBLISHERS

With much smaller budgets and very specific markets, specialized publishers might well assume that advertising is not an area of marketing relevant to them. Not necessarily. Even if you accept that space advertising is not always the most effective way to gain outright sales, there are still many reasons for continuing to advertise. Most call for a long-term view of selling to specific markets rather than short-term coupon counting. Consider the following.

Advertising is just one element in your marketing mix

The message you provide in your advertising reinforces other stimuli to purchase: mailshots, advance notices, reviews and word of mouth. Collectively, they boost your profile and lead to sales. Advertising can be used to update your sales message, remind the market of catalogues now available, pass on good reviews or sales figures, or refer to topical events that make your publications particularly relevant. One small independent publisher found that taking a weekly slot in a trade magazine with witty and informal information about itself paid real dividends: it had its best ever year.

Maintaining the public profile of your list and publishing house

Both your market and your authors need to know that you are actively publishing and selling titles, even if the announcement in the media results in no direct sales. For example, it is commonplace for advertising sales departments to sell space around editorial features, and if the educational press runs a special feature on a subject that is of central importance to your house you probably need to be seen advertising there. Similarly, a children's publisher about to set out for the Bologna Book Fair needs to advertise its presence in the special book fair edition; it will form a checklist of key children's publishers long after the fair is over.

Even if your list of titles in a particular area is small, if you advertise alongside your major competitors you rank yourselves with them. Advertising can thus provide a boost to your whole list as well as the possibility of attracting new authors.

A cost-effective way of reaching your market

For a magazine with a highly targeted readership, and a product relevant to that market, space advertising can be a very cost-effective way of spreading sales information. Bear in mind too that many very specific journals have a high pass-on factor, so the readership is much higher than the circulation figures imply. Per head of the market reached, space advertising usually compares very favourably with the costs of circulating a mailshot or employing a rep (but compare this with the cost per response). For some less specific books (eg women's reads), space ads in the right magazines can be the only way to reach the market – or at least some of it.

Backing up the sales efforts of your reps

The reps' ability to point to space advertising as a visible sign of promotional commitment increases their credibility with those they sell to. An occasional 'big splash' can impress both trade and end market.

To support a publication you want your books to be reviewed in

A large proportion of the revenue of magazine and journal publishers comes from advertising sales. If you don't provide advertising revenue, would readers be prepared to pay the higher cover price that might result? Is there a danger that without advertising revenue an important publication might fold and the outlet for reaching an influential market be lost?

To carry on a winning trend

Even if your product is the market leader, you need to carry on reminding potential purchasers of its success rather than assume saturation point has been reached. Previous purchasers still read advertisements for products they already own. The sales copy confirms their good judgment, and if they are satisfied with their purchase, they are interested to read about new developments.

It is worth noting here that many magazines are becoming conscious of the need to offer improved value for money spent on advertising to their customers. In a bid to improve the advertiser's feedback several now include reader-response cards or tick-box coupons to request further information.

ORGANIZING PROMOTIONS

> Promotion means putting together building blocks of awareness.
> Walter F Parkes, head of Steven Spielberg's DreamWorks studio

As already discussed, more and more publishers are trying out promotions, sometimes arranged on their own, sometimes in conjunction with promotions agencies which specialize in setting up mutually beneficial arrangements between non-competing organizations approaching the same target market. For the remainder of this chapter 'promotion' is used in the widest sense, meaning pushing or promoting to a higher position. The ideas that follow assume a broad market; there are specific sector references to be found in Chapter 11.

Features, reader offers and mock reviews

With limited formal review space available, many publishers are now concentrating their efforts on promotional campaigns that achieve a similar effect. For example, magazines that see a particular publisher's products as appealing strongly to their own readership may be keen to set up special features (often called 'sponsored editorial'), perhaps supplemented by reader offers of varying complexity. Since they are presented as media features rather than space advertisement, these gambits offer editorial endorsement, which impresses the market. Sometimes the publisher may be required to take – and pay for – advertising space to support the promotion.

Competitions and contests

A competition is a very good way of getting people involved with your product, whether in-house (a bottle of champagne for the best slogan for our new campaign) or out of house (how many words can your class make from the title of our new school dictionary?). Competitions are also an effective means of securing news and feature coverage in the media, particularly through local papers. There has to be some basic explanation of the book or product being promoted before the prizes and rules can be described. The competition is then trailed, takes place and the results are announced   it's a lot of coverage for relatively little effort (much of which will be done for you by the paper's promotions department). You can get substantially increased exposure if you tie a competition into an advertising package.

If you want a large response, keep the questions simple (tie-breakers tend to put people off) and ask the audience to e-mail or ring in with the answers. If you are using a competition to 'qualify' prospects, to find out whether they are really interested in buying what you have to offer, you may want to ask more difficult questions and get a smaller, quality list of potential customers.

What should you offer as a prize? In general, if you are promoting a book or other published product, your prizes can be copies of the product(s), or perhaps the winner's choice from your whole list. In this way the actual cost to you of providing the prizes will be substantially less than their perceived value to the winners. If you are using a competition to build a database of people interested in your product, for example for a high-priced multi-volume reference work, the prize should always be the product itself (otherwise you will be building a list of people attracted by a free holiday – or whatever else it is you are offering).

The prizes need not be enormous. Listen to local radio and you will find that small rewards are supplemented by the great pleasure of winning and being mentioned on the air. You could consider pursuing sponsorship if you want to offer bigger prizes, but this can be very time-consuming and the resulting media coverage will have to be shared.

If you offer an incentive and run out quickly, you will inevitably get letters from people who feel hard done by – 'I responded by the deadline but was not one of the first 50 out of the hat and feel very let down by your publishing house.' These may go to the managing director rather than to you. Stick to your plan; your promotional gambit has clearly worked as you have both thought of an attractive offer and increased its value in the marketplace. Such letters are a sign of success, not of alienation, and when your organization writes back (as you must), you could consider offering the person an opportunity to order at a reduced rate – or buy something else!

A few ideas for competitions

■ When organizing local radio interviews to boost new titles or in support of author tours, try offering a few copies of the book as prizes for correct answers to a quick competition. Not only do you get a good idea of how many people are listening (and it's usually very encouraging), you prolong the author's time on the air.

■ If you are promoting a book that lends itself to a quiz, mention on your press release that prizes are available if the media use the book's content as the basis for a competition. Consider supplying a page of sample questions and answers.

■ Offer a prize to booksellers for the best window or in-store display for forthcoming major titles/promotions. Chain bookshops regularly charge for window displays, so you may only get entries from the independent stores.

■ Schools always seem to be keen to increase their resources by taking part in competitions to win books; class project or quiz sheets that fill up small slots of teaching time are always popular and can encourage teachers to purchase more copies of your materials, or to fully appreciate their benefits by using them in new ways.

■ Even if you get only a few entries, celebrate the prize-winners. Get your nearest rep to present prizes and ask the local paper to cover the ceremony: most will be pleased to feature a good local story.

SPONSORSHIP

The pursuit of sponsorship is a vast subject in its own right, and can be an excellent way to get your firm or product's name in front of a specific audience. The key to really effective sponsorship arrangements is ensuring compatibility between the interests of all parties involved.

Consider both outgoing and incoming sponsorship. Supporting an event of interest to a market you want to reach (eg a children's publisher backing a children's theatre) is outgoing sponsorship. Accepting money or help in kind in return for promoting a sponsor's name in addition to your own product (eg books sponsored by supermarkets) is an example of incoming sponsorship.

Give careful consideration to what both parties expect out of the sponsorship deal, and put it in writing. You will get more attention if you approach potential sponsors with information on what they will get out of a joint collaboration rather than telling them how much you need the money. Sponsors have become accustomed to receiving requests for support from all sides, and expect more than a straight exchange of logo for cash. Most want to work together to capitalize on joint markets, media coverage and potential image building. A great many sponsors are also attracted by possible opportunities for corporate entertaining.

OFFERING INCENTIVES

Some publishers offer incentives to purchase with expensive products, for example laptop bags with business books or a free set of CDs with a music encyclopaedia. Such offers can encourage the order to come more quickly if a 'sell by' date is added. Giving the reader a choice of offers can be particularly effective; people's attention is directed to making a decision between several items they would like to own, and they may effectively assume they are going to buy the product.

Others use an offer to boost the size of order, for example a free item (or perhaps free postage and packing) if the order value is over a certain size. You can also use offers as a staging process, encouraging the potential purchaser to spend more: for example free postage and packing over a certain order value, with an additional gift in return for a larger spend.

Getting your product adopted as an incentive in a promotion

Regular incentive fairs are held where those producing products likely for selection as incentives in promotional campaigns can display their wares. It is worth attending just to see the kind of promotional deals that are set up.

Interestingly, promotional companies like using books as they imply quality and have a high perceived value (discounting of books is a relatively recent phenomenon). Of incentives to promote sales of a magazine, nothing apparently outpulls a free book plastic-wrapped onto the front cover. Publishers can offer either old stock or, if the print run of the magazine is sufficiently extensive and the promotional opportunity seen as valuable enough, produce a special edition. For example, for authors who have a long backlist, a reprint of an early title may renew enthusiasm for their work and give an added lift to sales of their forthcoming title.

Along similar lines, try offering training institutions bulk copies of books that are relevant to the courses they run. They may decide to incorporate a copy of your product into the course fee, thus enabling them to sell an added-value package to their customers – most delegates like to go home with a free book. Bulk sales of key reference materials can similarly be made to organizations that might distribute them to their workforce or customers, perhaps offering the opportunity to have their own logo printed on the spine. (For more information on bulk sales see Chapter 1.)

Produce free material

Prestigious national events (eg hosting the Olympic Games, or the introduction of new currency) can create opportunities for celebratory/commemorative materials. When the United Kingdom launched a new coin, I was working for an educational publisher. We sent free worksheets by the authors of our best-selling maths scheme with our regular schools mailing to every primary and junior school in the United Kingdom. The material showed how to incorporate the coin into giving change, receiving pocket money, purchasing and so on, and was very popular with schools. We were convinced it encouraged brand loyalty.

UPDATE YOUR WEBSITE/PRODUCE A NEWS SHEET

Again, these moves are excellent for customer loyalty. Even editorially outstanding or best-selling products can become boring to the market. So tell customers about the progress of further products from the same stable, report on how others are using your material, provide feedback on problems familiar to the market, or include 'human interest' stories. Have you noticed how the large supermarket chains all produce customer magazines? They are trying to present themselves as more human, to challenge a view of them as impersonal supermarkets which offer no warmth or advice.

ALLOW THE READER TO TRY YOUR PUBLICATION OUT

Fiction publishers produce early 'reading copies' for bookshops in the hope that they will generate excitement about forthcoming titles. Similarly, booklets containing extracts from new novels are made available to customers by the till-point: this is a good way of gaining market research on what is likely to sell, as well as promoting the next season's list. For the same reason, the sale of serial rights to magazines and newspapers is an excellent way to arouse interest and tempt readers to want the whole volume.

'Home interest' magazines find that printing recipes boosts their readership. If you are promoting a new cookery book try featuring a sample recipe in your advertisements.

STUNTS

From reading poetry through the loudspeaker system at a railway station, to releasing balloons from the top of a monument (and yes, both have been done) – it's up to you and your imagination. Two cautionary notes. First, make sure the stunts you arrange really are relevant to the main aim of press coverage (selling more stock). The punters should remember both the event and the product. Second, ensure you target stunts at the right people. Chocolate cakes sent to cookery feature editors to announce publication of a new cookbook may be very much appreciated, but if booksellers get to hear of it they may just conclude you have too much money to spend and demand more discount.

9

Organizing events

SALES CONFERENCES

Most publishing houses brief their key selling staff – representatives who call on shops, deal with key accounts or represent the house in other ways – at regular sales conferences. New titles are presented, feedback on previous promotions is sought, information on company news passed on and a friendly 'we're all part of the same team' atmosphere encouraged.

When they are held depends on the kind of list being promoted. Educational publishing houses may hold one in the school holidays before the start of each term, or perhaps one before the autumn selling cycle and another in the spring. A general publishing house will usually tie the conferences into the major selling and catalogue seasons: one mid-year to launch the Christmas list, another around the turn of the year for the season ahead.

At first trainee staff will probably be required only to sit and listen to those presenting. There is much you can learn for when your own turn to present comes around, both from your reactions to spending the majority of the day listening and the presentational style of those you hear.

If the organization of a sales conference falls to you, do remember what the real purpose is. While a sales conference offers a valuable opportunity for marketing and editorial staff to get together, and everyone enjoys a day out of the office, the real function is to brief those who sell on your behalf. These occasions give them the chance to tap the brains of those who commissioned and authorized the books they will try to sell over the next few months – and to find out all they can about them.

Checklist for a successful sales conference

Who should be there

Establish exactly who needs to come and to which sessions. Be firm about who should be there, and for what. You should consider (tactfully) excluding some people. For example, will the presence of the managing director and chairman inhibit reps from asking question they really want answered? Very large groups can jeopardize both the presenter's ease of delivery and the audience's willingness to respond out loud.

If political necessities mean the entire hierarchy is assembled for the formal presentation, consider organizing an informal get-together afterwards for questions. Alternatively, can you divide into two smaller groups (perhaps home and export staff) and present different subjects in different locations at the same time? This is harder work for the staff presenting titles, but worth the effort if improved recall results.

The venue

Is it convenient to get to (remote but beautiful could prove difficult if everyone is relying on the same taxi to get them from the nearest station) and is there enough space for the number attending? Is it reasonably priced? Bearing in mind whether it's a busy time of year and whether you are competing with other bookings, negotiate with the venue's manager about the room rate for the day(s); never accept the printed price list as absolute.

Find out about building renovation programmes in advance; they are very noisy. What is more, they never run to schedule, so if you are assured they will be over by the time you arrive, have it confirmed in writing. Is there air conditioning; how loud is it? If not, will opening the windows make it impossible to hear the speakers over the roar of passing traffic? Find out whose responsibility it is to check that everything is working (eg that all the bulbs in key lights are operating, and in particular the speaker's reading light for use if the room is darkened for slides). Make a note of their name and take their mobile number.

What those attending should take away with them

Provide the delegates with a folder containing copies of advance notices, leaflets and covers for all the titles to be presented at the conference. They can then make notes on these as they listen. If speakers are presenting by PowerPoint (see later) you can make a copy of their slides for the file.

Scheduling the programme

Keep the sessions short and vary the presenters (two short presentations are preferable to one long one by the same speaker). If the conference lasts over several days, try to avoid a long session on a Friday afternoon. Above all, stick to time (having an effective chair for the day is essential). Sitting absorbing information all day is much more tiring than you might think, and an awareness that yet another speaker is running late creates a tension that inhibits good listening!

Consider asking an author along to talk about a big book, but brief him or her very carefully – and don't let him/her talk for too long. What the reps really want are anecdotes that persuade the book buyer in stores to take more stock. Snippets of information from the author are often excellent for this, and getting enthusiasm going.

Breaks

Keep breaks prompt and ensure everyone gets back on time. Being back in the classroom seems to make everyone hungry, and special biscuits will be particularly appreciated. Don't offer alcohol at lunchtime. Drinking after the evening meal is an established ritual; try to supplement it with something more stimulating, perhaps an after-dinner talk provided it is amusing and not too heavy. Are there any sports facilities available nearby: tennis courts or a swimming pool?

Organizing the room

You may just be inheriting the layout everyone else has used, but if it is up to you, think about how you want the room arranged: as a conventional boardroom (with everyone sitting around in a circle, behind tables) or as an audience, with chairs in rows? Sitting without desks between speakers and the audience can mean people feel more obliged to take part and ask questions, but also means they can't make notes as easily.

What equipment do you need? Should there be a lectern at the front for speakers, or is there then a risk that they will hide behind it and feel isolated from the audience? Encourage speakers (if they feel sufficiently confident) to stand close to the audience, and to move around. If there is no lectern, there does need to be somewhere for speakers to put their papers and a glass of water. Any venue that offers conference facilities should have all the equipment you need, but do go for a preliminary visit to make sure.

How to present effectively at a sales conference

What to say

Provide yourself with a list of key points to mention for each title and practise talking around them. Talking from memory, while engaging eye contact, is much more persuasive than reading from a script. Even worse is reading aloud from the file of advance notices that the audience too have in front of them. Speak slowly, particularly at the beginning. You don't have to be word-perfect; this may encourage you to speak too quickly. Hesitations and occasional repetitions help to get the message across. Time yourself.

The audience needs to know the major selling points of the books being presented. They will have very little time to engage the attention of the book buyers they sell to, so pass on anything that is likely to be of use: anecdotes about the author or the project, a story from the press or news that shows the project is very current, feedback from market research, comparisons with the competition and so on. Choose three or four main points, then shut up.

Today it's very common for speakers to present their ideas as PowerPoint slides, but effective delivery of ideas through this medium is not as easy as it seems. Having all the slides in a matching format can look very branded and professional, but if all the slides look alike, it may inhibit those listening from distinguishing one title from another. It's also very hard for the audience to absorb what the speaker is saying and to read a packed screen at the same time. In a recent study of how the medium works, Professor John Sweller of the University of New South Wales commented, 'It is not effective to speak the same words that are written, because it is putting too much load on the mind and decreases your ability to understand what is being presented... It is difficult to process information if it is coming in the written and spoken format at the same time.' (http://www.smh.com.au/

news/technology/powerpoint-presentations-a-disaster/2007/04/03/1175366
240499.html). PowerPoint works best as support to the verbal presentation,
with keyword summaries appearing, not as a doubling up of content.

What to wear

Don't think it doesn't matter and that the books will be the real stars. The
audience will be appraising how you present yourself for the occasion. Stand
on both feet. Resist the temptation to fiddle with your tie or hair. Smile.

Involve the audience

Make eye contact, not just with those you know are sympathetic – allow
your gaze to move around the room so everyone feels included in what you
say. Ask questions and announce competitions, incentives and games for
anything from slogans to future sales.

Don't be afraid to ignore persistent or difficult questioners. They are
probably annoying everyone else in the room too. Suggest you discuss their
difficulties after the general session has finished.

Use props. Hold up book jackets and covers; turn the pages of flipcharts
you have prepared in advance. Commission some cartoons to illustrate
the points you are making; photocopy an article from the recent press that
confirms the need or topicality of your title. But don't distribute samples
of the hot-off-the-press promotional materials until you have finished
speaking!

PROMOTIONAL PARTIES AND BOOK LAUNCHES

Launch parties for new books used to be relatively commonplace but are
much more rationed these days. If you do get asked to organize one, here
are some guidelines.

What you seek to get out of it

The aim of a promotional party or book launch is usually media coverage
leading to more sales. You provide the opportunity for journalists and
gossip columnists to meet the author and hear more about the book. They

report it, the public read what they say and flock to buy the title. Even if the party does not result in specific features or news coverage, you can promote gossip and word of mouth and keep the author's profile high. At other times such a party is organized as a celebration, or to boost the company name. Sometimes the arrangement is purely political, to keep the author happy.

When to hold the event

Monday is a bad day if you want coverage in the Sunday papers; most Sunday journalists get the day off. Tuesday is too early in the week for them to be interested in covering for the following Sunday. Friday evening is best avoided as POETS day (push off early, tomorrow's Saturday). As regards timing, after work is convenient, say from 6.30–8.30 pm, on the assumption that people will be going elsewhere for supper. Alternatively, try lunchtime.

Who to invite

Ask enough of the author's friends and relations to make them feel comfortable and prevent the room from looking empty. Ask all the relevant journalists and 'media people' you want to cover the book. Try to ensure the event is not a restaging of the last office party as everyone who is working late comes along for a free drink.

Who else is interested in the book's subject matter? Members of Parliament, captains of industry, 'television personalities' – all can be invited. If there are well-known names who can't be there but are fully committed to the subject, ask them if they can provide a message of support which you can read out.

Send out the invitations three to four weeks ahead, accompanied by a press release giving more information on the title being launched. Provide your name and e-mail address/telephone number for RSVPs and make a list of all those invited/expected in alphabetical order by surname. On the day sit by the entrance and ask the names of all who arrive, tick them off and hand out pre-prepared name badges (if appropriate). If possible get someone experienced to stand next to you so you don't ask the company chairman for his or her name.

All members of the home team should carry a badge saying who they are: it has the added advantage of deterring them from talking to one another.

If you are expecting a VIP or main guest, ensure that someone is ready to receive and host him or her for the rest of the evening. 'Big name' or not, VIPs will probably still be nervous.

Book a photographer to take pictures of (preferably recognizable) guests enjoying themselves. Brief him or her on the combinations of people you want recorded. You can circulate the results afterwards to members of the press who failed to turn up, and still secure coverage in their papers. Try offering a picture to one paper as a scoop first, in return for a guarantee that it will be featured in a prominent place. Newspapers are much more aware of the artistic and intrinsic merits of the camera than they used to be. No longer do all photographs have to appear as illustrations to the text; a good photograph and caption can form a feature on their own.

When circulating a photograph, always send it with an effective caption: it can make the difference between the shot being featured and being ignored. Ensure you repeat the caption on the accompanying press release as a reminder to the people assembling the pages that there is one available.

See Chapter 7 for advice on getting images into the trade press.

The venue

The location should be relevant to the title being launched. If your subject matter is of interest to a particular section of the press, choose a location that is easy for them to get to, eg city venues for financial titles. If the venue is very special but difficult to reach, either lay on transport (eg a bus will collect from a particular place at a particular time, and run a shuttle service back) or forget it.

When to expect the guests

If you put 6.30 pm on the invitation, most will arrive around 7.00 pm and stay (depending on how good the party is) for about an hour. You can influence how long they stay by the timing of the welcome speeches: most will wait until they are over.

What to provide

Make the drinks as simple as possible. In general more white than red wine will be drunk, and many people will ask for soft drinks: the commonest mistake is not to provide enough. Guests are usually given a drink as they come though the door into the reception; thereafter glasses are most easily replenished by waiters (or staff) walking around with bottles and topping up. If you decide to provide more exotic drinks (eg cocktails or spirits) have them ready-mixed on trays; waiters can circulate and offer to exchange empty for full glasses. If you have a principal guest, let him or her know what you are proposing to provide and ask if he/she has any special requirements.

For early evening receptions most organizers work on the assumption that the guests will be going elsewhere to eat, so lay on cocktail party nibbles. Include vegetarian selections. Most people prefer to help themselves from passing trays rather than load a plate which they then have to juggle with a wine glass, and risk looking greedy.

For lunchtime launches, something more substantial may be needed. Offer a couple of choices (one vegetarian) but choose dishes that can be eaten with a fork, standing up.

When selecting the menu ask freelance cooks for their suggestions and costs. A hotel will give you a price list. Don't be ashamed to negotiate on price (perhaps by asking if there is anything simpler on offer), particularly if you are offering a hotel a booking at a time when it would otherwise be empty.

Speeches

After the party has been in full swing for about half an hour someone should thank everyone for coming and the author(s) for providing the occasion for the party, welcome any key guests and reporters and make a few pleasant remarks. The author may reply. You may find some resistance to formal speeches, but it is very important to concentrate people's minds on why they are there, to provide a focal point to the event. However, do ensure that the speeches are neither too long nor too many.

What to have to hand

Even though you have already sent out press releases with the invitations, keep a pile of printed materials to hand. There will almost certainly be journalists who want to go away and write the story up straight away but have forgotten to bring the necessary information. Copies of what is being promoted should be on display. They are very likely to be removed by guests (a traditional perk), so if the material is valuable the number available needs to be carefully controlled.

What to do afterwards

Follow up journalists who did not attend and offer them a photograph and a story. Make sure those who said they would feature the book do so. (For hints on getting media coverage for press conferences see Chapter 7).

Did the venue provide all it said it would; did all go smoothly? If not, negotiate.

PRESS CONFERENCES

A press conference calls together key members of the relevant press to impart a story or version of events. They should only be called if you have definite news to impart. If you call a press conference and there is no news story you will make journalists wary of accepting your invitation the next time you ask them.

You will need someone to chair the event: to coordinate questions and ensure that all the news points are raised. The book's editor or author may be the ideal person. Alternatively, consider asking someone with related interests who is a 'name' in their own right. If chairing your press conference links the person's name with a cause they support, they may do a particularly good job for you.

AUTHOR TOURS AND SIGNING SESSIONS

A promotional tour during which a popular or newsworthy author gives a series of talks, or perhaps signs copies of a new book, requires an immense amount of planning. On the other hand, the large number of literary festivals that are springing up offer similar opportunities to publishers, but with someone else doing the organizing. The public appetite for meeting their favourite writers, or simply those whose point of view they are interested to hear, is making this a growing trend, and as many of the festivals are either hosted or serviced by local booksellers, it draws more people into bookshops and improves sales. What is more, stock signed by the author tends not to be returned to the publisher's warehouse if it subsequently fails to sell; lots of it makes its way onto internet auction sites and adds value to the selling price.

Even though such events are usually organized in conjunction with a local bookshop, do a double-check that additional stock has been ordered to meet anticipated demand. It can be very frustrating for the author to have people wanting to buy the book and none available to purchase. Be sure the event is well publicized by yourself, the festival organizers or the bookshop in advance. Some festivals seek support from publishers through taking advertising space in the programme. If the event is being coordinated by publisher and bookshop, it is common practice for the publisher to share the cost of some preliminary space advertising – but you may be pleasantly surprised on the advertising rates charged by local papers.

On the day, a few shop staff should be available to crowd around the signing desk and get things off to a good start: nothing attracts punters like seeing a crowd.

EXHIBITIONS

Some firms instruct reps or have mobile exhibition teams who will provide everything needed if you inform them in good time of the nature of the exhibition and the stock required.

If you have to mount the display yourself, find out what will be available on site (screens, tables, chairs, platforms and so on) and from what time the exhibition room is available for assembly. Take enough additional promotional material to make your stand look interesting (posters, showcards and so on). A large cover for the table looks better than bare wood – a few yards of a crease-resistant polyester from the local department store is as good as anything. Whatever your company colours, if it is black it won't start to look grubby. All those who are to help run the stand need a name badge to identify them as part of the company.

Never underestimate how many people you need to help run an exhibition stand. It is far better to have several people taking stints than assign one poor soul for the whole day: by the end of it they will be incapable of selling a cold drink to a thirsty person.

Have a means of recording potential interest to hand, and a stapler for attaching the enquirer's business card. With this information you can contact each prospect after the exhibition to discuss their interests in further detail – and then move on to talk to the next potential customer.

You should have stock of your brochures and catalogues ready to hand out, but you want to ensure that they re-emerge from the ubiquitous exhibition carrier bag handed out to visitors as they enter. Can you mark the products you discussed with a highlighter pen? Staple your own business card to the front of the brochure to make recall more likely.

AWARD CEREMONIES AND LITERARY PRIZES

Literary prizes attract more attention today – the biggest are featured on the news pages (not in the book section) of the national press. Prizes offer both shortlisted and winning titles the promise of substantial extra sales. The publication of many novels is scheduled for what is seen as the most advantageous time for getting on to the shortlist for a particular prize.

If one of your titles is a front runner for a forthcoming prize you will be required to put together a plan of action to support and sustain media interest, and further capitalize on it if the books wins. For example you may have to produce (overnight) stickers to go on book jackets for circulation to booksellers saying 'Winner of X' and prepare attractive point-of-sale material.

Trade organizations issue lists of which prizes are run and when and how to enter titles for them.

10

The bottom line: how to look after a marketing budget

Marketing costs money. Even if you concentrate on the 'free' promotional techniques listed in Chapter 7 you will incur costs: your time, the electricity and telephone bills, the production cost of free copies given away for review or feature and not recoverable through sales. While most of these activities will be paid for out of the general company overheads, when it comes to drawing up a budget for the active promotion of a title, a firm decision must be taken on how much can be spent.

A glance at the title file of a forthcoming book should show you how many it has been estimated can be sold in the first year(s) after publication. The marketing budget will be designed to produce these sales and so generate enough revenue to first, pay for the direct outlay on the book (author advance, production, promotion costs and so on), second, make a contribution to company overheads, and third, produce a profit to invest in new publishing enterprises and remunerate shareholders.

These three considerations will be computed together as the eventual return on investment (ROI): how much the publisher invested in the project, and how much it got back. The period over which ROI is calculated, and eventually judged, will depend on the nature of the publishing project, its long-term significance to the house and the specific market being targeted.

WHERE MARKETING BUDGETS COME FROM

The budget assigned to the marketing department will be just one of a whole series of payments which senior managers of a publishing house have to allocate. For example, house overheads have to be provided for – both those that are attributable to specific departments (staff and freelance hours) and those that come from the company as a whole (audit fees, personnel department costs and the post room). The marketing department may see its need for a decent budget as paramount, but the level of spending cannot reasonably be substantially increased unless there is a strong probability of extra sales resulting. The marketing budget is but one element in the financial equation of the publishing business, as the following examples show.

These figures are not designed to show that any one type of publishing is intrinsically more profitable than any other; the amounts quoted as potential profit obviously depend on selling all the print run. For subsequent reprints

Table 10.1 New general hardback title (print run: 3,000)

	%	Amount	Balance
Published price			£25.00
Less discount to book trade	45	£11.25	£13.75
Less production costs[1]	18	£4.50	£9.25
Less royalties to author	9	£2.25	£7.00
Less marketing budget	6	£1.50	£5.50
Less publisher overheads[2]	20	£5.00	£0.50[3]
Potential profit on print run of 3,000			£1,500[4]

Notes

1. Origination, artwork, paper, binding etc.
2. Storage, despatch, representation and staff.
3. 2% of list price.
4. To make ends meet on the above kind of project, publishers are increasingly marketing a 'C format' version (hardback edition size and type of paper, limp binding) in between hardback and paperback editions.

Table 10.2 Subsequent mass-market paperback edition of the same title (print run: 30,000)

	%	Amount	Balance
Published price			£6.99
Less discount to book trade	50	£3.50	£3.49
Less production costs	10	£0.70	£2.79
Less royalties to author	7	£0.49	£2.30
Less marketing budget	5	£0.35	£1.95
Less publisher overheads	20	£1.40	£0.55[1]
Potential profit on print run			£16,500

Note
1. 7.9% of list price.

Table 10.3 New educational textbook (heavily illustrated, print run: 5,000, limp binding)

	%	Amount	Balance
Published price			£9.95
Less discount to book trade on 50%[1]	17.5	£0.87	£9.08
Less production costs	30	£2.99	£6.09
Less royalties to author	5	£0.50	£5.59
Less marketing budget	15	£1.49	£4.50
Less publisher overheads[2]	20	£1.99	£2.51[3]
Potential profit on print run			£12,550

Note
1. Assuming 50% direct sale to schools.
2. Storage, despatch, representation and staff.
3. 25.2% of list price.

some titles would show much healthier margins, once the basic origination, permissions, illustrations and marketing costs had been paid for.

The figures show that the increased cover price of a hardback book in comparison with a paperback is not due solely to increased production costs (as is generally believed), but to the lower print runs and hence higher unit costs for each book printed, as well as a higher royalty rate. The levels of discount given to different accounts will vary hugely according to a number

Table 10.4   New academic monograph (print run: 500, hardback)

	%	Amount	Balance
Published price			£40.00
Less discount to book trade	25	£10.00	£30.00
Less production costs	22	£8.80	£21.20
Less royalties to author	10	£4.00	£17.20
Less marketing budget	5	£2.00	£15.20
Less publisher overheads	20	£8.00	£7.20[1]
Potential profit on print run			£3,600

Note
1. 18% of list price.

of factors such as quantity taken, terms (firm sale or sale or return) and overall level of business between the two parties.

These examples show the complicated financial structure of publishing. Each title is in effect a separate business for which costs must be calculated, and the marketing allowance is just one part of that equation. If it is thought essential to award a larger than average marketing budget, or indeed to assign more money to any of the above costs (eg to give more discount to the book trade, or spend more on production) then either the unit sales must be greater to justify the increase or another variable must be altered. Options here include increasing the unit price, selling the content in another way (eg as a paid-for podcast, printing fewer copies, lowering the quality of materials and hence the production costs, paying reduced royalties, or looking for a co-publishing deal which makes production costs more favourable and eases cashflow). Marketing budgets cannot be seen in isolation.

DRAWING UP A BUDGET

A budget is a plan of activities expressed in money terms. Successful management of a budget means delivering, at an acceptable cost, all the promotional strategies detailed in the budget. It is not just a question of keeping promotional expenditure within the prescribed limit irrespective of how many of the planned activities are achieved.

The amount allocated to the marketing budget (and to other departmental budgets) is usually based on a percentage of the organization's (or section's) projected turnover for that year. What you can spend is dictated by what you will be receiving.

For each forthcoming title the marketing manager will estimate market size and the percentage likely to buy. Anticipated future income from new titles is added to other sources of revenue such as rights sales for content (both in the original and in additional formats such as online or partial), reprints and investment income. Projected turnover for the year ahead, and probably for the next three- or five-year period, is planned at high-level management meetings. Expectations are subsequently monitored against actual performance, usually on a monthly and annual basis. Comparisons are then made with previous years and long-term plans are updated.

The manager calculates what it will cost to reach potential buyers, aiming to reach as many as possible with the budget allocated and deciding where the available resources will have the most impact. Some companies have tried to improve sales by substantially increasing their level of promotional expenditure, but if it costs proportionally more to achieve the resulting extra sales the outcome can be financial ruin. Decisions to overspend on marketing may still be made, and sometimes the risks pay off, but it should not be forgotten that monitoring a budget is an essential part of drawing one up, and people do lose their jobs or firms go out of business for failing to implement what they have agreed to.

HOW MUCH IS SPENT

If the overall marketing budget is based on a percentage of anticipated turnover (different amounts being allocated to various titles according to need and ease of reaching the market), what kind of percentages are we talking about? The question depends entirely on the sort of list the house produces. On high-price reference works selling mainly direct to specialist markets, and on which little discount is given to the book trade, marketing budgets may be as high as 20 per cent of anticipated turnover, perhaps more to launch a major title in the first year after publication. If on the other hand the firm is selling educational titles with much lower prices through bookshops and wholesalers there is less room for spending large amounts; budgets will probably average 6 to 8 per cent of forecast turnover. On academic or highly specialized reference titles, the percentage spent on marketing may be no more than 5 per cent.

It used to be the case that publishers would try to recover promotional costs on the first edition of a new title; today they are frequently forced to take a longer-term view. Higher advances and increasing competition from large corporate publishing outfits, interest payments to finance production and overhead costs before any sales revenue is received, have ensured that sometimes a hardback is only made profitable through the subsequent publication of a paperback edition, or even the same author's second or third book with the house (hence the popularity of two- and three-book deals).

Other types of book require heavy spending on promotion at the time of publication: if sales do not take off well, they will be flops in the long term however much money is subsequently allocated. Directories (whether online/in print or both) are a good example of the type of resources needing large initial promotion budgets, perhaps for two or three years, until the sales strategy can become chiefly one of encouraging subscription renewals. The same goes for a new series launched by an educational publisher with a view to getting large-scale adoptions. Once the adoptions have been made and the scheme is being used in schools, less intensive selling will be needed. When promoting a new journal it may be cost-effective to spend the whole of the first year's individual subscription revenue on acquiring a subscriber. Once the subscription is recorded the subscriber should stay for a number of years to make the venture profitable.

Remember that even if you give identical budgets to all your titles, some will always outperform the others. If sales for one title disappoint and you have extra resources to spend, it is usually better to spend the additional funds on titles that are doing well than on trying to recover the position of the poorer sellers: it's better to back the winners.

HOW THE BUDGET IS DIVIDED UP

Four main categories of expenditure exist, in decreasing order of importance.

Core marketing costs

These are the regular marketing activities which are essential to the selling cycles of the publishing industry. I include here web and print resources: catalogues, advance notices and new book/stock lists. The total sum required for these items is usually deducted from the marketing budget before further allocations are made. These should only be cut as a very last resort.

Plans for individual titles

New titles or series, or perhaps works that are already published but need actively promoting, should have specific amounts of money allocated to their marketing. The allocation is not always made exactly in proportion to the anticipated revenue: some markets may be easier or cheaper to reach than others, and need less extensive budgets.

If it is your responsibility to draw up these preliminary allocations, decide on which titles or series the money could most usefully be spent, then look at actual costs of reaching the market. How many people are in it? How much would it cost to reach them? If you have the information, how much did it cost to reach them last year? Look at last year's actual costs and then add a percentage to cover inflation. Alternatively, ask the same suppliers to requote. What response do you need from the market to justify the sum you are proposing to ask for? Is this attainable? What backlist titles in the same subject area can be listed on promotional material to increase the possible chance or size of order?

Budgets for 'smaller' titles

Next comes the allocation of money to titles needing (or receiving) smaller budgets. This may mean you will only be able to promote them actively if you pool the budget with that of other titles and do a shared promotion. This is not necessarily an unwelcome compromise. Boosting a range of related titles together encourages an awareness of your publishing house as a particular type of publisher, and may attract both new purchasers and new authors. In the same way most editors have a responsibility for building a particular list. Cooperative promotions back up and give authority to your main title strategies, and can provide a useful push for the backlist books included.

Contingency

Last of all may come a contingency amount to be used at the marketing department's discretion on any title or group of titles as good ideas come up. It does not always reach the final budget: during the process of reconciling how much the marketing department would like to spend with how much is available, sacrifices are looked for. The contingency budget is often a casualty.

The sum of these four areas of spending is usually based on (or at least compared with) the percentage of the firm's anticipated turnover as discussed above. By drawing up a budget in this way the interdependence of all the titles in a list can be seen. If one title fails to achieve what it is budgeted to do, all the other titles in the list will have to work harder if the firm is to survive or profit margins are to be maintained.

Reasons for failure vary. Production time may be longer than anticipated; an author may produce the manuscript late or produce a text that needs substantial and time-consuming reworking before it can be published; copy-right clearance can take up to six months. Until a title is actually released for publication, recorded dues cannot be added to the sales figures. If this happens at a financial year end, sales will be lost from the year's figures.

If the manuscript cannot be remedied the sales will be lost altogether, a serious situation if money has already been spent on promotion.

WHEN TO SPEND IT

Once a basic marketing sum has been allocated, the next step is to budget for when it should be spent during the year. There are external constraints on you.

When the market wants to be told about new books

Promotion is usually a seasonal business; timings will vary according to the type of book being promoted and the market being approached. In markets where Christmas is a major holiday, roughly 40 per cent of the year's general sales in bookshops take place between the middle of October and 24 December. Most publishers for this market therefore time their main selling season so that the books are on the stockists' shelves ready to meet this bonanza. In the same way educational publishers promote titles to the schools market at the times when teachers are considering how to spend their budgets, and academic publishers aim to reach their market when reading lists for students are being compiled.

When the books themselves are scheduled

The production department will produce a list giving scheduled release (when stock goes out from the warehouse to the trade) and publication dates (when bookshops can start selling). Promotion schedules should be planned around these dates; with some types of book, timing is particularly important. Yearbooks and directories must be promoted early because they age and get harder to sell as the new edition approaches. Academic monographs too must be promoted ahead of publication: as much as 60 per cent of first-year sales can occur in the month of publication. If promotion plans have not been carried out and the dues recorded by the time of release, sales may never recover.

The need to promote early should be balanced against the risk of peaking too far ahead of publication date, with the danger that the effects will be lost. The fault may not be yours: the author may deliver the manuscript late, and production can take longer than anticipated.

When you have time to market them

Obviously, promotions that are not related to publication dates (for example relaunching old series or organizing a thematic push for the backlist) can be scheduled for less busy periods in the calendar, but again market acceptability must be considered. Publishing is most often a seasonal business, and you cannot really avoid this. You must just accept that you will be busier at certain times of the year.

HOW TO MONITOR YOUR BUDGET

Once the budget is established, stick to it – or only depart from it in a conscious fashion, with permission! In most houses once invoices have been passed by the person who commissioned the work (and it is generally that person who checks them against the quote), they are sent to the person in the accounts department who deals with promotion expenditure. In return, monthly reports are provided on spending levels. Even if you have this service, the figures you receive will be several weeks behind your actual expenditure, and I would recommend keeping a record yourself, with a running balance of how much has been spent (or committed but not yet billed) and what still remains from the title's budget.

It may be helpful to decide at the beginning of the year the percentages of the individual title budgets to be spent on print, design, copy, despatch and other key elements. That does not mean the proportions cannot be changed. I once printed 50,000 copies of a cheap flyer for a single title instead of the more usual 10,000 because the author had arranged lots of mailings and insertions that were to cost little or nothing. I therefore spent most of the despatch budget on printing.

I find it useful to look at costs per thousand for leaflet production lists and mailing charges. Unit prices for print reduce as numbers increase, mailing lists and despatch charges in general do not (or not by very much). Harness your promotion expenditure to your marketing responses and you start to get very sophisticated market information. If you compare the costs of producing a catalogue with the orders received directly from it (or perhaps received during the period over which it was being actively used for ordering), you can compile a figure for orders per page and an accurate indication of how profitable your endeavours have been. This is the way the rest of the retail trade is run (the key ratio is floor space to revenue).

HOW TO MAKE YOUR BUDGET GO FURTHER

Affording effective marketing in publishing is tricky: the purchase prices in general are low, and the quantities in which books sell are low too (15,000 units for a new paperback novel makes it a bestseller). It follows that being awarded enough marketing budget to enable each title to reach its full potential is not always possible. At the same time though, take comfort from the fact that there are more opportunities for the free coverage of books and their authors than any other product or service. Try the following money-saving techniques:

Take your budget personally

If you do this you are more likely to be efficient in its use. Circulate mailing results; analyse the progress of each promotion; record sales figures before and after promotions; make recommendations on how they could have been improved/why they were so good. There is a real reluctance within the industry to recording why marketing worked/did not work, largely because people are terrified of being associated with failure. Even if you decide not to share what you observe, keep a record for your own future instruction.

Get your timing right

This is crucial, as was noted above. Timely handling of the standard in-house procedures for book promotion is particularly important. Ensure the title is listed on the website and in catalogues for the season in which it is due to be published. Be sure that the advance notice is ready to appear at the right time, containing up-to-date information.

Explore viral marketing and social networking

It costs vastly less to inform a market via e-mail or through online discussion facilities than it does through sending out printed marketing materials. Ensure you have an effective website and that you update it regularly to give those returning to it something new to look at. Feed information on your titles to all possible carriers, association websites, those producing relevant newsletters and those active within enthuser groups that might regard the information as useful to members. See that it is featured in lists of titles available, and in the export editions of general trade search engines.

If you find a specific community that is particularly interested, encourage them to be ambassadors for your project; making a few available free for them to run a competition or offer as prizes may get them talking about it. Get them to endorse it for you and they may do even more. This is a particularly useful tactic for independent publishers, when you can justify a shared passion that unites both you and the wider group of people who share your enthusiasm!

Be proactive

There may be mailings going out that you could join in with if you ask; secondary markets may exist and prove highly profitable if you think of targeting them. Think laterally. Why not send all academics a catalogue request form in case they are interested in other areas for which you publish? There are certain well-known combinations of interest and profession (many academics like opera, and lots of politicians seem to be interested in bird watching); if you have products on your list likely to appeal, try them out.

Watch what your competitors are doing. One very effective way of doing this is to give each member of staff in the marketing department a competitor to 'adopt'. They then become responsible for watching out for the competitor's marketing and plans. Pool the information at a meeting and you can have a very helpful overall survey of your market.

Learn from other industries by developing a general interest in advertising and marketing. Above all, be interested in your products and who buys them.

Get better value for money for your spend on print

If you decide you need a leaflet, don't spend too much on production. Instead of sophisticated design, concentrate your attention on effective copy and buying reasons that speak directly to the market. Remember that over-complicated design can get in the way of effective communication.

Then try to circulate what you produce as widely as possible: through loose inserts to the subscribers to relevant journals; circulating at specialist meetings; putting in delegates' bags at conferences and so on. If you are sending printed information to standard outlets (eg bookstores and libraries), use shared mailings rather than bearing all the despatch costs yourself. In surveys most libraries, academics and schools say they don't care whether promotional material reaches them on its own or in company; it is the content that counts. If commercial opportunities do not exist, then consider forming partnerships with non-competing firms to share costs (assuming the mailing list can be used in this way). Can you take exhibition space in partnership too? These methods may attract slightly lower levels of response than individual mailings, but the cost of sales will also be substantially reduced. You will be able to reach more people for less money.

If you prepare a central stock list or standard order form, run on extra copies and use in mailings, include in parcels or send to exhibitions. If you use a new book supplement in your catalogue (perhaps inserted in the centrefold) can this too be reprinted for use in mailings? If your catalogue is designed as a series of double-page spreads, could these be turned into leaflets later on? With this in mind, if you are working in more than one colour, ensure that anything you may want to delete later on (such as page numbers) appears in black only, which is the cheapest plate to change. Can full-colour material be reprinted for a second mailing in two colours rather than four?

Sometimes you may not need formal marketing materials at all. A sales letter with a coupon for return along the bottom can be a very efficient way of soliciting orders. (The opposite does not apply, by the way: brochures always need a letter to go with them.) Update your information not by reprinting but by sending out accompanying photocopied pages of reviews or features that have appeared.

Use your authors

Supply authors with advance information sheets and leaflets; ask if they are members of societies that would circulate a flyer on a forthcoming book with its journal. Authors who have titles with several publishing houses might like a leaflet to list all their books, to use when they are speaking. You could pay a proportion towards production, much cheaper than paying for the entire piece yourself. Most authors have websites, so have yours link with theirs.

Use free publicity to the maximum possible extent

The pursuit of free publicity should not replace your standard promotional tools; rather, it should back them up. But don't end up paying for advertising space if the magazine would have printed a feature with a little persuasion. Many magazines are willing to make 'reader offers' – an editorial mention in return for free copies to give out (because it helps them cement the loyalty of their readership). Nor should you offer to pay for a loose insert if your author is on the editorial board and could have arranged for it to be circulated for nothing.

To make maximum use of free publicity you need to exploit the link between what you are promoting and why people are interested. Thus the fact that a book is coming out may be less interesting than the background of the author. Find out what interests the market, not you!

Negotiate as a matter of course

Always ask for discounts. There is a standard publisher's discount of 10 per cent for booking advertising space. Sometimes more can be squeezed for sending camera-ready artwork (although publications don't expect anything else), the fact that it's the first time you have advertised, or simply that the rate the medium quotes is too expensive for your budget. If you have the time, use it – the advertising sales representative will probably come back to you with a reduced price. Particularly good deals can be obtained just before a magazine goes to print – once it has gone to the printers the space has no value at all. If you go for a series of adverts you should get an additional discount, and likewise if you book a year's requirements in one go.

Do you have someone in the department who has previously worked in advertising sales? If so, ask them to handle negotiations for you, and you will almost certainly reduce your anticipated costs further still. Consider going on a negotiating skills course.

One final tip on dealing with discounted offers: decide where you want to advertise and then negotiate on price. If you allow yourself to get used to responding to the special offers available from magazines you are less than committed to appearing in (ie you would not have paid the full price), your marketing becomes much less targeted and you run the risk of seriously overspending. Remember that space costs are only one part of the total outlay. Continually saying 'no' can be an exercise to find out just how much can be negotiated off the list price.

Try to get money in more quickly

Books may be sent to trade outlets on a variety of different terms, some more beneficial to the publisher than others. Encouraging the trade to 'buy firm' rather than on 'sale or return' prevents unexpected returns which reduce sales and the overall profitability of particular titles.

Provide every opportunity for customers to buy direct and pay early, and in the most cost-efficient way for you. Some credit cards charge a higher percentage of the sales invoice than others. If you work for a small publishing house, state the reasons that customers should order from you rather than from an online retailer; encourage them to be loyal to something they believe in! For example:

> We are an independent publishing house and would appreciate the chance to fulfil your order directly. Apart from ensuring that the book gets to you more quickly, this offers us an important benefit – the chance to improve our margin – and hence to carry on producing the kind of books we know you value.

Asking individuals for payment with order rather than the chance to pay later with an invoice will depress the order response slightly, but improve your finances. Can you compensate by offering a cast-iron guarantee of satisfaction or their money back?

Institutions such as schools, colleges and libraries will need an invoice to pay against, but can they be encouraged to pay sooner rather than later? State your credit terms on the order form. For serial publications, directories and journals, offer customers the chance to complete a standing order. In return offer to hold the price for a second year, or perhaps give a discount.

Don't regard the wording on your company order forms to date as 'standard'. Study those you receive from other industries, and appropriate the best ideas. Experiment with different formats and styles, all with the intention of making yours as user-friendly and easy to understand as possible. Get people not connected with a promotion to fill in the order form before you pass it for press. Have they got enough room to write? (For more hints on developing order forms see Chapter 5 on direct marketing.)

Apply for all the free help you can get

Can your authors arrange for you to attend relevant meetings and run book exhibitions? Does your firm belong to any professional associations from whose collected wisdom you can benefit? Find out about the special interest publishing groups that are part of your professional organization, and try to get copies of the reports they publish; when you are more experienced it may be worth trying to attend. Read the professional press that your market reads (and the general press that covers it), and look out for helpful articles that improve your understanding of your customers. You may even spot useful quotes that you can use in your marketing materials.

Bulk sales

Are there any specific interest groups that offer the possibility for 'special sales': learned and professional societies and associations which may promote to their members? If they can offer their members a discount they look helpful and proactive. Never underestimate how useful it can be if an external organization helps you to meet your internal – and frequently highly political – targets.

HANGING ON TO A REASONABLE BUDGET

Finally, although I said that the marketing department budget is just one of many financial responsibilities of the company, it is certainly true that when times get hard, cutting the marketing budget is often considered the easiest way to reduce expenditure.

How can you best resist this tendency? The best plan is to combat difficulties with information, so you know why titles are selling badly and are making changes to market them more efficiently. Compare sales patterns of annual publications with the same period last year. Are any market changes responsible for the differences you see? If you are promoting to a selection of lists, did any one perform particularly badly? By contacting a new selection of different names you may be able to remedy the situation (although if you have had to market twice over to achieve your basic orders the gross margin will still be reduced). Telesales can tell you a great deal. Talk to the reps and customer services. Are products being returned because they do not meet the expectations of those they were marketed to? Is the offer unconvincing? Try another offer, or better still test one against another before you start on your main marketing push, and pick the best.

If cuts are the only option, the key skill is knowing which elements to axe while doing the least possible damage to sales. Understanding the reasons that particular promotions have either failed or succeeded will help you decide what to avoid in future, and how to plan better for next year. The very last elements you should cut are the regular tools of the trade: the advance information sheets and the catalogues on which so much of the publishing sales cycle depends.

11

Approaching specific interest markets

All definitions of marketing agree on the importance of the customer, an understanding of whom is vital for all forms of effective promotion. I make no apology therefore for returning to the subject again in this final chapter.

This chapter is an expansion of various sections in Chapter 1 about the importance of understanding those you are contacting before trying to sell them anything. All marketers need to be fascinated by their customers, the range of products they buy, how they choose, how and why they need them and how they choose to pay. The opening chapter gave you some general comments on the selling environment in general; this chapter includes more specific information for those pursuing particular markets.

THE 'GENERAL READER'

Countless pieces of publisher advance information list the 'general reader' or sometimes that more cultivated counterpart, the 'educated general reader'. Trying to pin down who we are talking about is more difficult. Marketing theoreticians talk about segmenting markets into individual sectors (by a variety of different factors including age, sex, expenditure and ownership patterns), and then there are lifestyle stages at which certain needs will be stronger.

Given this book is for international use, it is difficult to provide specific guidance on what individual sectors of general readers are like, other than how important it is to keep track of what is going on in society as a whole. You need to read a variety of newspapers, consult a variety of websites/ blogs and watch/listen to a variety of television and radio stations – and above all to listen to people talk about the concerns they have. Watching soap operas or observing which major films are coming out (and which ones are successes) is an excellent way of keeping track of current trends in society and learning to read them. My other main recommendation is that our ability to spot changes in society – and newly emerging markets – becomes more acute as we ourselves age, and a wider range of things happen to us. As generalizations, however, I would identify the following current trends:

■ Shortage of time. Time famine is established worldwide, and there are various forms of rage listed as proof of how much we hate waiting ('trolley rage', 'road rage' and the new 'car park rage'). To get more done in the time available we multi-task, texting while talking and surfing the web while chatting online.

■ Desire for better experiences, in friendships, sex, relationships and conversation. We want deeper, more fulfilling relationships – but quickly.

■ Restlessness; a desire for new horizons and the ongoing need for fulfilment and happiness. In relationships we see a greater desire for things to be better, yet show a reduced tendency to work at them to make them so.

■ Guilt. Every parent seems to suffer from this, and working mothers and single parents are particularly prone. Parents are constantly made to feel that society's ills are their fault.

■ Success. As a result of a culture that increasingly demands results, we extend this to every aspect of our lives. Boxes must be ticked and measures met; we want the provability of services to deliver what we want. (Hence the prevalence of testimonials and statistics to promote the effectiveness of products and services under consideration.)

■ Respect, or rather lack of it. All of us want to be treated with it, whatever our past relationships or behaviour, and we feel resentful if we are not. Rejection of the prevailing tone of voice can be instant (think how quickly we leave websites that get it wrong) and young people are particularly quick to claim that they have been patronized.

■ Concern about the environment. This is growing very fast, steered by environmentalists, but bandwagoned by politicians and championed by children, who are putting pressure on the generations above them.

Of course all these trends create opportunities for promoting and selling products and services, and in each case published products could be strong beneficiaries. Those marketing anything, from cosmetics to petrol need to build an awareness of the customers around them; of how it feels to be one as well as how the organization you are working for requires you to function in order to sell something. Remaining interested in your products and who buys them is the best starting point.

FINDING ENTHUSIASTS AND RECOMMENDERS FOR BOOKS AND WRITERS

How can publishers sustain their brand in a world that is getting increasingly frenetic? How can books and reading compete with so many other things to do with your time? One common response to the vast choice of activity available today is that life is becoming increasingly niche; people are intensively farming their time into small plots of things they want to do. Meanwhile, accessing products and services to sustain life's essentials is getting ever easier. Provided you have access to a computer, you can order what you need at any time of the day or night, and have it swiftly delivered to your door. And this deliverability of whatever we want, whenever we want it is making us increasingly demanding. We know our rights, and are intolerant of information that has been sent to us without our permission or that has been randomly targeted.

But ironically, it seems that this very accessibility is leaving a gap in our lives. Apparently with everything available, without struggle, we are missing the personal aspect of shopping: the involvement and enthusiasm that goes into making a choice and holding what we have bought immediately. Market analysts are pointing to the emergence of high-ticket, high-involvement Saturday morning purchases of products that we see as defining us. Among the demonstrations of this increased consumer activity are buying things from a delicatessen and discussing taste and origin, buying flowers and cleaning services to improve our environment – and browsing in bookshops.

This is a great opportunity for publishers. They have the chance to promote their products and services to a market that is looking for an individual and personal benefit. For example, people want the ability to present themselves as part of the current culture, having read the 'latest book' (in the same way as they might boast about having seen the latest play or film), and the opportunity to put questions (either live or online) to their favourite authors – and talk up the experience afterwards – or to attend events at which they speak. Literature festivals are packed with those who want to meet their heroes, to 'touch the hem' of those they have only so far read. Signing sessions provide an intimate and valuable contact (even for those who cannot be there, as titles bought in this way can be sold on eBay for large amounts of money).

The general public may know little about publishing, but given how widespread is the ambition to get a book in print, they are often fascinated by stories of those who either get published, or start a publishing company themselves.

Maintaining a company ethic, and ensuring that potential customers understand it, is a particularly useful practice for independent and small presses to develop. Tell your customers a story and they may buy into it, feeling they have discovered something worth supporting. Tell them how you came to set up the firm, why you do what you do, what you did before (even better if you left a corporate lifestyle to publish what you care about). Quality of life and work–life balance are issues that we all relate to today, and describing how you came to find yours may bring both customers and long-term recommenders of what you are doing. Interestingly, this recommendation may start from the moment you first find an enthusiast. It used to be believed that customers had to experience years of good service before they would start recommending a supplier, but recent research has shown that given the taste for the new in society, enthusiasts tend to pass on the name of their latest find immediately. How quickly can you start turning those who buy from you into advocates?

Here are my top tips for turning your brand into a community that other people want to belong to:

- Share your vision, for your organization and its future; particularly if you started the organization, describe how you came to set it up and what motivates you to do what you do.
- Have a visitors' book on your website to allow people to record their thoughts (most people like to see their name quoted).
- Similarly, host a blog or chatroom on your website to create a sense of community. Encourage feedback and post news that shows you respond to it.

- Encourage enthusiastic correspondents to add their comments to Amazon and other book review sites.
- Where relevant, offer reading copies of new books for book groups.
- Make occasional offers of free copies, run competitions and prize draws either through your mailings or on your website.
- Offer proof copies to selected people to encourage them to 'talk you up'.
- Most publishers send out manuscripts for review before committing to print. Widen this to form a reviewing community and encourage feedback. Then print the names of those involved in a special section within the book. Not only will this spread ownership, if the reviewers are children this can prompt lots of additional sales in schools and amongst grandparents, parents and other fond relatives.
- Offer branded goods that relate to your products, such as T-shirts and stationery. You can test market with a single item, and if there is positive feedback, roll this out. This was how Penguin's highly successful T-shirts of 'paperback originals' were born – produced for the reps at a sales conference, they had far wider appeal and were subsequently sold successfully through bookshops.
- Produce information sheets, either web-based or printed for specific needs, for example for book groups; guides to terminology or key place names for saga/fantasy addicts; bookmarks and window stickers for distribution through reps and shops.

SELLING BOOKS TO PUBLIC LIBRARIES

The words 'and libraries' often appear on the marketing plans for new titles, but it is worth spending a little time thinking about why libraries should be a key part of all promotional planning. In the past publishers have known relatively little about the public library world. There are very few job moves between the two professions, and publishers have tended to take library sales for granted. Now there are a growing number of initiatives to promote awareness and cooperation, to expand and change working practices, and many of these actively involve readers through library events and readers' groups. This is entirely pragmatic: with library budgets being cut and publishers struggling to sell, the mutual interests of librarians and publishers are undeniable.

Librarianship, especially in the public sector, is undergoing wide-ranging change, and the librarian's role is now far wider than just lending books.

Librarians offer the markets they serve access to the information they need; their prime function is access, not recommendation. Thus while you will find immense support from librarians in forwarding the information you send to the professionals most able to make a decision on it, their long-term loyalty is to the markets they serve, not to any particular format or publishing house. Public library book purchasing is also currently undergoing radical change, moving away from individual library authority purchasing to buying through consortia and centralized supplier selection from detailed profiles provided by library authorities. This is partly because of the impact of reduced budgets, but also a response to central governmental plans for national purchasing models (which cut down on administrative costs, and ensure best prices and hence value for money).

Overall book loans are down in public libraries, and the reasons for this are interesting. More accessible bookshops occupying prime retail sites, and publishers' initiatives to make books purchasable wherever the public has time and the inclination to spend (supermarkets, garage forecourts, garden centres and so on) have increased the public's willingness to buy rather than borrow. Cuts in the book purchasing funds for libraries, and reorganizations of how the money is both allocated and administered, have also had an effect – readers can lose interest if fewer titles by their favourite authors appear on the shelves. Purchasing budgets for libraries now have to cover information access through methods other than book purchase, and libraries are very involved in offering wider access to information, technology and entertainment, however the public wants to receive it, so there has been investment in the provision of internet access, audio, DVDs and downloads. Finally, perhaps the public has less time for reading these days because of the vast range of alternative distractions on offer that were not (widely) available 10 years ago. For example people spend time and money on the internet, interactive CD systems, and the customization that is now available for viewing and listening, so they can make a personal timetable rather than be forced to rely on the broadcaster's schedule.

Librarians will tell you their regular users are skewed towards those who are at home for at least part of the day: the retired, the unemployed and mothers with small children. Cuts in opening times have had an effect on borrowing. However some very interesting groups are spending more time in libraries. In the United Kingdom, the National Centre for Research in Children's Literature has revealed that children from ethnic minorities, and in particular girls, make vastly more use of local and school libraries.

Librarians also point out that their customers are today using libraries in new ways: local businesses as a wide-ranging resource for market information, job seekers who access the internet for job vacancies and updating their CVs, local and family historians for the specialist services available. All these activities result in active use of the library's resources but record no corresponding loans.

How to send information to public librarians

What librarians decide to stock is based on the information they receive and their wider understanding of what is available. Organizations that sell resources to libraries edit the range available and offer a selection. Some librarians rely on this, since they lack the time to look further afield; others make a point of keeping up to date with the wider range of material available, but this is usually a personal commitment rather than a job requirement.

Librarians read the professional and trade press to gain information on what is being launched; they also respond to their users' requests for specific resources. They acquire information on what their regulars want to read or use through experience and constant handling, checking and updating the stock, but they also have political initiatives to maintain, to do with widening access, increasing use and maintaining services. Most librarians retain a particular interest in searching for, and purchasing, locally available material likely to be of interest to the increasing numbers of people researching their family history.

When targeting librarians who are still able to purchase stock and are not yet bound into purchasing consortia, bear in mind that the profession is highly collaborative, in that decisions on what to buy are taken in consultation with colleagues. But it's vital to note that while decisions are discussed, most of the subsequent buying is done online. Thus while librarians may look at a synopsis and the cover, they don't get the chance to read a few paragraphs, or to handle a publication, before deciding whether or not to stock it. The information publishers provide is thus vital in creating the right kind of buying information for each title, and your reputation as a firm that maintains standards of a particular kind (whether good or bad) will support the decision making.

Information sent to librarians should make it clear who a particular product is for and what is in it, so that they can then make an appropriate decision about whom to pass it on to. It follows that the marketing materials they receive need to be robust enough to withstand circulation, or easily navigable as web pages. Direct mail and catalogues are probably best addressed to the stock/acquisitions officers in each of the different regional authorities (their names and addresses can be found in the annual professional publications/sites). But do ensure such information is well managed: as information provision experts it can be particularly annoying for librarians to receive catalogues without indices or where the navigable information is inconsistently set up. Increasingly information is now received via e-mail, either through the equivalent of one-off direct mailshots or through regular e-mail newsletters. While these can highlight the latest titles on or immediately before publication, they may also lose impact because of the number of e-mails everyone now receives!

Information to include in the copy

You should include all the main reasons for librarians to stock particular titles, such as author reputation (reviews of previous titles), subject matter and readership, but it is vitally important that all this is backed up by the appropriate bibliographical information. Librarians need to know:

- publication date;
- price;
- extent;
- size;
- format;
- ISBN;
- series and ISSN;
- intended audience;
- illustrations, diagrams and tables, in colour, and black and white;
- whether it is a new or re-issued title;
- binding and production details;
- indices and appendices;
- the time span for publishing part works.

Other points to emphasize to librarians

- Which courses/educational stages your title is relevant to: in particular, if your products relate to project work for specific educational stages. For example, the local children's libraries near where I live are well stocked with reference books for ten to eleven year-olds on Spain. This is because a local head teacher sets a project on the country for the final year of junior school.

■ Any significant overlaps between subject areas. This may enable them to pull money from several allocations. The wider the spread of interest groups they serve, and that you meet, the more likely your resources are to be purchased. Cross-curricular, interdisciplinary areas are particularly attractive.

■ Products that offer librarians the chance to enhance the prestige of their collection. Librarians tend to identify with the collection they look after and are proud of it. Products that offer prestige through ownership, giving the chance to enrich the collection as a whole and make an enhanced resource available to their users, are interesting to them.

■ Remember that librarians often have to order at the last minute or risk losing their budget for not just this year but the year ahead, so information that might make them choose your title in a hurry is valuable. A high-price product may therefore be a useful resource in that, provided it is an appropriate purchase for the library, it takes less time to order and enhances the range of resources available to the reader in one go.

■ Production details. Librarians are looking for resources that will last a long time, so they are keen to hear about product specifications that make it clear that care has been taken – acid-free paper, sewn rather than glued bindings, search engine usability etc.

■ Good covers matter enormously. Librarians are heavily involved in promoting as well as stocking books these days; many are displayed in the library face out, rather than spine on. Sometimes a book jacket does not do justice to a particular title, which won't encourage readers to pick it up and try it. While the quality of the writing matters more than the cover, overall product attractiveness plays a key part in attracting readers' attention and enhancing their enjoyment. Today many reading groups run under the auspices of libraries, and it is the librarians who choose books and purchase stock to support them. This can offer publishers the opportunity to use reading groups as 'focus groups', getting direct customer feedback on jacket design as well as the books' marketability.

Public Lending Right

Most territories now have some form of payment to authors for loans. The principle of the legislation is simple. Authors earn their living through the royalties on books sold; copies sold to libraries may have many readers but only one sale and one royalty payment. The loan payment acts as a compensation for these 'lost' royalties. The funding comes from the public purse. The arrangements for distributing the funds vary from country to country.

Such schemes have revealed interesting borrowing patterns, which do not always tie in with sales patterns through bookshops. The feedback provided is used extensively in public libraries. This includes subject breakdowns, lists of 'classic' authors, and comparisons of local, regional and national trends.

SELLING TO ACADEMIC LIBRARIES

There is a common assumption that whatever resources academics choose to use will end up being bought, on their recommendation, by the associated library, so there is no harm in sending the details of what is available directly to the librarian as well. It's time to update the notion of academic libraries as being passive purchasers of other people's recommendations. There has been a revolution in how information is delivered within increasing numbers of universities.

To start with the nomenclature has changed, but this reflects a change of role rather than mere political correctness. Academic libraries are now increasingly known as 'information resource centres', and the range of services under their management, and often roof, has expanded considerably. This is partly due to student preference – students demonstrably prefer accessing information online – and partly due to logistics, where it is most sensible and appropriate to locate relevant services. With a reduction in educational intimacy through the teaching experience (because of increased class sizes and the wider use of group assignments rather than individual essays), access to supporting information through their local resource centre is becoming an important part of the student experience. Surveys have found that many students visit the information resource centre every day, the vast majority at least once a week – and of course all can access information 24/7 through their computers.

This centrality to the student experience is strengthened now that the range of services available through information resource centres is expanding. In some universities all computer services are now part of information provision, from lecture delivery mechanisms offering handouts to discussion fora that support them. Through the information centre students can now access learning support agencies (offering advice on how to research and present academic assignments), careers information, help with finance and housing as well as with special educational needs such as dyslexia.

Nor do information resource managers only find out what is being taught once the reading lists appear. They are increasingly intimately involved with the educational objectives of what is being taught, as well as with planning and content of both course structure and assessment strategy. There are two main drivers of this trend.

First, employers increasingly demand graduates who are self-starters; who can investigate and explore issues themselves, and thus challenge and innovate in the workplace rather than simply replicate what has been done before. Their experience as students is fundamental to this personal development. The supported learning environment that information resource centres provide is a vital part of this.

The second driver is economic. With larger class sizes, and a wider geographical network of students (because of financial pressures many students now opt to live at home, travelling long distances to reach their local university), the resource centre becomes increasingly important to their student experience. Many information centres are also moving to a delivery model that suits the students and their working patterns, which are often intense and last-minute. While the online delivery mechanisms have long been accessible around the clock, the centres are now increasingly physically open 24 hours a day, as a haven where students can come to meet each other, research and write.

Another common view amongst publishers is that academic librarians work on percentages, dividing up the budgetary pot into amounts for books, journals and other resources such as the photocopier. Rather, information resource managers are increasingly involved from the very beginning of course development. Each curriculum area has an associated 'information specialist' who not only reviews the resourcing of existing areas, but also examines whether these resources provide a suitable basis for possible extensions and additions to the curriculum.

It's worth a quick digression to understand the value structure of the librarianship profession – which is often difficult for essentially entrepreneurial publishers to grasp. Publishers may spend just one or two years in each job, particularly at the beginning of their careers. Job hierarchies within information management tend to move much more slowly, and information staff often feel a deep sense of loyalty to the organization they work for.

The starting point for understanding the different ethic in information provision is that managers have a deep commitment to their user base – but they see themselves as conduits, providing access to what is available, rather than committed to housing any particular type of resource. They are increasingly unsentimental about books and the printed format. They want value for money for their institutional budgets and to hold resources that enhance the relevance and prestige of their collection.

So when finally deciding which resources to invest in, they look for a dynamic mixture that will best suit the academic needs. This may be part book, part purchase of licences, part printed journal – but the mixture chosen will match the learning needs, not any specific portions of the budget. The use of all resources is closely monitored, documented and discussed. Academic librarians are pragmatic and well informed – and above all do not want to tie up funds in resources that will not get used.

The other point to bear in mind is that resource managers are dealing, on a daily basis, with consumers who are vastly more technologically adept than publishers. Students today have grown up with screen access, and understand how to cut, paste, download – and fast. They are intolerant of system difficulties. There is fast-growing understanding within the student market that information as a commodity belongs to all and must be accessed quickly. At hearings for cases of 'academic misconduct' there is often a real confusion about the role of the author (whether of textbook or student essay) in creating ideas; the student view tends to be that what exists should be accessible to all. And while information managers have a clear grasp of copyright, and are meticulous about adhering to procedures that capture and reward ownership, it can be argued that the student desire for free access to what is available has more in common with the resource manager's determination to provide access for the market, than the publishers' hegemonistic view of their own material as superior to their competitors, and their brand as meaning something.

And increasingly, if information managers can't get what they want from publishers, they will go elsewhere, sometimes turning publisher and distributor themselves. There is an increasing tendency to put together resource packs to support student learning, taking material (by agreement) from a variety of different sources to provide students with the best possible learning support. Sometimes what they use is individual chapters from a variety of textbooks; sometimes a direct commission for new material from relevant scholars – remember that information specialists' knowledge of the curriculum, and who are the movers and shakers, is very strong. This saves the students' time, ensures they are relying on high-quality information

– and is a principle they are already used to from downloading individual chapters of books from publishers' websites and Google. Such a manual (which may be available online as well as in printed format) offers a wider viewpoint than just one textbook, and gives academics who are teaching the reassurance that students have at least some additional material to widen their understanding, can be incorporated in the course price, and enhances student appreciation (particularly if well packaged).

Because resource managers are motivated by access rather than profit, provision in this way can work out substantially cheaper for the universities than the purchase of textbooks. This is a process of re-intermediarization; it changes the traditional intermediaries on whom the system of information dissemination has up to now relied while still (or arguably better) meeting student needs. In the process information managers become competitors to publishers rather than merely absorbers of what publishers choose to produce. Underestimate their future significance at your peril!

If targeting university information resource managers with product details is part of your job, here is an important checklist of considerations:

■ Get the words right. Find out what the institutions and managers you are contacting are called, both their job titles and job functions, and target information appropriately. Ensure your in-house database/the organization you are renting mailing lists from is up to date too.
■ See them as an integral part of your marketing campaign, not an add-on. While there is probably little point (and insufficient marketing budget) for the preparation of separate marketing information for academics and information providers, you should bear in mind both their overlapping and different priorities, and send relevant additional information in an accompanying letter or e-mail.
■ Specify accurately the courses and areas of curriculum development to which your materials are relevant. If resources are relevant to a variety of different curriculum areas, it may be possible for information specialists to purchase by pulling from several associated budgets. They are hence very interested in cross-curricular, multi-disciplinary products.
■ They want to know the pedigree of what you are producing. Give them the details of staff involved in the development of your materials – at which institutions, supported by what kind of information delivery mechanisms? A whole new hierarchy of effectiveness in academia is emerging. So find out what kind of information provision there is within the universities of those who have been commissioned to write for your publishing house – and talk this up in the marketing information. Obtain

quotes and endorsements from information professionals and use them on your marketing information.

■ Information managers are increasingly aware of the important role they play in publishers' sales, so treat them as qualified professionals. Emphasize the shared commitment to your joint market – which they understand better than you do.

SELLING TO EDUCATIONAL MARKETS

Educational publishers produce materials for sale to schools: courses and textbooks; assessment and diagnostic materials; resources on educational theory, practice and implementation strategy for teachers; computer software, DVDs and audiotapes, and much more. There are substantial investment costs required in this market. Developing new materials in response to government-inspired curriculum changes is expensive, and with no guarantee of adoption, competition is fierce. Most publishers concentrate on producing texts and course materials for the major curricular areas, but there is a notable trend that all products must be surrounded by relevant additional resources, some paid for by schools, others 'brand-building' (and therefore free). In some areas of the curriculum, it's the books that are becoming incidental. Clare Malinchak, 5th grade special education teacher at Cedar Hill School, Bernards Township, New Jersey, USA, comments:

> We are seeing a trend to switch from traditional textbooks to hands-on 'kits' with supplemental textbooks. In some areas, especially science, we are turning away from traditional, formalized testing, to a more hands-on (performance-based) assessment. For example, to teach a unit about time we would encourage the children (my class consists of those aged 9–10) to learn about pendulums and water clocks and then for assessment give them materials and have them apply the information they have learned to create either time piece discussed, with numerous variables. Our district is involved in a 'technology boost' right now. We are in the process of ordering 'lcd projectors' for all classrooms, as well as purchasing 'smart-boards' for teachers interested in using such technology, and the school's annual Parent Teacher Organization fundraising benefit, which raised a substantial sum in just one night recently, will go towards funding it. So software, DVDs and so on are actually taking a back-seat to the hardware at this time.

> (quote from conversation with author)

Getting a title widely adopted in schools can take a long time. Teachers need to evaluate sample copies of new material and see how they relate to the syllabus and set texts; perhaps to try them out in the classroom and discuss the results with their colleagues (and in particular the staff member with responsibility for that area of the curriculum), the head teacher or principal and/or local educational advisers.

Publishers face competition not only from each other, but other interested parties. Of late there has been concern about initiatives from media organizations which see the development of educational materials, and in particular the hosting of revision sites, as an extension of their brand within the youth market. This is an impressionable group of consumers, who are increasingly monied in their own right.

But once schools have made their selection, and materials have been adopted, they cannot afford to change their minds; and if parents have to buy school books, as happens in many markets, and hence there is a resale market for second-hand copies, the pressure *not* to change a core text can be particularly strong. For the publisher who can produce materials that meets the needs of teachers and candidates for a subject that is popular at public examination level, and secure widespread adoption, the rewards can be substantial: a profitable course of updating, reprinting and the publication of related materials.

The long-term investment needed for this means that the major players in the educational market tend to be specialist publishing divisions within larger companies which can provide the funding necessary. Smaller companies tend to specialize in specific market areas, and have done particularly well of late in revision aids for examinations, where there is both school and parent pressure to improve results.

Recent changes in the educational market

Don't assume the schools market is the same as when you were in full-time education! In recent years there have been huge changes in the priorities and responsibilities of government education policy and a great deal of consequent restructuring. In general, these have involved a move towards national standardization, so that the same areas are being taught in all schools, and the approach is increasingly cross-curricular. Children learn the same topics from different viewpoints, so the child's general understanding of life is enhanced (eg reading skills are used in maths lessons to teach children how to read a timetable or make price comparisons in the marketing information from holiday firms). All this is supported by rigorous programmes of inspection and monitoring, and resulting league tables of school performance.

Parameters of learning are set out for teachers and parents, making teachers more accountable to their pupils and giving interested parents a clearer idea of the academic level their child should be at. Children are fully monitored by their teachers, and there is a comprehensive formal testing system to gauge pupils' progress. All schools are subject to review, and teachers have regular assessments of their performance. These changes have had a knock-on effect on parental attitudes to education and teachers. Seeing league tables makes them more conscious of their position as both funders of the system (through taxes they pay) and consumers (their children experience the system) – and hence more aware of, and inclined to lobby for, their rights.

Three important factors influencing educational publishing today are:

■ Large investment is taking place in the digital delivery of teaching materials. While educational publishers still find that the majority of their income comes from the sale of print – primarily textbooks and related resources – the major part of their investment is going into the development of digital delivery mechanisms, for which demand is growing all the time and for which schools are enthusiastic. However educational publishers are finding that switching to electronic delivery has not brought the economies of scale, and hence increased profits, that have been found from related developments in scientific and academic publishing, and several large publishing conglomerations have been reconsidering their long-term commitment to their educational divisions.

■ The increasing sophistication of educational marketing. Ten years ago most educational publishers sent out their marketing materials via low-cost shared mailings to schools. While this is still an option, there has been huge investment in the acquisition and maintenance of information about the educational market. Some publishers have built databases themselves, others rely on the investment of educational marketing companies. The resulting information banks (which must be fully data protected) record not only the named heads of department as well as senior school staff, but also which texts they have adopted, and even the results of recent school inspections. The availability of this information (obviously at a much increased cost) means that both calls by educational reps, and educational marketing materials sent, can be targeted, precise and personal – and can be expected to yield the best possible results.

■ There is an increasing closeness between the organizations that offer public examinations and educational publishers. There are obviously huge benefits for the educational publisher that can publish what the examiners consider to be the best resource for pupils taking their examination. And while interested bystanders may wonder what controls are in place to ensure best educational practice and avoid vested interests, this is becoming an important factor in what gets published, adopted and widely sold.

How schools spend their money

How much individual schools spend on publisher resources is entirely up to them. Educational publishers today see themselves as competing not just with other publishers but with a wide variety of organizations selling products to schools, for example firms selling security systems, training days or maintenance of the buildings and their general fabric (desks for classrooms, chairs for the staff/faculty room etc). One of the biggest costs for schools is entry of pupils in public examinations, for which the fees are heavy (to cover setting the papers and marking them). Most schools are spending more on these fees than on materials with which to teach. It is common to hear of schools attempting to save teachers' jobs by cutting back on maintenance and teaching materials, relying instead on photocopying or online materials.

The good news for educational publishers is that teachers continue to see publisher materials as the main agents of the school curriculum. What is more, they are for the most part very diligent in determining which published materials will be best for their school, trialling their hunches in the classroom before major capital expenditure is made.

Head teachers and department heads may talk to the local advisory staff and their colleagues in other schools. In most schools or departments, areas of priority for spending are outlined, perhaps at the end of a school year. Publishers' websites and catalogues are rigorously checked for price comparisons of both installing new materials and the renewable costs of replacing items that can only be used once, such as workbooks. Discussions – and lobbying – over what to buy take place in staff meetings. There is an increased concern with getting value for money, and teachers respond to the possibility of saving money on what they need as they would to any consumer offer – with interest.

How publishers keep in touch with the educational market

Educational publishing is a national market (English language teaching (ELT) will be considered separately), and good educational publishers need to keep up to date with many different trends in what is happening to education wherever they are based: government educational initiatives, predictions of future demographic developments, and new practices and fashions in teaching. They frequently employ editorial and subject advisers to scout developments and spot good teacher-produced materials being used in schools (the genesis of many a good textbook). They read the educational press (general and subject-specific), talk to local education advisers, school inspectors, examiners and lecturers in teacher training colleges, and attend exhibitions and meetings. They also keep in touch with their sales managers, and visit schools with the reps to hear at first hand how their materials are being received. They know exactly what their competition is producing, and can estimate market share.

Most schools order their materials either directly from publishers, from school suppliers who act as wholesalers for lots of different publishing houses, or via their local bookstores. Publishing houses are moving to supply schools direct, as doing so brings not only increased profit margins, but also useful information about ordering patterns and time frames (eg the best time to send out information on new titles).

How to reach the market

There are a number of well-established methods for promoting to educational markets:

■ an effective website;
■ mailings – to schools, advisers and so on;
■ e-mails to teachers;
■ representation within schools;
■ telemarketing;
■ despatch of inspection, approval and free copies;
■ mounting displays at exhibitions and conferences;
■ penetrating support mechanisms for teachers;
■ space advertising;
■ free publicity.

Website

An educational publisher needs an efficient website, giving both basic and additional information, whenever the teacher needs it – and providing a feedback mechanism for individual queries. The teaching day is heavily prescribed; there are only specific times at which teachers are free to find information, and so accessing via a website makes the best possible use of their time. A query can be sent and the answer received whenever the teacher is next free to pick it up – when there is not the time for a phone call. It should be easy to read, interesting, kept constantly up to date, and monitored so that feedback is dealt with efficiently. See Chapter 6 for more details.

Mailings

Printed brochures and catalogues are still the most common form of promotion to schools. This is because so many people tend to be involved in educational buying decisions. Teachers are natural collaborators; they have to discuss the materials they are considering buying, and printed marketing pieces are not only easier to discuss, they also give a flavour of the quality of the final product. So while e-mail alerts to individual teachers can work well to announce new materials, or tell them about materials they may buy for themselves, there is still a strong demand for printed information.

When to mail? Schools receive their annual budgets at the start of the new financial year, and educational publishers therefore tend to send their main information (usually their catalogues) a few months before this, when teachers are considering how to spend the next year's budget. This can be followed up with mailings at other times of the year, usually just before the budget arrives and at the start of the new school year. It's often a good time to send a reminder about six weeks before the end of the school year, as there may be money still in the pot which cannot be carried over to the next year.

What to send

Publishers producing materials for the youngest children usually produce an annual catalogue in full colour, and follow this up with specific e-mails, leaflets on major courses and other information sheets during the course of the year. Most publishers for secondary-age pupils produce a series of individual subject catalogues, one for each curricular area in which they publish and a complete catalogue listing everything. Again, these are followed up with specific promotions on major works. Extra stock of everything produced should be sent to the reps visiting schools for them to hand out as required (and additional information should be up on the website before the mailing goes out, so that those who want further details can find them).

Bear in mind though that teachers are as susceptible to feeling that they are reaching information overload as any other profession, but are perhaps more inclined to respond with an ethical objection. Repeated mailings of printed material may look (and be) wasteful. As schools tend to file the catalogues when received, only one physical mailing a year followed up with e-mails referring to the website or the catalogue is enough.

Whom to send to

Specialist marketing organizations have built the data with which to contact this market (and some publishers have built their own). Most educational marketing organizations offer a two-tier system. Publishers can pay a one-off fee to send out information to all schools of a particular type (eg secondary, primary, private). To receive a higher level of service, and for an annual subscription, publishers can gain access to a highly sophisticated programme recording each school's specific text adoptions, staff responsibilities and contact details, budget, feedback from the most recent school inspection – and much more. Of course such information is expensive to research and maintain, but it may well be worth it. For example, access to such a detailed profile before a rep's arrival in a school can make a considerable difference to the relevance of his or her presentation, and the key people within the school that he/she tries to meet during the visit. Primary publishers can note large schools that adopted a rival publisher's materials several years ago and may be considering a change – and hence might be receptive to the idea of a formal presentation to staff, after school hours.

When considering mass mailouts, primary publishers usually send their material to the head teacher/principal or head of subject. Mail addressed to the head is routinely opened by the school administrator and passed on. After a quick look through by the head – and perhaps a short note to the subject coordinator involved if something looks particularly interesting – the catalogue tends to be stored, along with material from other publishers, in the staff room or the head's office until the time comes for deciding how much to spend and on what.

In secondary schools the overall budget is divided between the various departments, and it is the department heads who have responsibility for spending. Specific mailings can be addressed directly to them (again names are available from list rental companies), but for the general despatch of catalogues, publishers often send a package consisting of separately marked items for different department heads to the school administrator, together with a letter asking for the contents to be divided up as appropriate. This is obviously considerably cheaper.

In some (not all) markets you have the choice whether to send your material yourself (bearing all the costs of postage and despatch) or to join with others and join a shared mailing, which is cheaper. Schools tend to say they don't care how the promotional material arrives, but if a catalogue reaches the school on its own it is perhaps more likely that a teacher will sit down and browse through straight away. Most people would be daunted by the simultaneous arrival of four – or more – catalogues, and put off looking through them until later. On the other hand, the fact that all publishers tend to send their material at the same times of year could adversely affect this theory.

If you do decide on a shared mailing:

■ Try to find out who else is to be included in the pack. There are bound to be certain of your major competitors with which you do not wish to join hands as you arrive in schools.
■ Do specify a position within the pack. If the mailing house is using plastic envelopes, find out whether your catalogue can go on the outer edge.
■ Don't forget other potentially interested parties, for example teacher training colleges, subject advisers, teachers' centres, school suppliers who may stock and promote your titles and so on. You can either rent the lists or build your own. As schools tend not to move or die it can be a good investment.

E-mailing teachers

The attitude to e-mail within schools varies. Some schools see teachers receiving information this way as a benefit – in that it reduces the amount of post entering the school; the time taken to open up shared mailings, divvy out the contents, as well as deal with all the personally addressed items. Others see it as a managerial issue, and would rather their staff were planning lessons/teaching/consulting with colleagues than reading e-mails.

A significant indicator is how individual schools encourage parents to correspond with teachers. Some see it as a quick and easy way of getting and giving feedback, others feel they must protect their staff, and feel that encouraging parents to get in touch through the regular mechanisms (letter, visit, phone call) helpfully cuts down the amount of time taken away from the classroom.

Educational marketing companies are however routinely collecting institutional e-mail addresses from teachers where they are provided, and other teachers pass on their home e-mail addresses when they attend exhibitions. Coverage is not yet uniform or entirely reliable, but will surely only increase. One teacher commented to me, 'E-mail is definitely the way to go! I rarely use the telephone during school hours because I do not have a telephone in my classroom, and the few phones accessible to me are in a noisy faculty room.'

For teachers who do like to receive information this way, e-mail alerts are useful, directing those who are interested to a website where they can request a sample copy. E-mail alerts also work well for titles they may consider purchasing for their own use, and paying for themselves.

Preparing your marketing approach to schools

When targeting information you have to bear in mind the different needs and priorities of those within schools who will benefit from your materials, and who may, or may not, be involved in the decision to purchase. The difficulty you face is that one set of information has to meet all these needs. For example, the financial responsibility may be with the head teacher/principal or head of department/grade level leader, but it is the classroom teachers who have to make the material work. A new maths course available to primary schools could offer the principal the benefits of cost-effectiveness, efficiency, longevity, satisfied teachers and classes. The class teacher meanwhile may appreciate the practical benefits of your material working well with mixed-ability classes, so that all children can be occupied on the same material at the same time, leaving the teacher free to concentrate on individual needs and problems. School administrators, who usually place the order, may be more interested in your ordering mechanisms and how efficient your firm is to deal with; they tend to have long memories for past problems.

What are teachers interested in? From my research, several major factors emerged:

■ Relevance to the curriculum/examination syllabus. Appropriate and attractive material, developed by teachers/examiners for real teaching needs, will always attract attention. Fiona Little, Head of English at Kingston Grammar School, says, 'It's a good idea to target new specifications and syllabus changes; these occur regularly. New strategies mean lots of new texts – and many of the old ones becoming redundant. Teachers feel quite insecure when something new is implemented and look for materials to support their teaching at these times.'

■ Digital delivery (whether in whole/part or through additional resources such as an effective website). Children actively prefer learning this way, and schools are starting to experiment with individual laptops for each child. Teaching resources that are delivered through a combination of online and traditional methods will now attract positive attention.

■ Value for money. Schools are perennially short of money, and there are long discussions at staff meetings over what to buy. Concentration is improved by the knowledge that whatever is selected prevents further spending in that subject area for a number of years. Special offers and money-saving gambits on quality materials undoubtedly attract attention. It follows that you should highlight all the special offers and promotions that you are making available to schools: library packs that incorporate a discount, starter packs for courses or an inspection copy system that can provide teachers with free copies of books. Similarly, lay out complete information on pricing and availability in a clear and consistent way. If you are promoting a scheme and the cost of installing yours is less than that of your competitors, provide installation and running costs. (Your reps may appreciate an expanded version of this with item by item comparisons for use when they are discussing prices in schools.)

■ Teacher support materials. Whereas many governments lay down what should be taught, in general they do not specify how. Back-up materials for teachers who spend increasing amounts of their time recording and assessing, and therefore have less time for actual lesson preparation, are thus increasingly important.

■ What's new. Teachers are interested in new materials for new needs. If they have been in teaching for a while and worked in several schools they probably know your backlist already; stress what they won't be familiar with.

■ And at what level. Indicate the level at which the material is aimed clearly and consistently. On web pages or in catalogues I feel the best way to achieve this is to have a series of 'running heads' along the top or perhaps down the side of the page so that the teacher can see at any one time the subject and age range of the material being looked at. Repeat the information, with any additional relevant details, under the individual title entry (eg header: 14–16; resources for which courses).

■ Series of titles. Teachers are in general more interested in complete series that can cater for pupils over a number of years than one-off books that require a hunt for new materials once the final chapter has been reached. Even if the series you are promoting is new and you have only two or three proposed covers of the first few stages available, draw a diagram indicating where the different stages will fit in; show planned materials by outlining covers. It will attract attention to a major new series.

■ Illustrate as much as possible. Use covers, illustrations from the books and specimen pages. Make the specimen pages large enough to read: it is better to have one that can be read than half a dozen that require a free magnifying glass to be mailed with every catalogue. Incidentally, I have heard many examples of teachers who do keep a magnifying glass handy for reading the sample pages in publishers' information – they should not have to!

■ Marketing information that they can access quickly. On websites and in catalogues ensure your searching capabilities are good and the structure logical. Every printed catalogue needs a contents list and an index, so users can find information in a hurry. On the contents page it is also a good idea to list new titles and provide page references. Some publishers produce new book supplements which appear in the centrefold of the catalogue; extra copies of these can be usefully run on for use at exhibitions or insertion in mailings.

■ Make it friendly. Have a professional and yet chatty introduction on your home page, or include a letter with your catalogue. Some publishers put a signed letter from the subject editor (and occasionally a photograph) on the inside front cover of the catalogue, and research shows it gets read. This can be a very useful place to remind teachers that you are interested in their suggestions for publication, which always bonds your interests.

■ Show your materials work. Include information on how particular schemes are working in certain schools, quotes from other teachers on the benefits of your materials, details on the progress of new materials under development. Lay out the scope and sequence of new materials in an easy-to-read manner; to help teachers quickly assess whether or not it will be easy to plot their lessons in between the hectic schedule of a school day which includes assemblies, field trips, presentations, birthday celebrations, meetings, etc. You are selling to a very specific market; write about what interests them.

■ Make it easy for recipients to reply. Print telephone numbers and website addresses large enough for them to be found in a hurry. Allow teachers to register for inspection copies via your website, and include freepost inspection copy request cards in your catalogues. Put them on a separate sheet or an extension of the back cover of the catalogue rather than the back cover itself: teachers are reluctant to destroy books, even promotional ones. Perforate where the tear has to be made to detach them. Include a stock list/order form in case schools have difficulty in ordering and a card asking for a representative to visit the school.

Representation within schools

In the struggle to get your materials adopted in schools, the reps who visit them are immensely valuable. The feedback in terms of sales figures and e-mails that result from mailings is statistical but largely impersonal – you do not know *why* your material was chosen or not chosen. It is the reps who get the eyeball-to-eyeball reactions to your pricing, subject coverage, durability of format and so on.

Your house may have its own sales team, or you may employ the services of an external agency. Typically separate teams concentrate on secondary and primary schools. Reps (who are often ex-teachers) are usually briefed by the editors and the marketing team at regular sales conferences, held twice or three times a year in preparation for the major selling seasons ahead. (More specific advice on presenting at sales conferences will be found in Chapter 9.)

Visits to schools are usually made after appointments have been set up; display materials and sample copies are carried in for presentation during morning and lunchtime breaks, preferably in the faculty or staff room. What the reps carry has become more complex in recent years. They travel in estate cars loaded with display boards, posters and boxes full of inspection copies, and write reports on every visit they make.

The sales manager who organizes the reps' activities won't want to set up a separate and time-consuming chain of command, whereby a host of additional people receive reports, but do make the most of your contact with them. You may get the chance to talk to them at sales conferences, but if you can, arrange to go out visiting schools for a day with them.

You will cramp their style: most reps value their independence and don't like being listened to. Make the most of the opportunity and learn from their swift delivery of sales benefits; there is not time to pass on all the background information you may consider relevant. It's a very useful lesson in copywriting; particularly for those who up to now have spent a lot of time thinking up bullet points on product benefits rather than understanding the practicalities of funding materials in schools.

Many publishing houses have used the difficult market as the justification for upping their sales effort, requiring reps to demonstrate products at faculty or staff meetings rather than just represent them. The stakes between winning and losing adoptions in schools are so high that detailed explanations of products by the reps after hours are increasingly common. Teachers can be asked from a variety of different schools in an area, perhaps with an editor in attendance to explain the background to the new scheme. Similarly when schools are involved in the development and piloting of new materials; the publishers not only demonstrate their commitment to practical and workable products but build up long-term loyalty.

Telemarketing

In-bound

The publisher's website can deal with many basic questions ('frequently asked question' (FAQ) sections are particularly useful), but in addition, most publishers offer a telephone helpline for information and direct orders. Most schools have an organizational credit card for ordering items people need in a hurry.

Out-bound

Bearing in mind the very limited times of the day that reps can talk to teachers, telemarketing can be an effective means of making direct contact with specific subject teachers. The telephone numbers of schools (and often e-mail addresses of teachers) are offered as an additional service by firms offering mailings to schools. There are some departments (eg music, art and any form of technology) that tend to have their own staffroom/kettle, and so tracking staff down to these locations, at the right times, can be a very good way of securing their attention.

Inspection copies

Teachers need time to look at material they are considering for adoption in their schools, so most educational publishers offer a system of supplying books 'on inspection'. Orders can be placed via the web, freepost reply cards are included in mailings for teachers to request the titles they would like to see, and reps are encouraged either to hand out inspection copies or order them for the staff members they talk to.

The rules for getting them vary slightly from company to company, but the principle is the same. A teacher may keep a book requested on inspection if multiple copies (usually 12–15) of the title are ordered for use in the school. In general a book available on inspection must be one capable of being adopted for class use. Other books are available 'on approval'; after the inspection period has elapsed they must be returned to the publisher in good condition or purchased. There is a grey area in between for some teaching practice-type titles, which could be sold in multiple copies through colleges of education to student teachers. In such cases the lecturer recommending the book may qualify for a free inspection copy.

In general, publishers spend too long describing the mechanics by which copies are available, and insufficient time encouraging teachers to really get to know the materials they request and discuss them with colleagues. Most books sent out for review will end up being pulped on return anyway, as they are 'un-saleable' (or it's just too expensive to put them back into stock). Teachers will be more likely to get to know a resource they are encouraged to look at than one they are frightened of damaging.

When you do despatch samples, send out a form with each one asking for the recipient's comments. Those that get returned will be an invaluable source of promotional quotations later on. It will not matter that the people commenting are not famous; first-hand feedback from practising teachers will be very convincing to the market.

Free copies to the educational press and other influential people

Educational publishers send materials to educational correspondents in the media; a positive review in the relevant press is a great asset for a marketing campaign to teachers. For similar reasons publishers sometimes mail new material free of charge to key people. The books are often sent in the expectation of a favourable recommendation that can then be used in the books' marketing.

Exhibitions and conferences

Professional conferences for teachers tend to occur outside term time, for regular exhibitions and conventions sometimes staff are given time off to attend. For example, teacher Clare Malinchak told me, 'In New Jersey we have a "teacher's convention" held annually in Atlantic City. All teachers in the state of New Jersey are given a four-day weekend in order for them to go to Atlantic City to attend workshops, presentations, and to receive free material and samples.'

Attending such events is a useful extension of the rep's activities. Some firms have mobile exhibition teams which mount large stands; others require the rep to do this as well. If you can, do get along to important meetings in your subject area. Not only do they provide a very useful opportunity for both editorial and marketing staff to meet school contacts made by the rep, and to explore current teaching trends, they also allow you to see at first hand what your competitors are up to!

Support mechanisms for teachers

There are other methods of getting information to teachers. Teacher training facilities, usually (but not always) within universities, offer a chance to impress trainee teachers with your materials when they impressionable and idealistic, and often long-term loyalties are formed in the process.

Many local education authorities have a teachers' centre where staff can meet one another, attend training sessions, use the library and much more. There are also various school advisers and troubleshooters who are available on various bases, from being suddenly parachuted in to support short-term crises, to offering support and advice on a long-term basis. All are qualified and experienced teacher/managers. The extent to which they are used or listened to depends on the views of the principal or head of department (some regard them as spies, others as offering extremely valuable fresh viewpoints) and the disposition of the advisers themselves. Contact lists are available by the subject/age of children on whom they advise. Keep them in touch with your publishing programme.

There are organizations that offer teacher training days in schools. All these are valuable marketing conduits for information on publishers' products.

Space advertising in relevant publications and on websites

Education has a supporting professional press, and there are certain publications in which you will find all your competitors advertising. You should consider doing so yourself. Even more valuable to you will be reviews or feature coverage in these papers.

The relationship between paying for advertising space and hence supporting an educational publication, and expecting coverage in return, is a complicated one. Advertising pays for editorial yet advertisers are not rewarded with automatic coverage. You do however have the right to have your materials at least considered for review.

Chapter 8 describes the organization of space for advertising and promotions, increasingly linked areas of marketing activity today. Chapter 7 deals with securing free publicity.

PROMOTING TO UNIVERSITY ACADEMICS

There has been a quiet revolution going on within universities in recent years. If you are tasked with promoting to this market, it is important that you understand what has happened.

A huge increase in student numbers

There is a worldwide move towards mass education at higher level (the 'massification' of higher education). Targets are various, but the intention is to have a much higher proportion of the population who have benefited from a university education.

The funding model has changed

The vastly increased numbers mean that old funding mechanisms have had to be changed too – because governments cannot afford to subsidize larger numbers of students. This has thrown the burden of funding higher education on to the students themselves (who are ultimately responsible) and their families. Most countries have a system of student loans, which recipients start repaying once their post-graduation income reaches a particular level. This is having a knock-on effect on applications. Students are in general opting to stay closer to the parental washing machine and support base, and there is a move away from expensive city centres where accommodation costs are high. Many students are holding down part (or full)-time jobs to pay the fees. There is very little money around for book buying.

Along with the changed responsibility for funding higher education has come a changed attitude of the students. They increasingly see themselves as consumers – rather than simply absorbers – of the learning on offer. Naomi Klein comments in *No Logo* (2002):

> Many professors speak of the slow encroachment of the mall mentality, arguing that the more campuses act and look like malls, the more students behave like consumers. They tell stories of students filling out their course-evaluation forms with all the smug self-righteousness of a tourist responding to a customer-satisfaction form at a large hotel chain... students slip into class slurping grande lattes, chat in the back and slip out. They're cruising, shopping, disengaged.

Academics who mark their work regularly report that students subsequently lobby for an increase, significantly on the grounds not that a specific piece of work deserves a higher mark, but that their overall average requires it. There has been a huge rise in plagiarism and cheating in exams.

A changed model of how education is delivered

The increase in student numbers has not been matched by a commensurate increase in staffing or facility improvements, and overall the character of the teaching experience has changed. Everyone is short of time. Academics are increasingly required to research and publish and not just teach. Some of the burden of classes has been moved onto research assistants, PhD students and part-time lecturers. Students are taught in larger classes, there is more use of group assignments, in part to avoid individual marking, and there has been a marked reduction in the former closeness of student–teacher relationships. Some would argue that this motivates students to become independent learners, others that higher education is fast becoming a process of transferring information.

Given that the academics are under so much time pressure, it is the information managers (formerly called librarians) who are increasingly taking a more active role in the provision of learning resources (print and electronic). Instead of course reading lists, which students lack the time or inclination to consult, course administrators may now put together course packs which pick and choose from the various materials available, and provide all the supporting material in one handy source. But the huge class sizes mean that libraries cannot possibly hold enough copies of supporting resources in print form, and hence they are looking to publishers to provide them with 'granular access': e-content licensing opportunities so they can secure the bits they want, much as happens with online journals and databases.

This demand for publishers to deliver *content* rather than a single format (even if backed up by an attractive website) is growing. A publishing house is much more likely to sell content if it can make the bibliographic details and print-on-demand facility available, quickly and in standard electronic formats. Many information managers are working with academic staff to build electronic profiles based on their interests, and they want to work with publishers/suppliers to access information about new titles through these profiling processes. All are becoming intolerant of time-wasting in the ordering process; gone are the days when anyone has time to go through paper slips or blurbs about new titles.

This pressure to change the delivery method is coming from the information managers; publishers in general are responding more slowly. In some markets, copyright restrictions prevent all textbook content being made available in digital format, and there are strict restrictions on how much librarians can make available online at any one time. Some publishers are starting to think about the development of standard 'content cartridge' models so that core content to support students can be loaded into the online learning tools used in universities, but in general publishers are reluctant to give up the textbook model, which has long yielded profits and which parents (who understand from their own time in education that books support learning) have been willing to underwrite. Rich profits have been made by publishers offering the single textbook that supports a popular course.

Arguably the old textbook model now needs reviewing for the online generation. The pressure to gain access to the resources they need will only grow, and students are becoming increasingly unwilling to buy print editions when they become out of date so quickly. (New editions appear annually in some markets, with little change apparent, but an insistence that the new edition be purchased.) Information managers are meanwhile dealing with students and staff who demand instant gratification for the resources they need to support learning. All expect Amazon-style delivery, and electronic access wherever possible. Significant too is the internationalization of higher education. Most universities have an international presence and these students, who pay higher fees, want electronic access to learning resources, not to know that there are 10 copies in the library, wherever that is.

A change in the role of the academic

In order to win promotion academics must publish their research. Lecturers with a lot of published research win the institutions they work for points and higher funding as centres of excellence. This has led to the emergence of a premier league of universities, with strong research departments, which are thus well placed to win further research funding.

Whereas at one time academics had job security for life, today their job security has become increasingly fragile. Many new appointments are made on the basis of a rolling contract that must be reviewed after three or five years. If the university (or a particular course) is not paying its way, then staff can be laid off. Research assistants and research fellows seldom have any job security at all, and no identifiable career path. Over the past few years there has been a strong trend towards the 'casualization' of the academic workforce; and in the United Kingdom today almost half are on part-time contracts. Regular reports say that academics' standard of living has declined in relation to comparable professions, but they are not a well organized lobby group and do not have public sympathy. In any case, the educational priority remains younger children. Politicians may say that education is a priority, but they usually mean basic skills such as reading and writing.

University departments are now required to bring income into the university, through carrying out research for industry and other parties willing to pay. There has been a massive growth in external income over the period. Academics often get no personal share of this external revenue (although part of it reverts to their department or school and they can often use a proportion in pursuit of their own research interests). Over the same period, administrative demands on staff have grown substantially, often through governmental increases in workload, for example teaching quality assessment and the research assessment exercise.

An increased pressure to retain students

Universities are expensive places to run, and there is a real pressure to both recruit students and to retain them once they have enrolled, particularly international students who bring even higher levels of fees. There are frequent complaints about pass marks being lowered to allow students to remain on the course, and softer (social sciences) options being chosen by students in preference to stricter disciplines (in the hard sciences).

A reduction in the value of the first degree

The undergraduate degree arguably now offers less academic depth, certainly less academic mentoring – and almost every job applicant has one. One response is the growing popularity of a higher degree, the MA/MSc, which many students (and their parents) are opting to fund, to try to differentiate applications in the workplace. Work experience has become much more significant on the CV than was formerly the case.

These points indicate the climate into which your marketing materials are being sent, and the trends that will become increasingly important. Here are some practical hints on how to manage the process of promoting publishers' products to academics on a day-to-day basis.

Promoting textbooks to the academic market

Textbooks are promoted to academics teaching at universities and colleges in the hope that they will be adopted. Adoption means that they will appear under the heading 'essential' at the top of the reading list that accompanies each course, and consequently be purchased in large numbers by both the students taking the course and the libraries serving them.

Promotions of textbooks are generally geared to getting a sample (or 'inspection') copy of the new book into the academic's hand. Each new academic year the local bookshops that serve college populations ask academics for details of what they will be recommending to students and the numbers likely to be taking the courses. They then stock copies according to their experience of what will sell: what the libraries will take, how many students will share a copy, and how many will have the motivation or cash to buy a copy of their own. These are stocked ready for the start of term.

So runs the theory, but since the last edition of this book appeared, I have myself become an academic, and teach marketing at Kingston University. My adopted textbook was the one chosen by the previous lecturer, who passed on a free copy. I based my lecture notes on it. Each week I receive e-mail alerts telling me about new textbooks that compete with the one I chose. They all make the same mistake: they talk about what they have to offer me, rather than why I might want to change the adopted book.

Why might academics *not* want to change their main resource?

- Time (always the biggest factor).
- They already have lecture notes based on the old one and can't be bothered to change.
- Familiarity. Lecturers teach the same subject once a year. Familiarity with the format of the relevant chapter is an obvious attraction.

From my experience, the factors that might prompt a change are:

- new resources that go with the book, eg PowerPoint slides that lecturers can use;
- really interesting case studies in the book – big brands excite the students, case studies about bicycle or umbrella manufacturers do not;
- a good price which students are likely to afford (small price differentials can make a big difference to how expensive a resource feels);
- a lecturer-only website that offers additional teaching materials (like sample exam questions and worked examples);
- a prize that students can be entered for – this is popular with the students, and the university's marketing department is always keen to cover prize-winners in its publications;
- a really attractive cover that will motivate students to want the book, and think the lecturer up-to-date for choosing it.

In short, when writing to academics, think about their needs and priorities, and not just about your publishing house and why you are pleased with your new title.

The best time to tell academics about new resources

Contacting the academic market is less time-specific now that different institutions organize their time in different ways. For example, there are traditional three-term years, three-term/two-semester years and two-semester years. Send advance information on forthcoming titles with guidance on how to get an inspection copy as soon as you have it, but always back this up with a realistic idea of when the title will be published. There is nothing more annoying for academics than planning to change the key course book only to be told it is not available until halfway through the first teaching term. If this has been their experience of your house, they will be wary of adopting your titles in future.

Distribution of free copies

It is usually worth distributing a number of copies of a new textbook free to key academics without requiring them to recommend it or show how many copies have been bought as a result. Likely recipients include heads of department where particularly large numbers of students may buy the book, or key respected academics within the book's subject area who may respond with a favourable quotation that you can use in your publicity material.

Most large academic publishing houses employ reps who visit universities on a regular basis, to find out who is teaching what, which resources are being used, spread information on their new titles – and pick up ideas for new products (courses that have large and growing student numbers but are inadequately resourced). Their visits are the ideal opportunity to hand out free copies of existing resources.

Academics tend to be well aware of their key role in the profitability of textbook publishing, and regard free copies as their right. If you look after a stand at an exhibition or conference you may have several soliciting free copies on the basis of the large student numbers they have it in their power to recommend to. To provide every university department with a free copy in the hope of securing sales could erode a book's basic profit margin, so be careful with your largesse. Never give away free copies of non-textbook titles. Profit on these titles is achieved with all the marginal sales – the odd ones here and there. If you have given these away, there will be no profit at all.

Summary books and study aids

Sales of these titles have become particularly strong in recent years, to the detriment of the standard (and it has to be said generally longer) course texts and background reading. Some are available as printed texts, others as websites or downloads.

These summaries are a guide to passing exams, listing all the key information candidates must have at their fingertips to pass. With students inclined to do less work but still keen to stay on their course, and academics keen to maintain student numbers to keep the course running and themselves in a job, such products have a widening market.

Also in this category are books aimed at the professional community which feature lists and double-page spreads. These may have higher prices, but their professional format and 'grown-up' appearance may make them attractive purchases for students and their parents. I am thinking in particular of business encyclopaedias and general reference books, which provide a short cut to wider understanding, often with a glossary containing all the right buzz words. Lecturers may find such resources equally useful for setting exam papers (each one needs a guide to marking, and lists of key areas to be covered are very useful). If you are promoting a title to a professional market, and feel it may have wider market in universities, it may be worth offering a student discount – or a bulk purchase to libraries.

Research monographs

The scholarly monographs promoted to academics are often the result of a PhD or other long-term research project. Markets for these titles are necessarily small, and most of the sales will be single-copy, to interested individuals or libraries. Print runs and promotion budgets therefore tend to be small too.

Although these titles may also end up on reading lists, they will usually be listed as 'further reading'. As multiple sales are unlikely, inspection copies are not offered; rather, they are generally available 'on approval'. After a period for examination they must either be returned in good condition or paid for.

Although marketing budgets are small, markets are highly specific and easy to target; extensive and costly campaigns are not required. It also pays to capitalize on all additional paths to the potential market. Much use can be made of penetrating the viral networks through which academics involved in particular subject areas communicate. With a print run of 500, sales of 200–300 can recover the costs; selling a further 50–100 gets a good margin, and profits on sales above that can be very substantial.

You have willing partners to promote such titles in information managers and librarians. Although they are determined to provide better access for their users to information from wherever it can be sourced, they still see books as of fundamental importance. Maxine Brodie, university librarian at Macquarie University Library, Sydney, Australia, says:

> The downside of the seductiveness of instant electronic access is, of course, that students have a tendency to think that if it's not on Google, it doesn't exist. One of our key strategies at the moment is to find ways of increasing the use of print by putting references to it in the places where students 'live' on the web. Books are not dead – but need to get better known; and anything that publishers can do to help us achieve this will also help their sales.

MARKETING CHILDREN'S BOOKS

Most general publishing houses have a children's division. Until comparatively recently their profile tended to be low, and they were seen as very much a subsidiary activity to the development of the firm's main list. Advances and royalties on children's titles were based on lower selling prices and so were worth less in cash terms to authors and illustrators. Children's authors attending events got less for their appearance than those writing titles for adults. The books received smaller promotion budgets and shares of company attention.

Today the area is vastly more active, a trend that is found in the book trade worldwide. The quality of children's books is better than ever, and they are reaching the market through an increasing variety of outlets. Children are also buying books for themselves, often through school bookselling operations.

Why has there been such a change? In part it is the product of increased competition. The founding of Walker Books by Sebastian Walker in 1978, as a company that would publish only for children, started a 'shake-up'. Larger advances were offered (dubbed 'cheque-book publishing' by his rivals) and titles were sold through new outlets such as supermarkets. Walker's fundamental legacy also lay in his insistence on the importance of producing excellent children's books; his company raised the profile of publishing for the young as an end in itself. Since then there have been some hugely successful titles – notably by JK Rowling and Philip Pullman – created originally for children and young people, but enthusiastically read by adults (what is dubbed the 'crossover market'), and this has had a big effect both on the popularity of reading and on sales. Other developments such as the growth of the mass market and the rise of character licensing have lifted children's books to be rated alongside toys and computer games as a first-class profit opportunity.

Opportunities for children's publishers today include the following.

The blockbuster novel for young people that becomes part of popular culture

In 2005, market research company Mintel reported that 'The *Harry Potter* series has become something of a crossover, popular with both children and adults, as has *The Curious Incident of the Dog in the Night-time*. This could perhaps mark the creation of a new genre of books, appealing to all ages' (Academic.mintel.com/Sinatra/academic/my_reports/display/id). Another survey, significantly commissioned by a supermarket, reported that 40 per cent of UK parents today think their children read more than they did at the same age, and recommend books to them (www.literarytrust.org. uk/database/stats/readchild/html). The specific vocabulary of these titles becomes part of popular culture – newspaper readers and crossword puzzle enthusiasts need to know what a 'muggle' or an 'aletheometer' is – and they consequently get read by all generations.

Huge sales of these titles forced the creation of a children's bestseller list, arguably because authors of adult titles felt uncomfortable seeing children's books selling better than theirs. Justine Larbalastier, US author of the *Magic or Madness* trilogy, says, 'Without her [JK Rowling] my career would not be possible. All children's and Young Adult authors owe her hugely.'

New selling locations to reach the mass market

Supermarkets experimented with own-brand books in the 1980s, but price competition over the more recent blockbuster novels was so keen that such stores used them as 'loss leaders' to draw shoppers in, and there has now been a rapid expansion of new places to buy children's books.

Today most large centres of population are ringed by out-of-town supermarkets and superstores where people with small children are more likely to shop and, crucially, find it more convenient to buy books. As well as selling books through supermarkets, books also sell well through superstores selling child-related merchandise, and can benefit from being displayed alongside non-book child-related products such as toys and prams. Through these outlets books are being sold to a much wider group of people, as many of the customers are probably not regular bookshop browsers. Purchases are often made on impulse, and there is huge demand for high-profile media-related properties of the kind publishers can offer.

Another new arena is the workplace selling of books, which has expanded dramatically in recent years. Firms involved in this (notably The Book People in the United Kingdom) buy large quantities of a limited range of stock, display the products in staff space and collect orders at the end of the week. Children's titles can work very well here, and in particular books on sport for boys, reference titles linked to the school curriculum and reading packs. Retailers can demand huge discounts but they are reaching customers who do not frequent bookshops (and hence are expanding the market), they buy firm (no stock gets returned) and their orders can often make a print project financially viable.

The traditional book trade has reacted in varied ways. In general the children's department is easier to find than it used to be, and children's titles are now part of the major promotions at the front of the store. Some major bookselling chains have experimented with dedicated children's shops, but the combination of excessive rents for high street sites and low-price products is a difficult one, and casualties have occurred. Shops that have done particularly well are often those that have become local centres of advice and encouragement on reading, with welcoming premises and detailed knowledge of their stock. From their shop front they can organize displays in schools and signing sessions in the store; advise children who visit in January with book tokens; arrange competitions and summer holiday reading schemes. For many of these activities they try to enlist the support of publishers.

Other booksellers have nurtured special markets, such as school bookshops (with a variety of well-thought-out recommended reading lists) and other junior markets, and are active in finding new ways to reach children. The organization of school book fairs and school book clubs is also an area of strong competition and activity. There is some special publishing for this market, book and activity kits.

Character licensing arrangements

With the wide availability of films for children, on DVD and various networks, and the marketing efforts of Disney Corporation, there has been considerable growth in demand for 'character' images created for a book or film to adorn a wide variety of specially designed merchandise – from nightdresses and bedroom slippers to rucksacks and school lunch boxes. With their backlist of character titles, publishers were well placed to take advantage of this opportunity.

Superstore purchasers shop thematically, following the child's interests; they may not be looking for anything as specific as a book or cutlery set, but a Pooh Bear or Thomas the Tank Engine item, and books can benefit enormously from being displayed in an accessible position alongside related merchandise. Some stores take this a stage further by launching specific boutiques within stores for certain characters that have a strong affinity with their own market.

Educational upheaval and parental anxiety

Changes in the educational environment and consequent parental anxiety have created an opportunity for children's publishers. Buying resources to practise for tests and assessments, for reading and project-based homework feels proactive and positive in a time of educational uncertainty. The rise of more non-fiction titles in particular is a response to an understanding that boys prefer reading fact books to stories, and there are greater concerns about boys' literacy than girls'.

Opportunities to meet authors

Another great boost to book buying has been increasing opportunities to meet authors through special appearances, literary festivals and book events.

The rise in literary festivals has been a notable trend worldwide. Each of them now has its own associated children's programme which often holds some of the most highly attended events – and at which huge numbers of titles can be sold. British author Jacqueline Wilson holds the record for the longest book signing – over eight hours. Children want to meet favourite authors, and these opportunities have become hugely profitable.

Marketing techniques for promoting children's titles

The new selling locations have necessitated a switch in marketing techniques. Instead of concentrating their energies on pursuing every possible opportunity for free coverage (how children's books used to be marketed), publishers must become increasingly aggressive to maintain these opportunities, which are under threat from both adult books and a variety of other merchandise with potentially higher stock turns and profits. Books often become more attractive when marketed in combination with toys and clothing, as a branded item appealing to a child with specific interests. Packaging that adds value to the product is particularly important: for example in warehouse clubs, catalogues and cash and carries, shoppers tend to be looking for a higher price and bulkier looking purchase (this is particularly important if the item is to be given as a present – customers want presents to look impressive!). For some outlets the publisher may produce own-brand items; packages that consist of 'books plus' may become part of the store's gift or hobby range rather than book range (and hence be stocked in greater depth).

Attractive printed material is still the mainstay of most children's marketing: something that will make an impression on the book buyer and give a taster of the quality of the product. For other markets where value for money is important, cheaply produced materials give a quick impression that there is plenty of choice, and limited price special offers, or deals so that purchases above a certain price attract free carriage, encourage a quick response.

The creation of interesting websites where children can find out more about their favourite characters is also very important. Children feel a character or title is more real if they can access information online to back it up. Such websites need to be sophisticated, interactive and regularly updated – publishers are marketing here to the most net-savvy generation. Similarly, non-fiction titles that offer checked web links can be welcomed by parents. Books have been through extensive processes of checking and so are more reliable than the web, but 'listing 1,000 checked websites' on the front of a reference title makes it look more appealing and up to date to the children they are buying for, and is reassuring and time-saving for parents (they don't have to check the sites themselves).

This raises an important issue in the marketing of children's titles. A marketing manager responsible for the promotion of a list of children's titles has to convince a middle market of the books' merits. Booksellers and wholesalers have to be persuaded to stock titles, and parents, relatives, teachers and librarians to buy on behalf of the children they represent. Even those promotions that are sent straight to children (eg school book club leaflets) rely on teachers to organize and parents to pay.

About 85 to 90 per cent of books are paid for by adults, including the use by children of book tokens or vouchers. The spread of adults (in demographic terms) buying for children is also extremely wide, making the targeting of marketing very difficult. For example many titles are bought by adults who are not responsible for children or by much older generations.

Each year publishers produce catalogues and leaflets detailing their new and existing titles. In addition they prepare a range of promotional material for display in shops, schools and libraries: posters, leaflets, balloons and so on. This must be attractive both to the adult (so it gets put up) and to the children who will see it. Appealing to 'the child in us all' is not as easy as it sounds. Children today are sophisticated and acutely conscious of being patronized. They can be persuaded that a book is not for them by a quick glance at the cover (particularly important when they are doing the buying through an online bookshop and that is all they see).

Their language also changes all the time, and while they will not expect to see the current hot terminology on the back of book covers, they can be very disparaging about words that sound out of date, and hence inclined to damn the product through association. Publishers do not need to talk like teenagers (they could not do it anyway) but they do need to have a sixth sense to spot terms that will date.

Just to illustrate this, here are the current terms used by three 14-year-old boys in specific locations in Kingston upon Thames, Melbourne and New Jersey (I say specific locations, because 10 miles down the road they would probably be different).

	Kingston	Melbourne	Randolph, New Jersey
good	sick	good	bad
very good	boom	awesome	mad
cool	safe	awesome	sweet
attractive	fit	hot	bangin'
bad	brass	sucks	nasty

This illustration is not designed to pass on their vocabulary, but to illustrate how rich and temporary it is.

The marketing manager for a children's list will also spend a good deal of time and money promoting the backlist, not just new highlights. Whereas a new general hardback fiction title will have its heaviest sales period in the months following publication, with another boost when the paperback appears, children's titles can take a much longer time to get established and go on selling for much longer than adult titles.

Children's publishing is probably the most price sensitive area of the book trade

Economies of scale are vital where high development costs on mass-market novelty formats necessitate high print runs and hence volume deals. Mostly this is done using a schedule of discounts, rising according to the quantity bought. At the same time costs must be kept as low as possible, and most authors are remunerated on the basis of net receipts rather than published price.

Children's books are highly price-responsive. There is a symbiotic relationship between retail price and volume in the mass market; adding an extra 10 per cent to a title can ruin its chances of success. Shoppers in out-of-town superstores are particularly price sensitive. People are often looking to spend a specific amount of money, and given that there is so much choice, will allow the pre-set budget to be the main criterion for decision making. When pricing new materials publishers need to look not only at competing books but also at toys, stationery and gift items that jostle for the same leisure spend. Money-off can be a significant marketing gambit at certain times of year (eg Christmas), but in general low retail prices mean there is less margin to play with. At the same time, consumers often have enhanced expectations of books compared with other products. They may expect a DVD to get scratched through over-use but will write angry letters to the publishers if a book falls apart after constant reading.

Finally, children themselves are very price conscious. Youth today has more disposable income – working parents who are not at home tend to compensate with bigger allowances – but with this has come an increased consumer confidence. They are used to shopping around, and an awareness that books in particular can always be found somewhere cheaper was fostered by the discounted prices available for the new *Harry Potter* titles they all wanted. 'It's out on x and cheapest at x' was a common request to parents.

Generating free publicity

Children's publishers often complain of the paucity of review space devoted to their books, although blockbusters such as *Harry Potter* have broken the mould, with reviews commissioned from children who have stayed up all night reading the new book appearing on the news pages. However hotly editors protest their independence from advertising, it is true that children's publishers in general spend little on space in anything other than trade magazines, and that is usually concentrated in the run-up to the Bologna Book Fair. But as the area becomes more profitable, and they advertise more, there will be more editorial features on children's books.

The result is that a great deal of the time of a children's marketing department is spent pursuing promotional initiatives that result in coverage. These may include the following.

■ Organizing promotional links with websites, magazines and newspapers read by parents and children: for example features that 'review' new titles, articles on key authors, and sponsoring competitions which feature the book as prize and hence promote word of mouth.

■ Producing free branded material for carriers such as posters, CDs and height charts. All of these offer some element of editorial endorsement and thus more column inches and clout in return for the money spent.

■ Arranging author tours, usually to a specific region for three to four days at a time: handling bookings from schools and libraries; liaising with the local press; arranging for copies of the relevant books for signing sessions.

■ Organizing the firm's material for national and international book trade events such as National Children's Book Week (now in its 31st year) and World Book Day, which provide the stimulus to many schools and libraries to organize book-related events.

■ Supporting specific local initiatives: perhaps supplying local booksellers with marketing material for a promotion they have organized or arranging for a character in costume to pay a special visit to a school.

■ Sponsorship of events relevant to the market.

■ Entry of titles for literary prizes. The resulting media coverage brings the winning titles to the attention of a wider public, as well as promoting reading and books in general.

Book fairs, exhibitions and conferences

At the Bologna Book Fair all the major players in the trade gather for the sale of rights and to display their wares. The trade press lists attendees, and this provides a useful summary of the main houses involved in children's books. Other book fairs around the world have specific exhibition space for children's publishers, and many publishers have an exhibitions team that can be despatched to mount displays at teachers' and librarians' conferences, teachers' centres, schools, local fairs and other events.

Exporting children's books

Gaining an export deal for a children's title is often the way of making it profitable, and if a title can be translated and exported, there is the opportunity to raise valuable revenue from co-editions, rights and royalties. A series of co-edition deals, secured at the right time, can be the key to successful publishing of a children's book, allowing the publisher to extend the initial print run and keep the price down. This revenue is, however, threatened by the development of the indigenous publishing industries in many former traditional markets.

MARKETING TO MEDICS

Here are a few salient facts to remember when promoting to doctors:

■ As part of their training, all doctors get to cut up and examine a complete cadaver (usually that of someone who has given their body to medical science). Week by week, in dissection practicals, they reduce it to bits (or do this virtually). It follows that they are robust people and absolutely not squeamish.
■ Perhaps fuelled by this, they tend to have a black sense of humour. There is a very high number of comedians and performers who are doctors or ex-doctors; at arts festivals 'revues' performed by medics are plentiful.
■ They are better educated and probably better off than the population in general.
■ They are entirely used to accessing information, extracting and digesting what they need to know and making quick decisions. A glance at databases offering drug information (to be found on the PCs of all

prescribing doctors) is useful background information on how to format information for doctors. It presents a no-frills approach that doctors are very comfortable with.

■ They are consumers of lots of things besides medical marketing. At a recent focus group I asked a group of doctors which advertising campaign had caught their attention in recent weeks. Of the six present, one said a political party, another Guinness, a third pet insurance, a fourth clothes and a fifth holidays. The only marketing aimed specifically at doctors to be mentioned was a spectacularly incomprehensible campaign from a drug company.

Medics like you to be specific

Medicine is a vast profession. Whereas the specific structure varies, in most systems the process of becoming a doctor begins with a degree at medical school, followed by two years' clinical training. Then there is a divide between those who opt to be general practitioners and those who choose further specialist training. It is a very hierarchical profession, and certain specialities attract more prestige than others. The more specialized the branch of medicine doctors are working in, the more specific the information sent to them should be. But this is a profession in which personnel move fast, and keeping track of such changes can be difficult. In the early stages of a hospital career, job moves may be particularly swift; certain branches of medicine move faster than others (eg oncology moves more rapidly than psychiatry). For this reason it is probably better to rely on a third-party database company to provide your contact lists rather than trying to do it in-house.

One common complaint from doctors is that they receive too much material. Although they are in general conscientious about opening it, there is simply not time to read in detail everything that is sent.

Many doctors give their home address for the delivery of post rather than their work address. A large and (growing) percentage of general practitioners work part time, and the majority of these doctors too receive their professional post at home. The medical marketing materials sent thus have to compete for attention with the domestic post. The scale of the post received in this way is enormous. As a recently retired doctor commented to me, 'When I retired I wrote to the Medical Mailing Company to delete me from their lists. Two months on the amount of mail we receive at home has dropped by two-thirds. I knew I received a lot of information, but had not registered quite how much it was.'

What is sent is not all direct competition in the form of other marketing leaflets. The post includes a wide range of free/paid-for magazines and journals, and samples. There is also the chance to receive medical and related books free from pharmaceutical companies, who purchase such titles from publishers and then give them away as promotional incentives, to encourage them to take an appointment from a representative or attend a presentation.

Marketing materials to send to medics

Adequate for the job

Remember that this is a market used to receiving lavish promotional materials – which they get from pharmaceutical companies all the time – supported by very good presentations from well qualified and trained representatives. While you should not waste money or produce over-costly materials, if you want to get noticed you must produce something that at least holds its own. At focus groups with doctors I have heard adverse comments about leaflets on thin paper, or in small sizes, as looking unimpressive, or not worthy of their attention.

Dignified

Medical marketing materials should have authority. Make it clear on the envelope that you are a publisher (not a drugs company), or use a blank outer envelope. Present your information clearly for what it is, rather than using bland promises of career enhancement or humour (an oblique approach often used by drugs companies). For example, 'New book information from Bloggs Medical Publishers' or 'Look inside for substantial savings on Bloggs Medical Books' is likely to be more effective than 'Getting to the top can be tough. Bloggs' new book makes it easier.'

Logical

Your text should be laid out in a concise and predictable order, with photographs of covers next to blurbs, information precise and free from adjectives and over-writing. Doctors can cut through the blurb and need to know quickly what is in it for them. It seems that unlike almost every other group to be targeted through direct marketing, doctors don't need accompanying letters to introduce a marketing idea. They are happy to work from precise information.

Be sure to include/emphasize current buzz words (at the time of writing 'evidence-based medicine' seems a very key phrase). If you are not sure about them, get them double checked by someone who does know. Getting them wrong is worse than not trying to be up to date. Make ordering mechanisms easy to use: doctors dislike wasting time.

Self-explanatory

Several doctors commented to me that any product worth buying has to make its case. There has to be enough information to enable the doctor to make a buying decision. One said, 'Too often, marketing information promotes a brand, and the accompanying brand image, but spends insufficient time early on in explaining the significance of the product. I don't want to have to hunt for this information, I want them to tell me.'

Don't think you can just provide brief information in a brochure and then refer the reader to your website for more information. Most doctors I have spoken to say they simply don't have time; the brochure should do it all.

Be sure to include the following information:

- Who has written this and where they are based. UK medicine is different from both continental Europe and the United States.
- Subject matter and level.
- Contents list (this is absolutely essential).
- Cover. All the doctors I have spoken to are seduced by the look and feel of a book. If the title you are promoting has a high price, make it look appropriately weighty – have your designer 'airbrush in' the spine and pages to look value for money. Many doctors reported that it was actually seeing a book at a medical conference that made them buy title(s) they had only previously heard of.
- Testimonials, from people who are known in the field rather than the names of the publications in which their comments appeared. Peer opinion is very important. Ask your authors to approach the right people.
- Sample pages, perhaps with captions highlighting particularly significant points.

Easy to read

It has long been a joke that doctors have terrible handwriting. Today computerized notes and printed prescriptions have reduced the problem, but it is definitely best to make allowances for poor eyesight. With too much information to wade through, do ensure that your text is in a large enough type size to be read, and that design features enhance your message rather than compete with it.

Remember that these days the medical community is very international and doctors take up exchange programmes and courses worldwide. So never assume that the recipient of your information is necessarily a native English speaker.

Avoidable (if they so desire)

Few people realize that in order to delete a name from a mailing list the original sender needs to know from which list that name was taken (usually identified by the code at the top of the address label). Ensure all your envelopes carry a return address in case they are undeliverable. Why not add a mini-questionnaire asking for additional information on whether the right person is being mailed at the same time?

Make it clear that if the envelope is returned without opening, you do not need a stamp to return it. Alternatively, instruct recipients to put the contents in a new envelope and return it to a freepost address. Otherwise they simply won't bother and you will not be aware that you are wasting money on mailing those who are not interested in your products, or should not be on the mailing list at all.

Cost-effective

Doctors are as susceptible to special offers as the rest of the population, so do remember to make some. Medical texts are very expensive, so added value to encourage them to buy more and save at the same time is good. Interestingly whereas the corporate and business markets can respond very well to offers to take up a multiple buys (coordinate an order that all your colleagues need and receive a special discount for doing so), this idea is resisted by doctors. They are too busy and this is too commercial.

The best time to promote to doctors

There is a year-round demand for medical services, and year-round services to match. Academic holidays can be a good time to reach academics (with no students around, they have more time to read what you send). General practitioners tend to find that the workload is lighter in the summer and that doctors in a practice are never all away at the same time, so have more time to read your material.

Conferences

Professional and association conferences are a wonderful place to sell to doctors. Many view these as a short holiday, away from their day-to-day duties. They have time to read in the evenings and meet their colleagues. Circulate information through delegates' packs, course administration, and associated exhibition space. Sales may be particularly good at conferences where participants don't know each other very well – delegates can wander round the stands at coffee time rather than make it obvious that they don't have anyone to talk to! Ask your authors which conferences they would recommend you attend or send information to.

The role of medical librarians

If doctors complain about getting too much information, then consider the poor medical librarian, besieged by information on every specialism offered by the institution in question. Librarians have to juggle the different demands of various departments and specialities in an environment where budgets never match requirements. For more information on contacting this market see the section on marketing to academic librarians (page 244).

Interestingly, many medical libraries are collections culled from various different sites. For example, the library at our local hospital has three names (based on who originally gave the funding), but they all are the same place. Cross-check the lists you are using to ensure you are not sending out more copies of your information than you need to.

SELLING INFORMATION TO PROFESSIONAL MARKETS

For those planning a long-term career in publishing, a role in supplying information to fast-developing professional markets is a pragmatic move. Professional people such as accountants, lawyers and financial services staff need information on which they can rely, and on which they can base a service to their own customers. They could compile and update the detail their staff need themselves, but instead often choose to rely on publishers, who after all are experts in the management and delivery of information, to handle the process for them. They have substantial budgets to spend on the information resources they need, and the more bespoke/value-added publishers can make their service, the more valuable it becomes – and the more they can charge for it. And because the profits can be high, and because marketing staff responsible for promotion tend to use direct marketing to reach customers, and can thus track and prove how effective their efforts have been, there is a tendency for them to be better paid than their colleagues in other areas of the profession.

There are several important things for those marketing in this area to understand.

■ Business and professional markets often buy supplier brand, rather than individual contributor. They are buying from publishers core and ongoing values like consistency, confidence and competence, often to a greater extent than the temporary brilliance (even if amazingly far-sighted) of an individual and perhaps maverick brain. Given that they will be relying on the service provider to access, store, update and anticipate the information on which both their professional service and their professional requirements of compliance are based, they want to be assured that they are buying from an organization that prizes quality and accuracy, cares about the responsibility that accompanies provision, and that they can trust. *Their* reputation will be based on the reliability of what *you* provide.

Publishing relationships through official professional associations or representative bodies can work particularly well in this market, as they reinforce that closeness to the profession. For example the publisher might become a publishing partner of one of the leading professional bodies or associations in sectors such as accountancy, finance, tax or law.

■ When working with this market, you are a supplier as well as a publisher. And these markets demand good service from their suppliers; fully aware of how much they are paying. They want to access competence quickly, in whatever format they find most useful. They want the systems to be easy to use and work when they need them (they are very intolerant of mistakes), the functionality to be smooth and easy to operate, indices that allow swift access to content, cross-referencing that is efficient and imaginative. And if they lose or destroy what you provided, they still want you to sort it out – and quickly. What is more, this deliverability of the supplier's promise will colour whatever information you send to them in future. Thus if they have an ongoing issue with your organization about a separate service that they are dissatisfied with, it will influence how they both view and talk about you to their colleagues and competitors, in the much longer term. They will not be impressed if they seek to tell you of a difficulty and you lay the blame (even if correctly) at the feet of another department. To them you are one supplier, and every aspect of delivery is your responsibility.

■ They are more interested in the uses to which the information can be put than in the information itself. Provision by the publisher of professional detail is a given, something they take for granted – it is what they can do with it that interests them. Thus they will appreciate an information source if it serves as a tool for effective strategic planning, or an imaginative use of cross-referencing and linkage that enables them to demonstrate an additional competence to their clients. The publisher's immediate absorption of, and comment on, the latest legislative or tax changes enables them to offer a more complete service to those they work for; to show that they understand the implications of changed provisions within nanoseconds of their being announced.

'Information publishing is of limited value if it simply serves to inform but does not form part of a profit and growth strategy for the customer. We need to understand our customers' relationships with their customers and help them achieve their objectives. Motives of fear, greed, self-esteem and social standing are powerful drivers in encouraging sales' says Robert McKay, director, CCH Information, Wolters Kluwer UK.

Publishers can charge a lot of money for the additionally managed availability of the service they provide. Consider advice and information telephone lines, staffed by real experts, after standard office hours, or advice sections featuring frequently asked questions, all provided in a format that makes it clear the information is tailored to the individual or organization subscriber, rather than to the profession/or client base at large.

■ This market expects you to know them; their working habits; worries and priorities. They identify you as being part of their market – rather than a distant supplier – and expect a high level of involvement in return for the high level of investment they provide. You need to know who they are, to be at their get-togethers, and have a sufficient grasp of their subject matter to be able to keep an intelligent conversation going. Editors and those managing content will most probably have a specialist subject knowledge of the relevant area; marketing staff may not, but it may not occur to your market to ask whether or not you are similarly qualified (they may just assume that you are). But even if they find out you are not equipped as they might expect, they will not expect you to talk up your long-term ambition to work on Stephen King novels instead of taxation resources.

■ They want the information delivered in the format that best suits their needs, irrespective of how you may prefer to deliver it, or what your other professional customers require. This may be as books, magazines, subscription products, electronic programmes, conferences and training, CDs and online. They may prefer delivery through their professional organization (see above) rather than directly from a publisher.

■ This is an area of publishing where only big players tend to do well. The major publishing players in this area are few in number but enormous in size, and highly concentrated in the areas in which they specialize. In a field of maybe no more than four competing services, they want to be first or second, not third. Whereas much of the publishing industry is grounded in friendly competition, with staff sharing information about markets, and joining in related camaraderie, this area is highly competitive and non-collaborative. Focus on the external competitors is total.

■ This is a market driven by change. Professions are constantly affected by change, through precedent, government intervention or the news agenda, and the information resources publishers develop and maintain must match. This means that new updates are constantly required – and of course updating offers a valuable (and chargeable) service to consumers. Publishers are judged by the speed with which they make changes to their product. They also need to be able to innovate, as the market can become bored with a long-familiar but inefficient system. Don't forget that professionals are not only involved in their working life; they see technological innovation in other aspects of their lives, from how they order food in restaurants to how their children download music for pleasure. Publishers need to be up to date on all delivery mechanisms and standards of customer service, not just those that have applied in their own industry up to now.

Format of published and marketing materials

There is a drive to provide all products for the business and professional communities online; print copies are expensive to produce, store and distribute. But whereas some markets have fully embraced technological access to information, not all are equally comfortable. (Lawyers often seem to prefer print – perhaps this relates to their financial models for charging out their services.) For markets like these, a model is emerging of an annual printed book, supported by an online information service that is updated all the time, so an individual can look in the latest edition, establish the principles of the subject, then go online to find out what has happened since it was passed for press.

In the longer term, as enhanced technology makes reading on screen easier, and new generations joining the professions are more comfortable with online than print, more and more resources are likely to be available in this way. This long-term move to online resources has enormous implications for the relationship between publisher and customer, as once a company has adopted a particular publisher's system, and rolled it out via its intranet to employees, changing the delivery mechanism to another publisher can be very problematic. Convenience is a substantial factor, and works in the existing supplier's favour simply because for many it is too much effort to change.

You might assume that online delivery of a service would mean that marketing information about why and how to subscribe to it is best delivered online too. Not so. If a decision to install a particular supplier's system needs to be discussed with colleagues, then printed marketing materials will most likely need to be supplied. People expect a service that has a high price tag to be presented professionally, and even if it is delivered entirely online, a high-quality marketing brochure explaining the benefits may be required, simply to convince customers that it is being offered by a professional service provider that considers all their needs. In other markets a series of customer contacts may be required, including a demonstration, and each of these stages must be supported by appropriate marketing materials. You should also consider how the competitors are promoting their service, and decide whether to match them – or be different. Your most basic guide for what materials to produce should be common sense supported by an understanding of the market and the emotion likely to be involved in purchase. A key question you should be asking yourself, at all times, is 'Would I buy from me?'

You will need to develop a specific writing style for this market, that is as up to date with the trends and fashions of the profession as its members are. (It's a good idea to recruit members of the market to comment on your marketing approach, perhaps in return for free resources.) The words you use need careful attention. You should consider presenting your company as 'providers/researchers/sourcers/investigators of information' rather than simply 'publishers' (which can sound a bit old fashioned). Similarly, high-priced products are best described as 'in-depth resources', 'one-stop points of reference', 'compendiums of advice' or 'dossiers of the latest research and advice' rather than 'titles' or 'books'.

It is similarly vital that the impression you provide affirms the overall organizational brand, from well-put-together sales information to personal contacts who are highly informed and professional in appearance. This market wants precision, so spelling mistakes, casual uses of English and an inappropriately 'matey' style will all undermine the image your organization seeks to create.

These are complex products, and no sales representative could be expected to answer all the questions a potential customer has. So your marketing information should answer all potential purchasers' likely questions, and anticipate and reassure by offering information about issues they had not thought to enquire about, but still need to know. Investment in a business's information provision is a very expensive area, and those making the purchasing decisions need to show that they have gained good value for money for their organization. Images should reaffirm the value on offer. If your resource provides access to a range of advisory services, can these be represented by showing how many volumes – or people – are involved?

Ultimately it is vital for those marketing products to this market to remember that their market has a choice, and because of the huge financial consequences of changing supplier, a decision to exercise that choice is very damaging for the rejected publisher. Sometimes quite small instances of annoyance or inefficiency – perhaps the product of an 'unreasonable' attitude on the part of the customer, or thoughtlessness on the part of a very junior member of the publisher team – can become long-held grudges which influence buying decisions years into the future. The more embedded supplier and customer can be, at all levels of their business relationship, the longer lasting their professional relationship will be.

Appendix: Useful contacts for further information

ORGANIZATIONS

Association of American Publishers: www.publishers.org
American Booksellers Association: www.bookweb.org
Australian Booksellers Association: www.aba.org.au
Australian Publishers Association: www.publishers.asn.au
Booksellers Association of Great Britain: www.booksellers.org.uk
Book Trust: www.booktrust.org
Book Trust Scotland: www.scottishbooktrust.com
European Booksellers Federation: www.ebf-eu.org;
Independent Publishers Group: www.ipgbook.com
Independent Publishers Guild: www.ipg.uk.com
International Association of Scholarly Publishers (IASP): Tel Austria 01 310 5356
International Association of Scientific, Technical and Medical Publishers: www.stm-assoc.org
International Booksellers Federation: www.ibf-booksellers.org
International Publishers Association: www.internationalpublishers.org
Publishers Association: www.publisher.org.uk
(includes a very useful list of national/regional publishing and bookselling associations)
Society of Young Publishers: www.thesyp.org.uk

BOOK INFORMATION AND INDUSTRY STATISTICS

Book Marketing Limited: www.bookmarketing.co.uk
Nielsen Book Data: www.nielsenbookdata.co.uk
RR Bowker LLC: www.bowker.com

TRAINING ORGANIZATIONS

Including distance learning:
Alison Baverstock and Associates: www.alisonbaverstock.com
Bloom Partners: www.bloompartners.com.au
Graham Smith Associates: www.gsatraining.co.uk
Institute of Direct Marketing: www.theidm.com
Publishing Training Centre: www.train4publishing.co.uk

Courses also run by:
Society of Freelance Editors and Proofreaders: www.sfep.org.uk
Society of Young Publishers: www.thesyp.org.uk
Women in Publishing: www.wipub.org.uk

OTHER USEFUL CONTACTS

American Library Association: www.ala.org
American Society of Journalists and Authors: www.asja.org
Association of Subscription Agents: www.subscription-agents.org
British Printing Industries Federation: www.britishprint.com
British Promotional Merchandise Association: www.bpma.co.uk
Chartered Institute of Library and Information Professionals: www.cilip.
   org.uk
Direct Mail Information Service: www.dmis.co.uk
Institute of Direct Marketing: www.theidm.co.uk
North American Serials Interest Group Inc: www.nasig.org
Press Association: www.pressassociation.co.uk/
Press Complaints Commission: www.pcc.org.uk
Public Lending Right: www.plr.uk.com
Reuters: www.reuters.co.uk
Society of Authors: www.societyofauthors.net

Society of Freelance Editors and Proofreaders: www.sfep.org.uk
UK Serials Group: www.uksg.org

PUBLISHING PRESS

The Bookseller (UK): www.bookseller.co.uk
Publishing News (UK): www.publishingnews.co.uk
Publishers Weekly (US): www.publishersweekly.com

USEFUL WEBSITES/PAPERS FOR THOSE SEEKING JOBS

UK

- www.thebookseller.com/jobs
- www.publishingnews.co.uk/pn/pnc
- Guardian Media: http://jobs.guardian.co.uk/browse/media/index.jsp (and Monday editions of the paper)
- CV Clearing House: http://www.bookcareers.com/cvonline/intro.htm is
- The Institute of Direct Marketing: www.theidm.com

US

Publishers Weekly: jobs.publishersweekly.com

Australia

- Weekly Book Newsletter (generally known as Blue Newsletter or Blue News): www.booksellerandpublisher.com.au
- The Australian media section – Thursdays
- www.seek.com.au
- mycareer.com.au – these are the job ads from *The Age* (Melbourne) and *Sydney Morning Herald*, and other Fairfax publications
- www.careerone.com.au
- www.meapcareers.com.
- Australian Direct Marketing Association: www.adma.com.au

For all markets, in addition to the nationals, remember:

■ Your local papers, whenever they come out.
■ Regionally based papers.

Glossary

Above and below the line   The traditional distinction between different sorts of advertising. 'Above the line' is paid for (eg space advertisements taken in newspapers). 'Below the line' marketing involves no invoice; it is normally negotiated in a mutually beneficial arrangement between two or more organizations (eg books presented on cereal packs). The usual result is an augmented offer to the consumer (more than just the product being sold), often with a time limit. The distinction between 'above' and 'below the line' is blurring as techniques are used in combination; some marketing agencies are now offering 'through the line' services.

Advance notice (or advance information sheet; AI)   A single sheet giving brief advance details of a forthcoming publication. Usually circulated six to nine months before publication, it is sent to anyone who needs the information: bookstores, reps etc.

Advertorial   Advertising copy that masquerades as an editorial item.

Affinity marketing   Marketing based on choices made by consumers that indicate they like/are likely to be attracted to related products and services to those for which plans are being made. Penguin's promotion of fiction titles on the back of Galaxy chocolate bars is an example of affinity marketing in that both products (a good read and a bar of chocolate) are assumed to appeal to the same person. The proposal becomes particularly effective if the two products can be enjoyed together (read while you eat chocolate).

Answers   Shorthand used on a publisher's or distributor's invoice to show the status of particular titles ordered by a bookseller and not immediately available. The most common abbreviations are:

nyp   not yet published
nk   not known
oo   on order

op   out of print; no plans to reprint
os   out of stock (reprint under consideration)
rp Jan   reprinting, will be available again in January

Arrears   See *dues*.

Artwork   Typesetting and illustrations were conventionally pasted on to board to form artwork which could then be photographed to make printing plates. Today most artwork is produced on computer and despatched online.

Author   The person whose name appears on the front of the product and who will be most closely identified with its creation; usually (but not always) the person who wrote it. Authors have often struggled for years to get a publishing deal, to craft their manuscript, and then see it reach a final format, and hence care passionately about how their work is presented. Publishers, who have more than one author or title to look after, can find such single-mindedness a little daunting. All authors tend to underestimate the role played by the publishing house in seeing a book prepared for publication (it's common to hear the process described as 'pushing a few buttons'), and to lose sight of the fact that publishing is a business, in which the publishing house is investing its money, not a social service, however ultimately life-enhancing or culturally enriching the product. Authors complain that publishers frequently underestimate the amount of effort required to write a book ('How long does it take you to churn one out?').

The relationship between authors and publishers, which is utterly symbiotic, works best if both parties understand and manage the expectations of the other. For example what kind of product is being produced, awarded what level of marketing budget and aimed at what kind of long-term sales/life? Authors tend to know little of the preparation and production processes of book publication, so guidance on what kind of supporting information is needed from them, and when, is good practice. (For example, information on their key contacts, or associations to which the product could be marketed, are needed well before publication.) Both authors and publishers tend to be creative people, and arguments and misunderstandings can brew quickly. Effective explanation should produce cooperation, more effective publishing and a longer-lasting relationship.

Backlist   Older titles on a publisher's list that are still in print.
Barcode   A machine-readable unique product code. The barcode usually appears on the back cover of a book, and is used for stock control and sales.

Benefits   In a marketing context, benefits are the advantages that come to the user/purchaser from a product or service's features. Too much publishing copy is feature- rather than benefit-orientated, but the market are far more interested in what the product will do for them than in how the publisher has set up its specifications. For example, product features of a guide book might be lavish illustrations or high-paper quality. The benefits to the reader however might be that it provides a lasting souvenir of the holiday, really gives a flavour of the place to be visited before they get there or stands up well to use throughout the trip because it is well made. Similarly a picture book for very young children may offer attractive illustrations by a well-known artist, but be appreciated by grandparents because it makes a welcome present that they can enjoy reading together.

Blad   Originally this meant a section of a book printed early to help in the promotion, and be shown as a sample. Today blads can consist of marketing information about, a random assortment of pages from, or a synopsis of a forthcoming publication, and do not necessarily constitute a distinct section.

Bleed   Printed matter that extends over the trimmed edge of the paper; it 'bleeds' off the edge. To obtain a bleed in a magazine ad, you have to book a full-page space.

Blog   A user-generated website where entries are made in journal style and displayed in reverse chronological order. The term 'blog' is derived from 'web log', but it is also used as a verb, meaning to run, maintain or add content to a blog.

Blurb   A short sales message for use in leaflets or jackets.

Body copy   The bulk of the advertising text; which usually follows the headline.

Bottom line   Financial slang referring to the figure at the foot of a balance sheet indicating net profit or loss. Has come to mean the overall profitability, for example 'How does that affect the bottom line?'

Brand   A product (or service) with a set of distinct characteristics that makes it different from other products on the market.

Break-even   The point at which you start making money. In a publishing context reaching break-even means that sufficient copies of a publication have been sold to recover the origination costs. The break-even point in a mailing is reached when enough copies have been sold to recoup the costs of the promotion.

Bromide   A type of photographic paper. Producing a bromide is a one-stage photographic process on to sensitized paper or film which is then developed. *PMTs* are routinely produced on bromide paper but alternatives now include acetate or self-adhesive paper.

Budget   A plan of activities expressed in monetary terms.

Bullet point   A heavy dot or other eye-catching feature to attract attention to a short sales point. A series of bullet points are often used in advertisement copy both to vary pace and to engage the reader's attention:

■ good for attracting attention;
■ uneven sentences and surrounding spaces draw in the reader;
■ bullet points allow you to restate the main selling points without appearing over-repetitious.

Buyer   The job title within a retail or wholesaling firm responsible for selecting/ordering stock. Large shops will have a different buyer for each department.

b/w   Abbreviation for black and white.

Camera-ready copy   Frequently abbreviated to **crc**. Artwork that is ready for photography, reproduction and printing without further alteration.

Card deck (also called business reply card mailing or cardex mailing)   A collection of business reply cards each offering a separate sales message to which the recipient can respond by returning the card concerned. Handily recipients often tend to pass on individual cards to others they know may be interested. Often used for selling technical, business and professional titles.

Cased edition   A book with a hard cover, as opposed to *limp* or paperback.

CD ROM   Short for compact disc, read-only memory. A high-density storage device that can be accessed but not altered by those consulting it.

Centred type   A line or lines of type individually centred on the width of the text below. Type on a blank title page can also be centred on the page width.

Character   An individual letter, space, symbol or punctuation mark.

Cheshire labels   Old-fashioned format for labels. Cheshire labels are presented as a continuous roll of paper which is cut up and pasted on to envelopes by a Cheshire machine. Still sometimes used for the despatch of items bought on subscription; ie where customer loyalty is established.

Closed market   Created when local selling rights are sold to a particular agent. Booksellers in an area that is part of a closed market must obtain stock of titles from the local agent rather than direct from the original publisher. This arrangement is under threat from the internet, which knows no geographical boundaries.

Coated paper   Paper that has received a coating on one or both sides, eg art paper.

Colour separations   The process of separating the colours of a full-colour picture into four printing colours, done with either a camera or an electronic scanning machine. The separated film may then be used to make printing plates.

Competitive differentials   What a company is good or bad at; the things that set it apart from its competitors.

Controlled circulation   A publication circulated free or mainly free to individuals within a particular industry; advertising sales paying for circulation and production costs. Much used in medicine and business.

Cooperative (or shared) mailing   A mailing to a specialized market containing material from several advertisers that share the costs between them.

Copy   Words that make up the message, often used of material prepared for advertising or newspaper features.

Cromalin proofs   See *digital proofs*.

Cut-out   An irregularly shaped illustration which will require handwork at the repro stage of printing.

Database marketing   Building up increasingly complex information about customers in order to serve their needs more precisely and sell more to them in the future. The long-term aim of *direct marketing*.

Database publishing   Publishing from information stored on a database. Can be a fast method of producing complex material or material that will date very quickly.

Desktop publishing   Producing camera-ready copy and artwork on computer screen (rather than the old method of pasting down on to board). This allows easy experimentation with different layouts and formats.

Die-cutting   A specialized cutting process used whenever the requirement for a cut is other than a straight line or right angle (ie when a guillotine cannot be used). A metal knife held in wood is punched down on to the item to be cut. Many old letterpress machines have been adapted to form die-cutting equipment.

Digital proofs   Digital proofs are of two broad sorts: high-res (short for resolution) or low-res. High-res proofs are made from the final printing files, normally PDFs. There are a number of quality levels. At one extreme, they may be little more than the sort of colour prints you would get from an office laserjet printer, and though they may look fine they won't necessarily represent the printed product very faithfully because they are produced in a fundamentally different way from it. To get closer to this ideal, most printers use special laser printers which are calibrated to the platesetter (the device that exposes the printing plate) in a very direct manner. Digital cromalins are these sort of proof: high-res, calibrated proofs which can be used to check for colour before the item is printed. Low-res proofs by contrast are for position and content only, and are made using standard office equipment.

Direct costs   Costs attributable to a specific project, as opposed to general overheads or indirect costs. For example, the printing bill for producing a particular title is a direct cost; the photocopier used to copy proofs that are circulated is an indirect one.

Direct marketing   The selling of services directly to the end consumer – including e-mail, direct mail, telemarketing and house-to-house calling.

Direct response advertising   Advertising designed to produce a measurable response, through e-mail, mail, telemarketing, space advertisements etc. This compares with direct promotion, whereby material is sent directly to the market which may, or may not, produce a direct response back.

Disintermediarization   An interruption in the former process of doing things. For example, authors who offer their content direct to users, by self-publishing or publishing through their websites are changing the usual sequence of intermediaries (publishers, distributors and booksellers); this is a process of disintermediarization.

Display type   Large type for headlines, usually 14 points or more.

Dues (also called **arrears**)   Orders for a new (or reprinting) publication before it is released. Publishers record the dues and fulfil orders as soon as stock is available. Checking the dues of forthcoming titles is a good way of finding out how well the reps are subscribing particular titles in bookshops and hence estimating sales.

Dumpbin   Container to hold, display and stock in retail outlets; usually supplied by the manufacturer to encourage the retailer to take more stock than might otherwise be the case. Most are made from cardboard, to be assembled in the shop. Supplied free but on condition that a stock order to fill it is received too.

Duotone   A half-tone shot printed in two colours. This is a more expensive way of printing a photograph than simply using a single printing colour, but can add depth and quality to the image presented. It is usually printed in black plus a chosen second colour. An alternative effect can be produced by using a tint of the second colour behind a black and white half-tone.

ELT   English language teaching (see Chapter 11 on the education market).

Embargo A date before which information may not be released; often used on press releases to ensure that no one paper scoops the rest. Sometimes ignored by the media to secure just such a competitive advantage.

EPOS Electronic point of sale. Machine-readable code that can be read by a terminal at a shop checkout to establish price, register any appropriate discounts and reorder stock.

Extent Length of text. For example, for a book, extent: 192 pp (192 pages); for a leaflet, extent: 4 pp A4 (four sides of A4 paper).

FE Further education: education that is beyond school but not within university (those still at school under the age of 19 receive secondary education). FE can be academic (eg GCSEs and A levels) or vocational (eg GNVQs), carried out in the student's own time or supported by an employer.

Features The specifics of a product or service that distinguish it from other products and services produced (eg extent, illustrations, level of content). See also *benefits*.

Firm sale The orders placed by a bookstore from which the publishers expect no returns. In practice most publishers have to be flexible and allow at least a credit for unsold titles, to ensure goodwill and the stocking of their titles in the future.

Flush left (or **justified left**) Type set so that the left-hand margin is vertically aligned, the right-hand margin finishing raggedly wherever the last word ends.

Flush right (or **justified right**) Type set so that the right-hand margin only is aligned vertically.

Flyer A cheaply produced leaflet, normally a single sheet for use as a handout.

Font The range of characters for one size and style of type.

Format The size of a book or page. In the United Kingdom this is usually expressed as height × width, in the United States and most of Europe as width × height.

gsm (or **g/m²**) The measure by which paper is sold: short for grams per square metre.

Half-life The point at which the eventual outcome of an experiment can be predicted.

Half-tone An illustration that reproduces the continuous tone of a photograph. This is achieved by screening the image to break it up into dots. Light areas of the resulting illustration have smaller dots and more surrounding white space to simulate the effect of the original. A squared-up half-tone is an image in the form of a box (any shape), as opposed to a cut-out image.

Hard copy   Copy on printed paper as opposed to copy on a computer or other retrieval system (which is soft copy).

HE   Higher education. Study at university level and above.

Headline   The eye-catching message at the top of an advertisement or leaflet, usually followed by the body copy.

House ad   An advertisement that appears in one of the advertiser's own publications or promotions.

House style   The typographic and linguistic standards of a particular publishing house. For example, there may be a standard way of laying out advertisements, standard typefaces that are always used and standard rules for spelling and the use of capital letters. Most publishing houses provide their authors with a sheet of instructions on the house style.

Hype   Short for hyperbole, it literally means exaggerated copy not to be taken seriously. It has come to mean over-praising, and is part of the generation of interest in titles that appeal to the mass media.

Impression   All copies of a publication printed at one time without changing the printing plates. Several impressions may go into the making of a single edition.

Imprint   The name of the publisher or the advertiser that appears on the title page of a book, or at the foot of an advertisement. One publishing house may have several imprints, eg Grafton is an imprint of HarperCollins, Puffin of Penguin.

Indent   1. To leave space at the beginning of a line or paragraph; often used for subheadings and quotations. 2. To order on account; to 'indent for'.

In-house and out-of-house work   Jobs that are carried out using either the staff and resources within the firm or those of external companies or freelances.

In print   Currently available. Telephone enquirers will often ask whether a particular title is still 'in print'.

Insert   Paper or card inserted loose in a book, journal or brochure, not secured in any way.

Inspection copy   Copy of a particular title (usually a school text or other educational book) supplied for full examination by a teacher in the hope that a class set will be bought or the title will be recommended as essential on the course reading list. If the title is adopted and a certain number purchased, the recipient may usually keep the inspection copy. Books for which a multiple sale is unlikely are generally available 'on approval': after inspection they must be either returned or paid for.

ISBN International standard book number: a system of providing each edition of a book with an individual identifying number. The appropriate ISBN should appear on any piece of information to do with the book: it is essential for bookshop and library ordering, stock control, despatch and more.

ISDN International standard data number, use of a telephone line for the exchange of data between computers.

ISSN International standard serial number, a similar system to ISBN for identifying serial publications. The number allocated refers to the serial in question for as long as it remains in publication. It should appear on the cover of any periodical and in any promotion material. Libraries catalogue and order titles by ISSN.

Jacket rough A design for a book jacket prepared for the approval of author, editor and marketing department.

Justified type Type set so that both left- and right-hand margins are aligned vertically.

Lamination A thin film available in matt or gloss applied to a printed surface; often used for book jackets, glossy brochures or the covers of catalogues which can expect a lot of use. Varnishing has a similar effect and is becoming less expensive; it adds less to the bulk than lamination, but is not as durable.

Landscape A horizontal oblong format, ie wider than it is deep (as opposed to *portrait*).

Letterpress A printing process whereby ink is transferred from raised metal type or plates directly on to paper. All newspapers used to be printed by this method.

Limp (or **C format**) A format midway between hardback and perfect bound paperback; the spine is usually sewn but encased in card covers rather than boards.

Line work Illustrations such as drawings that consist of lines only rather than the graduated tones of photographs. The cheapest kind of illustration to reproduce.

List All the publications a particular publisher has for sale. Also used for a group of new publications, eg spring list.

Litho   Short for lithographic. A printing process which works on the principle of greasy ink sticking only to those parts of the wet plate that are to be printed. Most usually ink is transferred (offset) from a printing plate on to an intermediary surface ('blanket') and then on to the paper. How most marketing materials are printed.

Logo   Short for logotype. An identifying symbol or trade mark.

Mark up   1. To prepare a manuscript for the typesetter by adding the instructions needed such as type specification, width of setting, indentations, space between paragraphs and so on. 2. To increase the price of a particular title above that shown in the list price. Examples of use include when individual copies rather than class sets of school books are ordered (this is also called double pricing) or when selling expenses are likely to be high, perhaps with an export order.

Measure   The width of text setting, usually measured in pica 'ems' (the m is chosen because it is the widest letter for setting).

Merchandise   Branded goods.

Merchandising   In a publishing context, this means persuading retail outlets and those who supply them to stock branded goods related to a key title, for example a stationery range that relates to a key children's title. Merchandising is a key function of the reps in bookshops, now that so much buying is done centrally.

Monograph   A single-subject study by an author or group of authors, usually of a scholarly nature.

Negative option   A practice often used by book clubs whereby, unless a member responds to say a particular title is not required, it will be sent – eg the 'book of the month' is often a negative option. The process will have been part of the terms and conditions of membership.

Net   The final total. In the case of a price or sum to be paid, the net price means that no further discount or allowances are to be made; net profit is the surplus remaining after all costs, direct and indirect have been deducted, as opposed to gross profit which is the total receipts, only allowing for the deduction of direct costs. For a mailer, asking for a list of net names means that several lists are run against each other to eliminate duplicates so the final mailing list, while containing names from several sources, will only include each individual once.

Nix(ies)   Addresses on a mailing list that are undeliverable by the carrier. If these amount to more than a certain percentage of the total list supplied, a reputable list owner or broker will provide a refund or credit.

Online   Connected to a telecommunications system. More and more publishers' products are available this way; with customers gaining access through a telecommunications link to the continuously updated publishing information database.

Over-run   1. Type matter that does not fit the design and must either be cut or the letter and word spacing reduced in size until it fits. 2. Extra copies printed, over and above the quantity ordered from the printer (see ***overs***).

Overs   Short for over-run. The practice of printing a slightly larger quantity than ordered to make up for copies spoilt during either printing or binding. It is commercially acceptable for the printer to allow 5 per cent over or under the quantity ordered unless otherwise specified. You will be charged for the overs.

Ozalid   A contact paper proof made from the film and usually used as a last-minute check on positioning on more complex jobs. A final check before printing, unless a printed proof is requested.

Perfect binding   The most common binding for paperbacks. The different sections of the book are trimmed flush and the pages glued to the inside of the cover. This is more expensive than ***saddle stitching*** but cheaper than sewing.

PMT   Short for photo mechanical transfer. The production of a PMT is a two-stage process: the creation of a photosensitive negative which is then developed with a chemically sensitive carrier. The line image produced provides artwork.

Podcast   A series of electronic media files, such as audio or video, that are distributed over the internet by means of a web feed, for playback on portable media players and personal computers, at a time that suits the listener. Used to mean either the content or the method by which it is made available (although this is also referred to as podcasting).

Point of sale   Eye-catching promotional material to be displayed with the product where purchases are made. For example publishers produce showcards, posters, bookmarks, balloons, single-copy holders, dumpbins and counter packs for display by the till point.

Point system   A typographic standard measure based on the pica, eg 12 pt.

Portrait   An upright oblong format, ie taller than it is wide (see also ***landscape***).

Pos   Abbreviation for positive, eg pos film, or point of sale.

Positioning   A marketing term for how you want your designated customer to feel about the product or service you are offering; the emotional relationship you want them to have with it.

Print on demand   As printing technology becomes cheaper and specialist publishers increasingly target highly niche markets, it may be cost-effective to print only the number of copies you have actual orders for. This can work particularly well for a high-price product relevant to a very small market, for example a market research report. Don't forget, however, that before any printing on demand can begin the origination costs must be covered. It follows that this is not as cheap an alternative to conventional production as is often imagined!

Print run   The number of copies ordered from a printer (see *overs*).

Pro forma invoice   One that must be settled before goods are despatched, often used for export orders or where no account exists.

Progressive proofs   A set of printed proofs showing each colour individually and then in combination.

Promotions   This originally referred to mutually beneficial arrangements between non-competing organizations approaching the same target market (now often referred to as affinity marketing); today the term is used more generally, to refer to general pushing or promoting of titles to a wider prominence.

Proofreading   Reading typeset copy for errors. There is a standard series of proofreaders' marks which should be made both by the mistake and in the margin. Typesetter's mistakes should be noted in red, and author's and publisher's in black or blue.

Publication date   The date before which stock may not be sold, to ensure no one seller saturates the market before all have the same opportunity. Sometimes ignored to secure a competitive advantage. (See also *release date*.)

Reading copies   Copies of a forthcoming title distributed before publication date to key people in the trade (notably booksellers and wholesalers) to create enthusiasm and promote word of mouth. Done on the grounds that those who sell books are more likely to enthuse to customers about titles they have themselves read and enjoyed.

Recto   The right-hand page of a double-page spread (with an odd page number). The opposite of *verso*.

Register   Trim marks that appear on the artwork supplied to a printer, should reappear on the plates made, and need to be matched up when printing to ensure the whole job will be in focus or register. If the plates have not been aligned according to the register marks or the marks were placed incorrectly the job is said to be 'out of register'.

Release date   Date on which stock is released from the publisher's warehouse for delivery to booksellers in anticipation of the *publication date*.

Some booksellers complain release dates are far too early and they end up warehousing the books instead of the publisher. This can fuel the temptation to sell early.

Remainder To sell off unsold stock at a cheaper price, often to 'remainder shops' such as discount bookstores.

Repro Short for reproduction; the conversion of typeset copy and photographs into final film and printing plates.

Response device How the order or response comes back to the mailer, for example link to the website to place an order, reply card or envelope.

Retouching Adapting artwork or film to make corrections or alter tonal values.

Return on investment (ROI) The eventual profit received by a publisher on a project; based on a calculation of how much the publisher invested in the first place, and how much it subsequently got back, after the deduction of associated costs. The period over which ROI is calculated, and eventually deemed acceptable or unacceptable, will depend on the nature of the publishing project, its long-term significance to the house and the specific market being targeted.

Returns Unsold stock of particular titles that may be returned to the publisher by the bookseller with prior agreement. Reps often use the authorization of returns as a bargaining point in persuading booksellers to take new titles.

Reverse out To produce text as white or a pale colour 'reversed out' of a darker background colour, as opposed to the more usual practice of printing in dark ink on a pale background. This technique can be very effective in small doses, but for lengthy passages of text it can be very hard to read. Never reverse text out of a photograph or illustration – it's impossible to read.

Review copy You will hear this term used widely to mean 'free copy', and probably receive many calls and e-mails requesting one. In precise terms, a review copy is a title sent to a potential reviewer (or review editor) in the hope of their featuring it in the media. Early copies released this way end up for sale in second-hand bookshops, and through online bookselling mechanisms, often before publication, and this practice is an ongoing source of tension between publishers and the media.

Review slip The enclosure in a book when it is sent out for review by a publisher. It should include details of title, author, ISBN, price and publication date, as well as a request for a copy of any review that appears.

Rights The legal entitlement to publish a particular work. Permission is given by the copyright holder (usually the author or editor) to reproduce the work in one particular format.

Subsidiary rights (for other formats (eg paperback, online), film, merchandising deals and so on) are then sold by either the firm's rights manager or the author's agent. The major occasion for selling rights is the annual Frankfurt Book Fair.

Roman Upright type (not bold), as opposed to italic.

Royalty The percentage of list price or net receipt paid on each copy sold to the copyright holder, usually the author. There are national variations in the period over which royalties must be paid. In the United Kingdom, royalties are paid to the author's estate for 70 years after his or her death; the manuscript is then deemed to be out of copyright and may be reproduced by anyone without paying royalties.

Rrp Short for recommended retail price. Usually set by the manufacturer, this is the basis for calculating the discount given to the retailer. The actual selling price is decided by the retailer, who may choose to lower prices and take a reduced profit margin in the hope of selling a greater quantity.

Run of paper Refers to the position of an advertisement that will appear in a particular journal or paper wherever there is room, at the editor's or designer's discretion. This is usually cheaper than specifying a particular (or preferred) position.

Saddle stitching A method of binding pamphlets or small books (48–64 pages is probably the limit for saddle stitching successfully). Wire staples or thread are used to stitch along the line of the fold. Also called wire stitching.

Sale or return Bookstores or wholesalers take titles 'on sale or return' on the understanding that if they have not been sold after a specified period (usually 6–12 months after ordering), and provided the titles are still in print, they may be returned for a credit. This leaves the long-term financial risk with the publisher. The opposite of *firm sale*.

School supplier (also called **educational contractor**) A firm that seeks to supply both schools and local education authorities with books and other educational products.

Screen 1. The process used to convert continuous tone photographs into patterns of dots, in order to reproduce the effect of the original when printed (see also *half-tone*). A coarse screen is used in the preparation of illustrations for newsprint and other less demanding jobs. 2. Short for silk screen printing.

See safe Bookstores or wholesalers usually take books on a 'see safe' basis. They are invoiced immediately for the total taken; those they do not sell may be returned for a credit or exchange. While the immediate financial outlay is thus with the shop, they are protected by the practice of *sale or return*.

Self-mailer   A direct mail piece without an envelope or outer wrapping. Often used to refer to all-in-one leaflets, which combine sales message and response device. Space for copy is limited so this format works best when the recipient already knows of the product being advertised.

Serif, sans serif   A serif typeface has 'handles' on the letters, like the typeface used in this book; a sans serif face does not.

Showthrough   How much ink on one side of a printed sheet of paper can be seen through on the other side.

Spam   Unsolicited or unwanted electronic advertising messages sent in bulk and received as e-mails.

Specs   1. Short for type specifications. Designers may refer to 'doing the spec' by which they mean laying down the parameters of text design, choosing a typeface and size. 2. The specifications for printing a job are all the production details (format, extent, illustrations, print run etc) sent to printers for a quote.

Split infinitive   'Splitting the infinitive' means dividing the two words that make up the infinitive in English (eg to love). So you would always write 'to love passionately' not 'to passionately love' – which splits the infinitive. The principle is based on the 19th-century British educationalists' obsession with Greek and Latin. So because in those languages, and incidentally in all modern European languages, the infinitive is never separated, because it is one word (amare, aimer, lieben mean to love in Latin, French and German), we should never do this in English either. It's pedantic and nonsense, but still something of an obsession for the English. The Americans seem to care less – one of the most famous split infinitives is the opening of *Star Trek*, which announces the mission of the Star Ship Enterprise 'to boldly go'.

Subscribe   To secure orders from bookshops and wholesalers before publication date, either by phone or through a rep visiting. The results are recorded by the publishing house as *dues*.

Tag line (or **strap line**)   A line of copy that sums up the product or the general philosophy of the company. Often displayed on the front cover of books.

Telemarketing, teleselling   Using the telephone to sell. While it is often thought of as the making of calls to promote products, effective telemarketing means considering the way incoming calls are handled as well as the way outgoing calls are made.

Terms The discount and credit conditions on which a publisher supplies stock to a bookseller or wholesaler. Terms will vary according to the amount of stock taken, the status under which it is accepted, what the competition are doing and how much customers want the book. (See *see safe*, *firm sale* and *sale or return*.)

Tint A pattern of dots that when printed reproduces as a tone. Using tints is a good way to get value from your printing inks. For example, even if you have only one printing colour, try putting the text in solid, and using a 10 per cent tint of the same colour to fill in and highlight certain boxes around copy. Further variations can be achieved if you are using more printed colours.

Trade discount The discount given by publishers to booksellers and wholesalers on the price at which they will subsequently sell. The amount of discount given usually varies according to the amount of stock taken or the amount of promotion promised. 'Short discounts' are low-scale discounts on products that are either very expensive (often those that are extensively promoted by the publisher directly to the end user) or those that are sold in sets (eg school textbooks).

Trim Short for 'trimmed size' of a printed piece of paper, ie its final or guillotined size.

Turnover The total of invoice value over a specified period for a particular company's sales.

Type area The area of the final page size that will be occupied by type and illustrations, allowing for the blank border that will normally surround text.

Typeface The style of type, eg Garamond, Helvetica.

Typescript The hard copy (usually a printout) of the manuscript or copy to be reproduced and printed.

Typo Short for typographical error; a mistake in the setting introduced by the typesetter.

Unjustified type Lines of type set so that the right-hand margin does not align vertically and thus appears ragged. This can also be described as 'ranged left' or 'ragged right'.

Upper and lower case Upper-case characters are CAPITALS, as opposed to lower case.

Verso The left-hand side of a double-page spread (even page numbers). The opposite of *recto.*

Viral marketing and **viral advertising** Marketing techniques that use social networks that already exist to produce an increase in awareness. Because they use pre-existing (and usually online) social networks, and encourage the spread of word of mouth as a personal communication, they can be a very useful and effective means of reaching a large number of people quickly.

Visual A mock-up or rough layout. A layout of planned printed work showing the position of all the key elements: headlines, illustrations, bullet points, body copy and so on. Blank 'dummy' books are often created before finished copies are available for promotional photographs.

Website A collection of web pages, videos and other digital assets hosted on a particular domain or subdomain on the World Wide Web. A web page is a document, typically written in HTML, that is almost always accessible via HTTP, a protocol that transfers information from the website's server to display in the user's web browser. All publicly accessible websites are seen collectively as constituting the World Wide Web. (Source: Wikipedia.)

Weight of paper Paper is sold in varying weights defined in gsm or g/m^2: grams per square metre. Printers can offer you samples of various papers in different weights.

Wholesaler An organization that purchases books in bulk, and stores them, in order to supply retail outlets quickly and efficiently, often securing higher than usual discounts in return for the large quantities taken.

The national bookshop chains, and outlets with large designated markets (eg library suppliers and school suppliers) will similarly demand substantial discounts from the publisher for large quantities of stock taken.

Bibliography

Baverstock, Alison (1993) *Are Books Different?*, Kogan Page, London

Baverstock, Alison and Douglas, Cathy (1999) *Effective Copywriting by Distance Learning*, available from Publishing Training Centre (www.train4publishing.co.uk), London

BML (2007) Books and the Consumer, ongoing survey (2005–07) [online] www.bookmarketing.co.uk (accessed 15 July 2007)

Clark, Giles (2001) *Inside Book Publishing*, Routledge, London

Crompton, Alastair (1987) *The Craft of Copywriting*, 2nd edn, Random House Business Books, London

Gombrich, Ernst (1995) *The Story of Art*, 16th edn, Phaidon, London

Klein, Naomi (2002) *No Logo*, Picador, London

McManus, Sean (2001) *Small Business Websites That Work* (www.sbwtw.com), Prentice Hall, London

McManus, Sean (2006) *Journalism Careers – Your questions answered* [e-book] www.journalismcareers.com (accessed July 2007)

Ogilvy, David (2007) *Ogilvy on Advertising*, Prion, London

Shipley, David and Schwalbe, Will (2007) *Send: The how, why, when – and when not – of email*, Canongate, London and Edinburgh

Solomon, Nicola (2007) quoted in Alison Baverstock, *Marketing Your Book: An author's guide*, A&C Black, London

Wimbs, Diana (1999), *Freelance copywriting*, A&C Black, London

Index